Plays on a Human Theme

Cy Groves

Head of English
Central Memorial High School
Calgary

MARTY

A RAISIN IN THE SUN

INHERIT THE WIND

McGRAW-HILL RYERSON LIMITED
Toronto   Montreal   New York   St. Louis   San Francisco
Auckland   Beirut   Bogotá   Düsseldorf   Lisbon
London   Lucerne   Madrid   Mexico   New Delhi
Paris   San Juan   São Paulo   Singapore   Sydney   Tokyo

PLAYS ON A HUMAN THEME

© THE RYERSON PRESS, 1967

Copyright © McGraw-Hill Ryerson Limited, 1979
First paperback edition

ISBN 0-07-082962-4

19 20 KP 99

PRINTED AND BOUND IN CANADA

Cover Design: Brian F. Reynolds
Cover Photo: Bob Wood

Canadian Cataloguing in Publication Data

Main entry under title:

Plays on a human theme

Contents: Chayefsky, P. Marty.—Hansberry, L. A raisin in the sun.—
Lawrence, J. Inherit the wind.

ISBN 0-07-082962-4 pa.

1. American drama—20th century. I. Groves, Cy, date. II. Chayefsky,
Paddy, 1923-   Marty. III. Hansberry, Lorraine, 1930-   A raisin
in the sun.   IV. Lawrence, Jerome, 1915-   Inherit the wind.

PS634.P532 1979   812'.052   C79-094228-3

ACKNOWLEDGMENTS

Random House, Inc., and the authors for *Inherit the Wind* by Jerome
Lawrence and Robert E. Lee, © Copyright 1955 by Jerome Lawrence
and Robert E. Lee and Random House, Inc., and Robert Nemiroff as
Executor of the Estate of Lorraine Hansberry for *A Raisin in the Sun* by
Lorraine Hansberry, © Copyright 1959 by Lorraine Hansberry.

Simon and Schuster, Inc., for *Marty* from *Television Plays,* copyright
1954 by Paddy Chayefsky.

Contents

INTRODUCTION TO DRAMA

Why read a play?

Plays were written to be acted. Why then, read through an anthology of plays or sit through a play reading? For most of us there is little opportunity to be part of a live audience, regularly watching first class plays. Access to the world of live theatre, the cost of theatre tickets, availability of free evenings, these are just a few of the reasons that theatre-going is still reserved for the fortunate few. Even city dwellers miss excellent plays since few theatre companies bring back a production once it has enjoyed a successful season. There are many excellent plays no longer being acted because of high production costs or changing box-office appeal.

For those who can never see a play, the cinema or television is the usual substitute. But the two-dimensional screen lacks the flesh and blood reality of the live, stage performance. The television screen play has the added disadvantages of commercials, a small screen, and inevitable home distractions. However, a play written specially for television and acted live can be most effective.

Reading or hearing a play brings the world of the theatre into one's living room or classroom *provided that one brings an alert dramatic imagination.* This is the secret of reading and enjoying the script of a play. It is true that not being able to watch a live performance means a loss of direct, visual appeal. But with a minimum of imagination, movement, facial expressions, appropriate settings, mood lighting, and above all the conflicts of real flesh and blood characters, can be seen with a dramatic, inner eye that "sees" the action unfold on an imagined stage.

Perhaps the most important reason for reading plays is that new worlds of experience are excitingly revealed. The reader has the opportunity to enter into someone else's skin and live his or her life within the condensed time limit of a couple of hours. Unlike the novel, the play can almost always be read at a single sitting. We rapidly become stimulated by thought-provoking ideas, excited by deliberately heightened action and conflict, moved deeply by deliberately created, vivid characters.

As we read, or hear others act out, the lives of these vivid characters, we go through a certain onrush of emotional release. At the end of the play we know, thankfully, that the characters in the play were not us. We sympathized, we were angry, we felt satisfaction or injustice; in some way we were moved. And then it is all over. What have we gained? We thought, we felt, we lived through a dramatic life experience. If the play was truly effective, then the audience or the reader feels a certain pleasure at having lived a little more, if only vicariously. Somehow we always feel a little better for having widened our life experience.

Why read these particular plays?

The three plays in this anthology have been specially chosen because they all present important fundamental ideas. *Marty* poses the question of what happens to the physically unattractive people in this world who seek, but cannot find, someone who will love and be loved. *Inherit the Wind* makes us wonder whether the right to think freely is truly assured every man in present day society. *A Raisin in the Sun* takes a hard look at the "American Dream" of materialistic success and makes us wonder whether the dream is worth it.

No one can guarantee that these plays will live forever—but their ideas will! The problem of Marty is as perennial as any ugly duckling portrayed in life or in literature, whether he be Quasimodo in Hugo's *The Hunchback of Notre Dame* or the clubfooted Philip Carey in Maugham's *Of Human Bondage*. There will always be people who suffer through some physical or social handicap. The question of the freedom to think in *Inherit the Wind* is as old as the death of Socrates and as new as the "book people" in Bradbury's *Fahrenheit 451*. The striving for materialistic success and status in *A Raisin in the Sun* is as old as the Parables and as new as *The Status Seekers*.

Because the characters in these plays are readily identifiable, the basic ideas that they represent seem far more realistic. We are left with an inevitable question: could this happen to me?

How to study a play.

(i) At the easiest and simplest level of enjoyment:
What was the play about?
Why did I enjoy it?

(ii) For deeper understanding and fuller enjoyment:
What was the author trying to communicate to me?
How did the author get his point across?

What was the main conflict and how was it resolved?

Which characters were most memorable? Why?

Which moments were most suspenseful? Why?

(iii) For the highest level of understanding of form and content:

To what extent were the characters believable or unbelievable? Why?

How did the characters stand as symbols for basic ideas?

To what extent was the outcome of the play satisfying or unsatisfying?

How was the setting appropriate to the events, to the characters, to the basic mood of the play?

Who would most enjoy, least enjoy, this play? Why? (that is, what is the play's audience appeal?)

How, if at all, would you improve the play?

Was the play's climax truly effective? In what way?

How did the author create interest in the often dull, exposition section?

To what extent was the play a mirror of life?

Seeing or reading a play is not the end: much of the pleasure comes later when you can talk, discuss, argue, listen—either amongst friends or over the breakfast table when the morning paper brings the critic's report on the performance you saw the night before.

MARTY
BY PADDY CHAYEFSKY

Above: *Mama, Thomas and Marty.* (PHOTO: UNITED ARTISTS)
Below: *MOTHER: Catherine, I want you come live with me in my house with Marty and me.* (PHOTO: UNITED ARTISTS)

INTRODUCTION/*Marty*

Paddy Chayefsky wrote *Marty* as a realistic alternative to the stereo-typed love stories in pulp magazines, televised soap operas, and Hollywood's glossy romances. Instead of the handsome and the beautiful, here is the unattractive, small, fat man who is convinced that "whatever it is that women like, I ain't got it," and the plain girl at whom no man would look once. Instead of the usual happy ending, we are left to ponder the happiness chances of the sad, little bachelor who finally plucks up enough courage to telephone the girl he would like to marry.

The plot is simple. Marty, a fat, plain, 36-year-old bachelor is under pressure from his family and friends to get married. He is convinced, after painful rejections, that he is not husband material and sadly accepts his unfulfilled, bachelor life. When he finally does meet a shy girl whom he likes, his friends disapprove of her appearance and his mother disapproves of her not being Italian. In an anguish of frustration, Marty goes against the wishes of his friends and family and telephones the girl he would like to marry.

Marty lends itself to the medium of television. The intimacy of the screen makes possible the quiet conversation, the facial closeup of inner torment, the small world that seems to close in on the lonely. It is significant that the motion picture of *Marty* was filmed in black and white and without the magnitude of the wide-screen process. The whole emphasis seemed to be on the intimate, the quiet, the unassuming.

The original television play starred Rod Steiger in the title role. Later it was adapted for the screen on a shoestring budget with Ernest Borgnine (Best Actor Award) and Betsy Blair in the lead roles. The unheralded film won the Best Film Award (1956) both in the U.S.A. and at the Cannes International Film Festival. The television play won the Sylvania Television Award as the best television script of the year.

What were the reasons for the acclaim given to *Marty*? Could it be that Chayefsky gave us an intimate image of "the little man" who is a part of each one of us? *Marty* brought back to audiences the feeling that there is a whole world of ordinary, plain people who never hit the newspaper headlines, who never live lives of great tragedy or achievement, who, like Charles Chaplin's "little man," are longing for love, understanding, and recognition. Many of the modern films claim to mirror everyday realism but all too often they depict only the unusual, the rebellious, the extreme. Marty is every man who is plain and unexciting, who wants love but cannot find it, who suffers rejection and becomes a "professor of pain."

As you read the play notice:

* The conflict between generations in the same family circle.
* The pressures of society to conform.
* The wasteland of the "so what do you feel like doing tonight?" crowd.
* The implied standards for selecting a partner with social prestige.
* The problem of the unwanted, elderly relative.
* The prejudice based on educational and religious differences.
* Man's fears of rejection.
* The in-law problem.

MARTY

CHARACTERS

MARTY PILLETTI	CRITIC
CLARA DAVIS	BARTENDER
ANGIE	TWENTY-YEAR-OLD
MARTY'S MOTHER	ITALIAN WOMAN
AUNT CATHERINE	SHORT GIRL
VIRGINIA	YOUNG MOTHER
THOMAS	STAG
YOUNG MAN	FORTY-YEAR-OLD

ACT ONE

Fade in: A butcher shop in the Italian district of New York City. The butcher is a mild-mannered, stout, short, balding young man of thirty-six. His charm lies in an almost indestructible good-natured amiability.

The shop contains three women customers. One is a young mother with a baby carriage. She is chatting with a second woman of about forty at the door. The customer being waited on at the moment is a stout, elderly Italian woman who is standing on tiptoe, peering over the white display counter, checking the butcher as he saws away.

ITALIAN WOMAN   Your kid brother got married last Sunday, eh, Marty?

MARTY (*Absorbed in his work*) That's right, Missus Fusari. It was a very nice affair.

ITALIAN WOMAN   That's the big tall one, the fellow with the mustache.

MARTY (*Sawing away*) No, that's my other brother Freddie. My other brother Freddie, he's been married four years already. He lives down on Quincy Street. The one who got married Sunday, that was my little brother Nickie.

ITALIAN WOMAN   I thought he was a big, tall, fat fellow. Didn't I meet him here one time? Big, tall, fat fellow, he tried to sell me life insurance?

MARTY (*Sets the cut of meat on the scale, watches weight register*) No, that's my sister Margaret's husband Frank. My sister Margaret, she's married to the insurance salesman. My sister Rose, she married a contractor. They moved to Detroit last year. And my other sister Frances, she got married about two and a half years ago in Saint John's Church on Adams Boulevard. Oh, that was a big affair. Well, Missus Fusari, that'll be three dollars, ninety-four cents. How's that with you?

The Italian woman produces an old leather change purse from her pocketbook and painfully extracts three single dollar bills and ninety-four cents to the penny and lays the money piece by piece on the counter.

YOUNG MOTHER (*Calling from the door*) Hey, Marty, I'm inna hurry.

MARTY (*Wrapping the meat, calls amiably back*) You're next right now, Missus Canduso.

The old ITALIAN WOMAN *has been regarding* MARTY *with a baleful scowl.*

ITALIAN WOMAN   Well, Marty, when you gonna get married? You should be ashamed. All your brothers and sisters, they all younger than you, and they married, and they got children. I just saw your mother inna fruit shop, and she says to me: "Hey, you know a nice girl for my boy Marty?" Watsa matter with you? That's no way. Watsa matter with you? Now, you get married, you hear me what I say?

MARTY (*Amiably*) I hear you, Missus Fusari.

The old lady takes her parcel of meat, but apparently feels she still hasn't quite made her point.

ITALIAN WOMAN   My son Frank, he was married when he was nineteen years old. Watsa matter with you?

MARTY   Missus Fusari, Canduso over there, she's inna big hurry, and . . .

ITALIAN WOMAN   You should be ashamed of yourself.

She takes her package of meat, turns, and shuffles to the door and exits. MARTY *gathers up the money on the counter, turns to the cash register behind him to ring up the sale.*

YOUNG MOTHER   Marty, I want a nice big fat pullet, about four pounds. I hear your kid brother got married last Sunday.

MARTY   Yeah, it was a very nice affair, Missus Canduso.

YOUNG MOTHER   Marty, you oughtta be ashamed. All your kid brothers and sisters, married and have children. When you gonna get married?

Close-up: MARTY. *He sends a glance of weary exasperation up to the ceiling. With a gesture of mild irritation, he pushes the plunger of the cash register.*

Dissolve to: Close-up of television set. A baseball game is in progress. Camera pulls back to show we are in a typical neighborhood bar—red leatherette booths, a jukebox, some phone booths. About half the bar stools are occupied by neighborhood folk. MARTY *enters, pads amiably to one of the booths where a young man of about thirty-odd already sits. This is* ANGIE. MARTY *slides into the booth across from* ANGIE. ANGIE *is a little wasp of a fellow. He has a newspaper spread out before him to the sports pages.* MARTY *reaches over and pulls one of the pages over for himself to read. For a moment the two friends sit across from each other, reading the sports pages. Then* ANGIE, *without looking up, speaks.*

ANGIE   Well, what do you feel like doing tonight?

MARTY   I don't know, Angie. What do you feel like doing?

ANGIE   Well, we oughtta do something. It's Saturday night. I don't wanna go bowling like last Saturday. How about calling up that big girl we picked up inna movies about a month ago in the RKO Chester?

MARTY   (*Not very interested*) Which one was that?

ANGIE   That big girl that was sitting in front of us with the skinny friend.

MARTY   Oh, yeah.

ANGIE   We took them home alla way out in Brooklyn. Her name was Mary Feeney. What do you say? You think I oughtta give her a ring? I'll take the skinny one.

MARTY   It's five o'clock already, Angie. She's probably got a date by now.

ANGIE   Well, let's call her up. What can we lose?

MARTY   I didn't like her, Angie. I don't feel like calling her up.

ANGIE   Well, what do you feel like doing tonight?

MARTY   I don't know. What do you feel like doing?

ANGIE   Well, we're back to that, huh? I say to you: "What do you feel like doing tonight?" And you say to me: "I don't know, what do you feel like doing?" And then we wind up sitting around your house with a couple of cans of beer, watching Sid Caesar on television. Well, I tell you what I feel like doing. I feel like calling up this Mary Feeney. She likes you.

MARTY *looks up quickly at this.*

MARTY   What makes you say that?

ANGIE   I could see she likes you.

MARTY   Yeah, sure.

ANGIE (*Half rising in his seat*) I'll call her up.

MARTY   You call her up for yourself, Angie. I don't feel like calling
her up.

*ANGIE sits down again. They both return to reading the paper
for a moment. Then ANGIE looks up again.*

ANGIE   Boy, you're getting to be a real drag, you know that?

MARTY   Angie, I'm thirty-six years old. I been looking for a girl
every Saturday night of my life. I'm a little, short, fat fellow,
and girls don't go for me, that's all. I'm not like you. I mean,
you joke around, and they laugh at you, and you get along fine.
I just stand around like a bug. What's the sense of kidding
myself? Everybody's always telling me to get married. Get married. Get married. Don't you think I wanna get married? I
wanna get married. They drive me crazy. Now, I don't wanna
wreck your Saturday night for you, Angie. You wanna go somewhere, you go ahead. I don't wanna go.

ANGIE   Boy, they drive me crazy too. My old lady, every word outta
her mouth, when you gonna get married?

MARTY   My mother, boy, she drives me crazy.

*ANGIE leans back in his seat, scowls at the paper-napkin con-
tainer. MARTY returns to the sports page. For a moment a silence
hangs between them. Then . . .*

ANGIE   So what do you feel like doing tonight?

MARTY (*Without looking up*) I don't know. What do you feel like
doing?

*They both just sit, ANGIE frowning at the napkin container,
MARTY at the sports page.*

*The camera slowly moves away from the booth, looks down the
length of the bar, up the wall, past the clock—which reads ten
to five—and over to the television screen, where the baseball
game is still going on.*

*Dissolve slowly to: The television screen, now blank. The clock
now reads a quarter to six.*

*Back in the booth, MARTY now sits alone. In front of him are
three empty beer bottles and a beer glass, half filled. He is sitting there, his face expressionless, but his eyes troubled. Then
he pushes himself slowly out of the booth and shuffles to the
phone booth; he goes inside, closing the booth door carefully
after him. For a moment MARTY just sits squatly. Then with*

some exertion—due to the cramped quarters—he contrives to get a small address book out of his rear pants pocket. He slowly flips through it, finds the page he wants, and studies it, scowling; then he takes a dime from the change he has received, plunks it into the proper slot, waits for a dial tone . . . then carefully dials a number. . . . He waits. He is beginning to sweat a bit in the hot little booth, and his chest begins to rise and fall deeply.

MARTY (*With a vague pretense at good diction*) Hello, is this Mary Feeney? . . . Could I please speak to Miss Mary Feeney? . . . Just tell her an old friend . . . (*He waits again. With his free hand he wipes the gathering sweat from his brow.*) . . . Oh, hello there, is this Mary Feeney? Hello there, this is Marty Pilletti. I wonder if you recall me . . . Well, I'm kind of a stocky guy. The last time we met was inna movies, the RKO Chester. You was with another girl, and I was with a friend of mine named Angie. This was about a month ago. (*The girl apparently doesn't remember him. A sort of panic begins to seize* MARTY. *His voice rises a little.*) The RKO Chester on Payne Boulevard. You was sitting in front of us, and we was annoying you, and you got mad, and . . . I'm the fellow who works inna butcher shop . . . come on, you know who I am! . . . That's right, we went to Howard Johnson's and we had hamburgers. You hadda milk shake . . . Yeah, that's right. I'm the stocky one, the heavy-set fellow . . . Well, I'm glad you recall me, because I hadda swell time that night, and I was just wondering how everything was with you. How's everything? . . . That's swell . . . Yeah, well, I'll tell you why I called . . . I was figuring on taking in a movie tonight, and I was wondering if you and your friend would care to see a movie tonight with me and my friend . . . (*His eyes are closed now.*) Yeah, tonight. I know it's pretty late to call for a date, but I didn't know myself till . . . Yeah, I know, well how about . . . Yeah, I know, well maybe next Saturday night? You free next Saturday night? . . . Well, how about the Saturday after that? Yeah, I know . . . Yeah . . . Yeah . . . Oh, I understand, I mean . . .

He just sits now, his eyes closed, not really listening. After a moment he returns the receiver to its cradle and sits, his shoulders slack, his hands resting listlessly in the lap of his spotted, white apron. . . . Then he opens his eyes, straightens himself, pushes the booth door open, and advances out into the bar. He perches on a stool across the bar from the BAR-TENDER, *who looks up from his magazine.*

BARTENDER   I hear your kid brother got married last week, Marty.

MARTY (*Looking down at his hands on the bar*) Yeah, it was a very nice affair.

BARTENDER   Well, Marty, when you gonna get married?

MARTY *tenders the* BARTENDER *a quick scowl, gets off his perch, and starts for the door—untying his apron as he goes.*

MARTY   If my mother calls up, Lou, tell her I'm on my way home.

Dissolve to: MARTY'S *mother and a young couple sitting around the table in the dining room of* MARTY'S *home. The mother is a round, dark effusive little woman. The young couple—we will soon find out—are* THOMAS, MARTY'S *cousin, and his wife,* VIRGINIA. *They have apparently just been telling the* MOTHER *some sad news, and the three are sitting around frowning.*

The dining room is a crowded room filled with chairs and lamps, pictures and little statues, perhaps even a small grotto of little vigil lamps. To the right of the dining room is the kitchen, old-fashioned, Italian, steaming, and overcrowded. To the left of the dining room is the living room, furnished in same fashion as the dining room. Just off the living room is a small bedroom, which is MARTY'S. *This bedroom and the living room have windows looking out on front. The dining room has windows looking out to side alleyway. A stairway in the dining room leads to the second floor.*

MOTHER (*After a pause*) Well, Thomas, I knew sooner or later this was gonna happen. I told Marty, I said: "Marty, you watch. There's gonna be real trouble over there in your cousin Thomas' house." Because your mother was here, Thomas, you know?

THOMAS   When was this, Aunt Theresa?

MOTHER   This was one, two, three days ago. Wednesday, and I came home. And I come arounna back, and there's your mother sitting onna steps onna porch. And I said: "Catherine, my sister, wadda you doing here?" And she look uppa me, and she beganna cry.

THOMAS (*To his wife*) Wednesday. That was the day you threw the milk bottle.

MOTHER   That's right. Because I said to her: "Catherine, watsa matter?" And she said to me: "Theresa, my daughter-in-law Virginia, she just threw the milk bottle at me."

VIRGINIA   Well, you see what happen, Aunt Theresa . . .

MOTHER   I know, I know . . .

VIRGINIA   She comes inna kitchen, and she begins poking her head over my shoulder here and poking her head over my shoulder there . . .

MOTHER   I know, I know . . .

VIRGINIA   And she begins complaining about this, and she begins complaining about that. And she got me so nervous, I spilled some milk I was making for the baby. You see, I was making some food for the baby, and . . .

MOTHER   So I said to her, "Catherine . . ."

VIRGINIA   So, she got me so nervous I spilled some milk. So she said: "You're spilling the milk." She says: "Milk costs twenny-four cents a bottle. Wadda you, a banker?" So I said: "Mamma, leave me alone, please. You're making me nervous. Go on in the other room and turn on the television set." So then she began telling me how I waste money, and how I can't cook, and how I'm raising my baby all wrong, and she kept talking about these couple of drops of milk I spilt, and I got so mad, I said: "Mamma, you wanna see me really spill some milk?" So I took the bottle and threw it against the door. I didn't throw it at her. That's just something she made up. I didn't throw it anywheres near her. Well, of course, alla milk went all over the floor. The whole twenny-four cents. Well, I was sorry right away, you know, but she ran outta the house.
  Pause.

MOTHER   Well, I don't know what you want me to do, Virginia. If you want me, I'll go talk to her tonight.
  THOMAS *and* VIRGINIA *suddenly frown and look down at their hands as if of one mind.*

THOMAS   Well, I'll tell you, Aunt Theresa . . .

VIRGINIA   Lemme tell it, Tommy.

THOMAS   Okay.

VIRGINIA   (*Leaning forward to the* MOTHER) We want you to do a very big favour for us, Aunt Theresa.

MOTHER   Sure.

VIRGINIA   Aunt Theresa, you got this big house here. You got four
bedrooms upstairs. I mean, you got this big house just for you
and Marty. All your other kids are married and got their own
homes. And I thought maybe Tommy's mother could come here
and live with you and Marty.

MOTHER   Well . . .

VIRGINIA   She's miserable living with Tommy and me, and you're
the only one that gets along with her. Because I called up
Tommy's brother, Joe, and I said: "Joe, she's driving me crazy.
Why don't you take her for a couple of years?" And he said:
"Oh, no!" I know I sound like a terrible woman . . .

MOTHER   No, Virginia, I know how you feel. My husband, may God
bless his memory, his mother, she lived with us for a long time,
and I know how you feel.

VIRGINIA   (*Practically on the verge of tears*) I just can't stand it no
more! Every minute of the day! Do this! Do that! I don't have
ten minutes alone with my husband! We can't even have a fight!
We don't have no privacy! Everybody's miserable in our house!

THOMAS   All right, Ginnie, don't get so excited.

MOTHER   She's right. She's right. Young husband and wife, they
should have their own home. And my sister, Catherine, she's my
sister, but I gotta admit she's an old goat. And plenty-a times in
my life I feel like throwing the milk bottle at her myself. And I
tell you now, as far as I'm concerned, if Catherine wantsa come
live here with me and Marty, it's all right with me.

VIRGINIA *promptly bursts into tears.*

THOMAS   (*Not far from tears himself, lowers his face*) That's very
nice-a you, Aunt Theresa.

MOTHER   We gotta ask Marty, of course, because this is his house
too. But he's gonna come home any minute.

VIRGINIA   (*Having mastered her tears*) That's very nice-a you, Aunt
Theresa.

MOTHER   (*Rising*) Now, you just sit here. I'm just gonna turn onna
small fire under the food.
She exits to the kitchen.

VIRGINIA   (Calling after her) We gotta go right away because I promised the baby-sitter we'd be home by six, and it's after six
now . . .
She kind of fades out. A moment of silence. THOMAS *takes out
a cigarette and lights it.*

THOMAS (*Calling to his aunt in the kitchen*) How's Marty been lately, Aunt Theresa?

MOTHER (*Off in kitchen*) Oh, he's fine. You know a nice girl he can marry? (*She comes back into the dining room, wiping her hands on a kitchen towel.*) I'm worried about him, you know? He's thirty-seven in January.

THOMAS   Oh, he'll get married, don't worry, Aunt Theresa.

MOTHER (*Sitting down again*) Well, I don't know. You know a place where he can go where he can find a bride?

THOMAS   The Waverly Ballroom. That's a good place to meet girls, Aunt Theresa. That's a kind of big dance hall, Aunt Theresa. Every Saturday night, it's just loaded with girls. It's a nice place to go. You pay seventy-seven cents. It used to be seventy-seven cents. It must be about a buck and a half now. And you go in and ask some girl to dance. That's how I met Virginia. Nice, respectable place to meet girls. You tell Marty, Aunt Theresa, you tell him: "Go to the Waverly Ballroom. It's loaded with tomatoes."

MOTHER (*Committing the line to memory*) The Waverly Ballroom. It's loaded with tomatoes.

THOMAS   Right.

VIRGINIA   You tell him, go to the Waverly Ballroom.

There is the sound of a door being unlatched off through the kitchen. The MOTHER *promptly rises.*

MOTHER   He's here.

She hurries into the kitchen. At the porch entrance to the kitchen, MARTY *has just come in. He is closing the door behind him. He carries his butcher's apron under his arm.*

MARTY   Hello, Ma.

She comes up to him, lowers her voice to a whisper.

MOTHER (*Whispers*) Marty, Thomas and Virginia are here. They had another big fight with your Aunt Catherine. So they ask me, would it be all right if Catherine come to live with us. So I said, all right with me, but we have to ask you, Marty, she's a lonely old lady. Nobody wants her. Everybody's throwing her outta their house . . .

MARTY   Sure, Ma, it's okay with me.

The MOTHER'S *face breaks into a fond smile. She reaches up and pats his cheek with genuine affection.*

MOTHER   You gotta good heart. (*Turning and leading the way back to the dining room.* THOMAS *has risen.*) He says okay, it's all right Catherine comes here.

THOMAS   Oh, Marty, thanks a lot. That really takes a load offa my mind.

MARTY   Oh, we got plenty-a room here.

MOTHER   Sure! Sure! It's gonna be nice! It's gonna be nice! I'll come over tonight to your house, and I talk to Catherine, and you see, everything is gonna work out all right.

THOMAS   I just wanna thank you people again because the situation was just becoming impossible.

MOTHER   Siddown, Thomas, siddown. All right, Marty, siddown . . .

She exits into the kitchen. MARTY *has taken his seat at the head of the table and is waiting to be served.* THOMAS *takes a seat around the corner of the table from him and leans across to him.*

THOMAS   You see, Marty, the kinda thing that's been happening in our house is Virginia was inna kitchen making some food for the baby. Well, my mother comes in, and she gets Virginia so nervous, she spills a couple-a drops . . .

VIRGINIA   (*Tugging at her husband*) Tommy, we gotta go. I promised the baby-sitter six o'clock.

THOMAS   (*Rising without interrupting his narrative*) So she starts yelling at Virginia, "Waddaya spilling the milk for?" So Virginia gets mad . . . (*His wife is slowly pulling him to the kitchen door.*) She says, "You wanna really see me spill milk?" So Virginia takes the bottle and she throws it against the wall. She's got a real Italian temper, my wife, you know that . . .

He has been tugged to the kitchen door by now.

VIRGINIA   Marty, I don't have to tell you how much we appreciate what your mother and you are doing for us.

THOMAS   All right, Marty, I'll see you some other time . . . I'll tell you all about it.

MARTY   I'll see you, Tommy.

THOMAS *disappears into the kitchen after his wife.*

VIRGINIA   (*Off, calling*) Good-by, Marty!

Close in on MARTY, *sitting at table.*

MARTY   Good-by, Virginia! See you soon!

He folds his hands on the table before him and waits to be served. The MOTHER *enters from the kitchen. She sets the meat plate down in front of him and herself and takes a chair around the corner of the table from him.* MARTY *without a word takes up his knife and fork and attacks the mountain of food in front of him. His* MOTHER *sits quietly, her hands a little nervous on the table before her, watching him eat. Then . . .*

MOTHER   So what are you gonna do tonight, Marty?

MARTY   I don't know, Ma. I'm all knocked out. I may just hang arounna house.

The MOTHER *nods a couple of times. There is a moment of silence. Then . . .*

MOTHER   Why don't you go to the Waverly Ballroom?

This gives MARTY *pause. He looks up.*

MARTY   What?

MOTHER   I say, why don't you go to the Waverly Ballroom? It's loaded with tomatoes.

MARTY *regards his mother for a moment.*

MARTY   It's loaded with what?

MOTHER   Tomatoes.

MARTY   (*Snorts*) Ha! Who told you about the Waverly Ballroom?

MOTHER   Thomas, he told me it was a very nice place.

MARTY   Oh, Thomas. Ma, it's just a big dance hall, and that's all it is. I been there a hundred times. Loaded with tomatoes. Boy, you're funny, Ma.

MOTHER   Marty, I don't want you to hang arounna house tonight. I want you to go take a shave and go out and dance.

MARTY   Ma, when are you gonna give up? You gotta bachelor on your hands. I ain't never gonna get married.

MOTHER   You gonna get married.

MARTY   Sooner or later, there comes a point in a man's life when he gotta face some facts, and one fact I gotta face is that whatever it is that women like, I ain't got it. I chased enough girls in my life. I went to enough dances. I got hurt enough. I don't wanna get hurt no more. I just called a girl this afternoon, and I got a real brush-off, boy. I figured I was past the point of being hurt, but that hurt. Some stupid woman who I didn't even wanna call up. She gave me the brush. That's the history of my life. I don't wanna go to the Waverly Ballroom because all that ever happened to me there was girls made me feel like I was a bug. I got feelings, you know, I had enough pain. No, thank you.

MOTHER Marty . . .

MARTY Ma, I'm gonna stay home and watch Sid Caesar.

MOTHER You gonna die without a son.

MARTY So I'll die without a son.

MOTHER Put on your blue suit . . .

MARTY Blue suit. I'm still a fat, little man. A fat, little, ugly man.

MOTHER You not ugly.

MARTY (*His voice rising*) I'm ugly . . . I'm ugly! . . . I'm UGLY!

MOTHER Marty . . .

MARTY (*Crying aloud, more in anguish than in anger*) Ma! Leave me alone!

He stands abruptly, his face pained and drawn. He makes half-formed gestures to his mother, but he can't find words at the moment. He turns and marches a few paces away, turns to his mother again.

MARTY Ma, waddaya want from me? Waddaya want from me? I'm miserable enough as it is! Leave me alone! I'll go to the Waverly Ballroom! I'll put onna blue suit and I'll go! And you know what I'm gonna get for my trouble? Heartache! A big night of heartache!

He sullenly marches back to his seat, sits down, picks up his fork, plunges it into the lasagna, and stuffs a mouthful into his mouth; he chews vigorously for a moment. It's impossible for him to remain angry long. After a while he is shaking his head and muttering.

MARTY Loaded with tomatoes . . . boy that's rich . . .

He plunges his fork in again. Camera pulls slowly away from him and his mother, who is seated—watching him.

FADE OUT

ACT TWO

*Fade in: Exterior, three-story building. Pan up to second floor . . .
bright neon lights reading "Waverly Ballroom" . . . The large, dirty
windows are open; and the sound of a fair-to-middling swing band
whooping it up comes out.*

*Dissolve to: Interior, Waverly Ballroom—large dance floor crowded
with jitterbugging couples, eight-piece combination hitting a loud
kick. Ballroom is vaguely dark, made so by papier-mâché over the
chandeliers to create alleged romantic effect. The walls are lined
with stags and girls, waiting singly and in small murmuring groups.
Noise and mumble and drone.*

*Dissolve to: Live shot—a row of stags along a wall. Camera dollies
slowly past each face, each staring out at the dance floor, watching in
his own manner of hungry eagerness. Short, fat, tall, thin stags. Some
pretend diffidence. Some exhibit patent hunger.*

Near the end of the line, we find MARTY *and* ANGIE, *freshly shaved
and groomed. They are leaning against the wall, smoking, watching
their more fortunate brethren out on the floor.*

ANGIE   Not a bad crowd tonight, you know?

MARTY   There was one nice-looking one there in a black dress and
  beads, but she was a little tall for me.

ANGIE   (*Looking down past* MARTY *along the wall right into the
  camera*) There's a nice-looking little short one for you right
  now.

MARTY   (*Following his gaze*) Where?

ANGIE   Down there. That little one there.

  *The camera cuts about eight faces down, to where the girls are
  now standing. Two are against the wall. One is facing them,
  with her back to the dance floor. This last is the one* ANGIE *has
  in mind. She is a cute little kid, about twenty, and she has a
  bright smile on—as if the other two girls are just amusing her
  to death.*

MARTY   Yeah, she looks all right from here.

ANGIE   Well, go on over and ask her. You don't hurry up, somebody
  else'll grab her.

  MARTY *scowls, shrugs.*

MARTY   Okay, let's go.

  *They slouch along past the eight stags, a picture of nonchalant
  unconcern. The three girls, aware of their approach, stiffen, and*

their chatter comes to a halt. ANGIE *advances to one of the girls along the wall.*

ANGIE   Waddaya say, you wanna dance? *The girl looks surprised— as if this were an extraordinary invitation to receive in this place—looks confounded at her two friends, shrugs, detaches, herself from the group, moves to the outer fringe of the pack of dancers, raises her hand languidly to dancing position, and awaits Angie with ineffable boredom.* MARTY *smiling shyly, addresses the* SHORT GIRL.

MARTY   Excuse me, would you care for this dance?

The SHORT GIRL *gives* MARTY *a quick glance of appraisal, then looks quickly at her remaining friend.*

SHORT GIRL   (*Not unpleasantly*) Sorry. I just don't feel like dancing just yet.

MARTY   Sure.

He turns and moves back past the eight stags, all of whom have covertly watched his attempt. He finds his old niche by the wall, leans there. A moment later he looks guardedly down to where the SHORT GIRL *and her friend are. A young, dapper boy is approaching the* SHORT GIRL. *He asks her to dance. The* SHORT GIRL *smiles, excuses herself to her friend, and follows the boy out onto the floor.* MARTY *turns back to watching the dancers bleakly. A moment later he is aware that someone on his right is talking to him. . . . He turns his head. It is a young man of about twenty-eight.*

MARTY   You say something to me?

YOUNG MAN   Yeah. I was asking you if you was here stag or with a girl.

MARTY   I'm stag.

YOUNG MAN   Well, I'll tell you. I got stuck onna blind date with a dog, and I just picked up a nice chick, and I was wondering how I'm gonna get ridda the dog. Somebody to take her home, you know what I mean? I'd be glad to pay you five bucks if you take the dog home for me.

MARTY   (*A little confused*) What?

YOUNG MAN   I'll take you over, and I'll introduce you as an old army buddy of mine, and then I'll cut out. Because I got this chick waiting for me out by the hatcheck, and I'll pay you five bucks.

MARTY (*Stares at the young man*) Are you kidding?

YOUNG MAN No, I'm not kidding.

MARTY You can't just walk off onna girl like that.

The YOUNG MAN *grimaces impatiently and moves down the line of stags. . . .* MARTY *watches him, still a little shocked at the proposition. About two stags down, the* YOUNG MAN *broaches his plan to another* STAG. *This* STAG, *frowning and pursing his lips, seems more receptive to the idea. . . . The* YOUNG MAN *takes out a wallet and gives the* STAG *a five-dollar bill. The* STAG *detaches himself from the wall and, a little ill at ease, follows the* YOUNG MAN *back past* MARTY *and into the lounge.* MARTY *pauses a moment and then, concerned, walks to the archway that separates the lounge from the ballroom and looks in.*

The lounge is a narrow room with a bar and booths. In contrast to the ballroom, it is brightly lighted—causing MARTY *to squint. In the second booth from the archway sits a girl, about twenty-eight. Despite the careful grooming that she has put into her cosmetics, she is blatantly plain. The* YOUNG MAN *and the* STAG *are standing, talking to her. She is looking up at the* YOUNG MAN, *her hands nervously gripping her Coca-Cola glass. We cannot hear what the* YOUNG MAN *is saying, but it is apparent that he is introducing his new-found buddy and is going through some cock-and-bull story about being called away on an emergency. The* STAG *is presented as her escort-to-be, who will see to it that she gets home safely. The* GIRL *apparently is not taken in at all by this, though she is trying hard not to seem affected.*

She politely rejects the STAG'S *company and will get home by herself, thanks for asking anyway. The* YOUNG MAN *makes a few mild protestations, and then he and the* STAG *leave the booth and come back to the archway from where* MARTY *has been watching the scene. As they pass* MARTY, *we overhear a snatch of dialogue.*

YOUNG MAN . . . In that case, as long as she's going home alone, give me the five bucks back. . . .

STAG . . . Look, Mac, you paid me five bucks. I was willing. It's my five bucks.

They pass on. MARTY *returns his attention to the* GIRL. *She is still sitting as she was, gripping and ungripping the glass of Coca-Cola in front of her. Her eyes are closed. Then, with a little nervous shake of her head, she gets out of the booth and stands—momentarily at a loss for what to do next. The open fire doors leading out into the large fire escape catch her eye. She crosses to the fire escape, nervous, frowning, and disappears outside.*

MARTY *stares after her, then slowly shuffles to the open fire-escape doorway. It is a large fire escape, almost the size of a small balcony. The* GIRL *is standing by the railing, her back to the doorway, her head slung down on her chest. For a moment* MARTY *is unaware that she is crying. Then he notices the shivering tremors running through her body and the quivering shoulders. He moves a step onto the fire escape. He tries to think of something to say.*

MARTY   Excuse me, Miss. Would you care to dance?
The GIRL *slowly turns to him, her face streaked with tears, her lips trembling. Then, in one of those peculiar moments of simultaneous impulse, she lurches to* MARTY *with a sob, and* MARTY *takes her to him. For a moment they stand in an awkward embrace,* MARTY *a little embarrassed, looking out through the doors to the lounge, wondering if anybody is seeing them. Reaching back with one hand, he closes the fire doors, and then, replacing the hand around her shoulder, he stands stiffly, allowing her to cry on his chest.*

Dissolve to: Exterior, apartment door. The MOTHER *is standing, in a black coat and a hat with a little feather, waiting for her ring to be answered. The door opens.* VIRGINIA *stands framed in the doorway.*

VIRGINIA   Hello, Aunt Theresa, come in.
MOTHER   (*In a low voice, as she pulls her coat off*) Is Catherine here?
VIRGINIA   (*Helps her off with coat, nods—also in a low voice*) We didn't tell her nothing yet. We thought we'd leave it to you. We thought you'd put it like how you were lonely, and why don't she come to live with you. Because that way it looks like she's doing you a favor, insteada we're throwing her out, and it won't be so cruel on her. Thomas is downstairs with the neighbors . . . I'll go call him.
MOTHER   You go downstairs to the neighbors and stay there with Thomas.

VIRGINIA   Wouldn't it be better if we were here?

MOTHER   You go downstairs. I talk to Catherine alone. Otherwise, she's gonna start a fight with you.

A shrill, imperious woman's voice from an off-stage room suddenly breaks into the muttered conference in the foyer.

AUNT   (*Off*) Who's there? Who's there?

The MOTHER *heads up the foyer to the living room, followed by* VIRGINIA, *holding the* MOTHER'S *coat.*

MOTHER (*Calls back*)   It's me, Catherine! How you feel?

At the end of the foyer, the two sisters meet. The AUNT *is a spare, gaunt woman with a face carved out of granite. Tough, embittered, deeply hurt type of face.*

AUNT   Hey! What are you doing here?

MOTHER   I came to see you. (*The two sisters quickly embrace and release each other.*) How you feel?

AUNT   I gotta pain in my left side and my leg throbs like a drum.

MOTHER   I been getting pains in my shoulder.

AUNT   I got pains in my shoulder, too. I have a pain in my hip, and my right arm aches so much I can't sleep. It's a curse to be old. How you feel?

MOTHER   I feel fine.

AUNT   That's nice.

Now that the standard greetings are over, AUNT CATHERINE *abruptly turns and goes back to her chair. It is obviously her chair. It is an old, heavy, oaken chair with thick armrests. The rest of the apartment is furnished in what is known as "modern" —a piece from* House Beautiful *here, a piece from* Better Homes and Gardens *there.* AUNT CATHERINE *sits, erect and forbidding, in her chair. The mother seats herself with a sigh in a neighboring chair.* VIRGINIA, *having hung the* MOTHER'S *coat, now turns to the two older women. A pause.*

VIRGINIA   I'm going downstairs to the Cappacini's. I'll be up inna little while. (AUNT CATHERINE *nods expressionlessly.* VIRGINIA *looks at her for a moment, then impulsively crosses to her mother-in-law.*) You feel all right?

The old lady looks up warily, suspicious of this sudden solicitude.

AUNT   I'm all right.

VIRGINIA *nods and goes off to the foyer. The two old sisters sit, unmoving, waiting for the door to close behind* VIRGINIA. *Then the* MOTHER *addresses herself to* AUNT CATHERINE.

MOTHER   We gotta postcard from my son, Nickie, and his bride this morning. They're in Florida inna big hotel. Everything is very nice.

AUNT   That's nice.

MOTHER   Catherine, I want you come live with me in my house with Marty and me. In my house, you have your own room. You don't have to sleep onna couch inna living room like here. (*The* AUNT *looks slowly and directly at the* MOTHER.) Catherine, your son is married. He got his own home. Leave him in peace. He wants to be alone with his wife. They don't want no old lady sitting inna balcony. Come and live with me. We will cook in the kitchen and talk like when we were girls. You are dear to me, and you are dear to Marty. We are pleased for you to come.

AUNT   Did they come to see you?

MOTHER   Yes.

AUNT   Did my son Thomas come with her?

MOTHER   Your son Thomas was there.

AUNT   Did he also say he wishes to cast his mother from his house?

MOTHER   Catherine, don't make an opera outta this. The three-a you anna baby live in three skinny rooms. You are an old goat, and she has an Italian temper. She is a good girl, but you drive her crazy. Leave them alone. They have their own life.

The old AUNT *turns her head slowly and looks at her sister square in the face. Then she rises slowly from her chair.*

AUNT   (*Coldly*) Get outta here. This is my son's house. This is where I live. I am not to be cast out inna street like a newspaper.

The MOTHER *likewise rises. The two old women face each other directly.*

MOTHER   Catherine, you are very dear to me. We have cried many times together. When my husband died, I would have gone insane if it were not for you. I ask you to come to my house because I can make you happy. Please come to my house.

The two sisters regard each other. Then AUNT CATHERINE *sits again in her oaken chair, and the* MOTHER *returns to her seat.*

The hardened muscles in the old AUNT'S *face suddenly slacken, and she turns to her sister.*

AUNT   Theresa, what shall become of me?

MOTHER   Catherine . . .

AUNT   It's gonna happen to you. Mark it well. These terrible years. I'm afraida look inna mirror. I'm afraid I'm gonna see an old lady with white hair, like the old ladies inna park, little bundles inna black shawl, waiting for the coffin. I'm fifty-six years old. What am I to do with myself? I wanna make dinner for my children. I wanna be of use to somebody. Am I an old dog to lie in fronta the fire till my eyes close? These are terrible years, Theresa! Terrible years!

MOTHER   Catherine, my sister . . .

The old AUNT *stares, distraught, at the* MOTHER.

AUNT   It's gonna happen to you! It's gonna happen to you! What will you do if Marty gets married? What will you cook? What happen alla children tumbling in alla rooms? Where is the noise? It is a curse to be a widow! A curse! What will you do if Marty gets married? What will you do?

She stares at the MOTHER—*her deep, gaunt eyes haggard and pained. The* MOTHER *stares back for a moment, then her own eyes close. The* AUNT *has hit home. The* AUNT *sinks back onto her chair, sitting stiffly, her arms on the thick armrests. The* MOTHER *sits hunched a little forward, her hands nervously folded in her lap.*

AUNT   (*Quietly*) I will put my clothes inna bag and I will come to you tomorrow.

The camera slowly dollies back from the two somber sisters. Fade-out.

Cut to: Close-up, intimate, MARTY *and the* GIRL *dancing cheek to cheek. Occasionally the heads of other couples slowly waft across the camera view, temporarily blocking out view of* MARTY *and the* GIRL. *Camera stays with them as the slow dance carries them around the floor.*

GIRL   . . . The last time I was here the same sort of thing happened.

MARTY   Yeah?

GIRL   Well, not exactly the same thing. The last time I was up here was about four months ago. Do you see that girl in the gray dress sitting over there?

MARTY   Yeah.

GIRL   That's where I sat. I sat there for an hour and a half without moving a muscle. Now and then, some fellow would sort of walk up to me and then change his mind. I just sat there, my hands in my lap. Well, about ten o'clock, a bunch of kids came in swaggering. They weren't more than seventeen, eighteen years old. Well, they swaggered down along the wall, leering at all the girls. I thought they were kind of cute . . . and as they passed me, I smiled at them. One of the kids looked at me and said: "Forget it, ugly, you ain't gotta chance." I burst out crying. I'm a big crier, you know.

MARTY   So am I.

GIRL   And another time when I was in college . . .

MARTY   I cry alla time. Any little thing. I can recognize pain a mile away. My brothers, my brother-in-laws, they're always telling me what a good-hearted guy I am. Well, you don't get good-hearted by accident. You get kicked around long enough you get to be a real professor of pain. I know exactly how you feel. And I also want you to know I'm having a very good time with you now and really enjoying myself. So you see, you're not such a dog as you think you are.

GIRL   I'm having a very good time, too.

MARTY   So there you are. So I guess I'm not such a dog as I think I am either.

GIRL   You're a very nice guy, and I don't know why some girl hasn't grabbed you off long ago.

MARTY   I don't know either. I think I'm a very nice guy. I also think I'm a pretty smart guy in my own way.

GIRL   I think you are.

MARTY   I'll tell you some of my wisdom which I thunk up on those nights when I got stood up, and nights like that, and you walk home thinking: "Whatsa matter with me? I can't be that ugly." Well, I figure, two people get married, and they gonna live together forty, fifty years. So it's just gotta be more than whether they're good-looking or not. My father was a real ugly man, but my mother adored him. She told me that she used to get so miserable sometimes like everybody, you know? And she says my father always tried to understand. I used to see them sometimes, when I was a kid, sitting in the living room, talking and talking, and I used to adore my old man because he was so kind. That's one of the most beautiful things I have in my life, the way my father and my mother were. And my father was a real ugly man. So it don't matter if you look like a gorilla. So you see, dogs like us, we really ain't such dogs as we think we are. *They dance silently for a moment, cheeks pressed against each other. Close-ups of each face.*

GIRL   I'm twenty-nine years old. How old are you?

MARTY   Thirty-six.

They dance silently, closely. Occasionally the heads of other couples sway in front of the camera, blocking our view of MARTY *and the* GIRL. *Slow, sweet dissolve.*

Dissolve to: Interior, kitchen, MARTY'S *home. Later that night. It is dark. Nobody is home. The rear porch door now opens, and the silhouettes of* MARTY *and the* GIRL *appear—blocking up the doorway.*

MARTY   Wait a minute. Lemme find the light. (*He finds the light. The kitchen is suddenly brightly lit. The two of them stand squinting to adjust to the sudden glare*). I guess my mother ain't home yet. I figure my cousin Thomas and Virginia musta gone to the movies, so they won't get back till one o'clock, at least. (*The* GIRL *has advanced into the kitchen, a little ill at ease, and is looking around.* MARTY *closes the porch door.*) This is the kitchen.

GIRL   Yes, I know.

MARTY *leads the way into the dining room.*

MARTY   Come on inna dining room. (*He turns on the light in there as he goes. The* GIRL *follows him in.*) Siddown, take off your coat. You want something to eat? We gotta whole halfa chicken left over from yesterday.

GIRL   (*Perching tentatively on the edge of a chair*) No thank you. I don't think I should stay very long.

MARTY   Sure. Just take off your coat a minute.

He helps her off with her coat and stares down at her. Conscious of his scrutiny, she sits uncomfortably, her chest rising and falling unevenly. MARTY *takes her coat into the dark living room. The* GIRL *sits patiently, nervously.* MARTY *comes back, sits down on another chair. Awkward silence.*

MARTY   So I was telling you, my kid brother Nickie got married last Sunday. . . . That was a very nice affair. And they had this statue of some woman, and they had whisky spouting outta her mouth. I never saw anything so grand in my life. (*The silence falls between them again.*) And watta meal. I'm a butcher, so I know a good hunka steak when I see one. That was choice filet, right off the toppa the chuck. A buck-eighty a pound. Of course, if you wanna cheaper cut, get rib steak. That gotta lotta waste on it, but it comes to about a buck and a quarter a pound, if it's trimmed. Listen, Clara, make yourself comfortable. You're all tense.

GIRL   Oh, I'm fine.

MARTY   You want me to take you home, I'll take you home.

GIRL   Maybe that would be a good idea.

She stands. He stands, frowning, a little angry—turns sullenly and goes back into the living room for her coat. She stands unhappily. He comes back and wordlessly starts to help her into her coat. He stands behind her, his hands on her shoulders. He suddenly seizes her, begins kissing her on the neck. Camera comes up quickly to intensely intimate close-up, nothing but the heads. The dialogue drops to quick, hushed whispers.

GIRL   No, Marty, please.

MARTY   I like you, I like you, I been telling you all night I like you . . .

GIRL   Marty . . .

MARTY   I just wanna kiss, that's all . . .

He tries to turn her face to him. She resists.

GIRL   No . . .

MARTY   Please . . .

GIRL   No . . .

MARTY   Please . . .

GIRL   Marty . . .

He suddenly releases her, turns away violently.

MARTY   (*Crying out*) All right I'll take you home! (*He marches a few angry paces away, deeply disturbed. Turns to her.*) All I wanted was a lousy kiss! What am I, a leper or something?

He turns and goes off into the living room to hide the flush of hot tears threatening to fill his eyes. The GIRL stands, herself on the verge of tears.

GIRL (*Mutters, more to herself than to him*) I just didn't feel like it, that's all.

She moves slowly to the archway leading to the living room. MARTY is sitting on the couch, hands in his lap, looking straight ahead. The room is dark except for the overcast of the dining-room light reaching in. The GIRL goes to the couch, perches on the edge beside him. He doesn't look at her.

MARTY   Well, that's the history of my life. I'm a little, short, fat, ugly guy. Comes New Year's Eve, everybody starts arranging parties, I'm the guy they gotta dig up a date for. I'm old enough to know better. Let me get a packa cigarettes, and I'll take you home. *He starts to rise, but doesn't . . . sinks back onto the couch, looking straight ahead. The GIRL looks at him, her face peculiarly soft and compassionate.*

GIRL   I'd like to see you again, very much. The reason I didn't let you kiss me was because I just didn't know how to handle the situation. You're the kindest man I've ever met. The reason I tell you this is because I want to see you again very much. Maybe, I'm just so desperate to fall in love that I'm trying too hard. But I know that when you take me home, I'm going to just lie on my bed and think about you. I want very much to see you again.

MARTY stares down at his hands in his lap.

MARTY (*Without looking at her*) Waddaya doing tomorrow night?

GIRL   Nothing.

MARTY   I'll call you up tomorrow morning. Maybe we'll go see a movie.

GIRL   I'd like that very much.

MARTY   The reason I can't be definite about it now is my Aunt Catherine is probably coming over tomorrow, and I may have to help out.

GIRL   I'll wait for your call.

MARTY   We better get started to your house because the buses only run about one an hour now.

GIRL   All right. (*She stands.*)

MARTY   I'll just get a packa cigarettes.

He goes into his bedroom. We can see him through the doorway, opening his bureau drawer and extracting a pack of cigarettes. He comes out again and looks at the GIRL for the first time.

They start to walk to the dining room. In the archway, MARTY *pauses, turns to the* GIRL.

MARTY   Waddaya doing New Year's Eve?

GIRL   Nothing.

They quietly slip into each other's arms and kiss. Slowly their faces part, and MARTY'S *head sinks down upon her shoulder. He is crying. His shoulders shake slightly. The* GIRL *presses her cheek against the back of his head. They stand . . . There is the sound of the rear porch door being unlatched. They both start from their embrace. A moment later the* MOTHER'S *voice is heard off in the kitchen.*

MOTHER   Hallo! Hallo! Marty? (*She comes into the dining room, stops at the sight of the* GIRL.) Hallo, Marty, when you come home?

MARTY   We just got here about fifteen minutes ago, Ma. Ma, I want you to meet Miss Clara Davis. She's a graduate of New York University. She teaches history in Benjamin Franklin High School.

This seems to impress the MOTHER.

MOTHER   Siddown, siddown. You want some chicken? We got some chicken in the icebox.

GIRL   No, Mrs. Pilletti, we were just going home. Thank you very much anyway.

MOTHER   Well, siddown a minute. I just come inna house. I'll take off my coat. Siddown a minute.

She pulls her coat off.

MARTY   How'd you come home, Ma? Thomas give you a ride?

The MOTHER *nods.*

MOTHER   Oh, it's a sad business, a sad business.

She sits down on a dining-room chair, holding her coat in her lap. She turns to the GIRL, *who likewise sits.*

MOTHER   My sister Catherine, she don't get along with her daughter-in-law, so she's gonna come live with us.

MARTY   Oh, she's coming, eh, Ma?

MOTHER   Oh, sure. (*To the girl*) It's a very sad thing. A woman, fifty-six years old, all her life, she had her own home. Now, she's just an old lady, sleeping on her daughter-in-law's couch. It's a curse to be a mother, I tell you. Your children grow up and then what is left for you to do? What is a mother's life but her

children? It is a very cruel thing when your son has no place
for you in his home.

GIRL   Couldn't she find some sort of hobby to fill out her time?

MOTHER   Hobby! What can she do? She cooks and she cleans. You
gotta have a house to clean. You gotta have children to cook
for. These are the terrible years for a woman, the terrible years.

GIRL   You mustn't feel too harshly against her daughter-in-law. She
also wants to have a house to clean and a family to cook for.

The MOTHER *darts a quick, sharp look at the* GIRL—*then looks
back to her hands, which are beginning to twist nervously.*

MOTHER   You don't think my sister Catherine should live in her
daughter-in-law's house?

GIRL   Well, I don't know the people, of course, but, as a rule, I don't
think a mother-in-law should live with a young couple.

MOTHER   Where do you think a mother-in-law should go?

GIRL   I don't think a mother should depend so much upon her children for her rewards in life.

MOTHER   That's what it says in the book in New York University.
You wait till you are a mother. It don't work out that way.

GIRL   Well, it's silly for me to argue about it. I don't know the
people involved.

MARTY   Ma, I'm gonna take her home now. It's getting late, and the
buses only run about one an hour.

MOTHER   (*Standing*) Sure.

The GIRL *stands.*

GIRL   It was very nice meeting you, Mrs. Pilletti. I hope I'll see you
again.

MOTHER   Sure.

MARTY *and the* GIRL *move to the kitchen.*

MARTY   All right, Ma. I'll be back in about an hour.

MOTHER   Sure.

GIRL   Good night, Mrs. Pilletti.

MOTHER   Good night.

MARTY *and the* GIRL *exit into the kitchen. The* MOTHER *stands,
expressionless, by her chair watching them go. She remains
standing rigidly even after the porch door can be heard being
opened and shut. The camera moves up to a close-up of the*
MOTHER. *Her eyes are wide. She is staring straight ahead. There
is fear in her eyes.*

FADE OUT

ACT THREE

Fade in: Film—close-up of church bells clanging away. Pan down church to see typical Sunday morning, people going up the steps of a church and entering. It is a beautiful June morning.

Dissolve to: Interior, MARTY'S *bedroom—sun fairly streaming through the curtains.* MARTY *is standing in front of his bureau, slipping his arms into a clean white shirt. He is freshly shaved and groomed. Through the doorway of his bedroom we can see the* MOTHER *in the dining room, in coat and hat, all set to go to Mass, taking the last breakfast plates away and carrying them into the kitchen. The camera moves across the living room into the dining room. The* MOTHER *comes out of the kitchen with a paper napkin and begins crumbing the table. There is a knock on the rear porch door. The* MOTHER *leaves her crumbing and goes into the kitchen. Camera goes with her. She opens the rear door to admit* AUNT CATHERINE, *holding a worn, old, European carpetbag. The* AUNT *starts to go deeper into the kitchen, but the* MOTHER *stays her with her hand.*

MOTHER (*In low, conspiratorial voice*) Hey, I come home from your house last night, Marty was here with a girl.

AUNT   Who?

MOTHER   Marty.

AUNT   Your son Marty?

MOTHER   Well, what Marty you think is gonna be here in this house with a girl?

AUNT   Were the lights on?

MOTHER   Oh, sure. (*Frowns suddenly at her sister*) The girl is a college graduate.

AUNT   They're the worst. College girls are one step from the streets. They smoke like men inna saloon.

The AUNT *puts her carpetbag down and sits on one of the wooden kitchen chairs. The* MOTHER *sits on another.*

MOTHER   That's the first time Marty ever brought a girl to this house. She seems like a nice girl. I think he has a feeling for this girl.

At this moment a burst of spirited whistling emanates from MARTY'S *bedroom.*

Cut to: MARTY'S *bedroom—*MARTY *standing in front of his mirror, buttoning his shirt and adjusting his tie, whistling a gay tune.*

Cut back to: The two sisters, both their faces turned in the direction of the whistling. The whistling abruptly stops. The two sisters look at each other. The AUNT *shrugs.*

MOTHER   He been whistling like that all morning.

The AUNT *nods bleakly.*

AUNT   He is bewitched. You will see. Today, tomorrow, inna week, he's gonna say to you: "Hey, Ma, it's no good being a single man. I'm tired running around." Then he's gonna say: "Hey, Ma, wadda we need this old house? Why don't we sell this old house, move to a nicer parta town? A nice little apartment?"

MOTHER   I don't sell this house, I tell you that. This is my husband's house, and I had six children in this house.

AUNT   You will see. A couple-a months, you gonna be an old lady, sleeping onna couch in your daughter-in-law's house.

MOTHER   Catherine, you are a blanket of gloom. Wherever you go, the rain follows. Some day, you gonna smile, and we gonna declare a holiday.

Another burst of spirited whistling comes from MARTY, *off. It comes closer, and* MARTY *now enters in splendid spirits, whistling away. He is slipping into his jacket.*

MARTY   (*Ebulliently*) Hello, Aunt Catherine! How are you? You going to Mass with us?

AUNT   I was at Mass two hours ago.

MARTY   Well, make yourself at home. The refrigerator is loaded with food. Go upstairs, take any room you want. It's beautiful outside, ain't it?

AUNT   There's a chill. Watch out, you catch a good cold and pneumonia.

MOTHER   My sister Catherine, she can't even admit it's a beautiful day.

MARTY, now at the sink, getting himself a glass of water—is examining a piece of plaster that has fallen from the ceiling.

MARTY   (*Examining the chunk of plaster in his palm*) Boy, this place is really coming to pieces. (*Turns to mother.*) You know, Ma, I think, sometime we oughtta sell this place. The plumbing is rusty—everything. I'm gonna have to replaster that whole ceiling now. I think we oughtta get a little apartment somewhere in a nicer parta town. . . . You all set, Ma?

MOTHER   I'm all set.

She starts for the porch door. She slowly turns and looks at MARTY, *and then at* AUNT CATHERINE—*who returns her look.* MOTHER *and* MARTY *exit.*

Dissolve to: Church. The MOTHER *comes out of the doors and down a few steps to where* MARTY *is standing, enjoying the clearness of the June morning.*

MOTHER   In a couple-a minutes nine o'clock Mass is gonna start— in a couple-a minutes. . . . (*To passers-by off*) Hallo, hallo. . . . (To MARTY) Well, that was a nice girl last night, Marty. That was a nice girl.

MARTY   Yeah.

MOTHER   She wasn't a very good-looking girl, but she look like a nice girl. I said, she wasn't a very good-looking girl, not very pretty.

MARTY   I heard you, Ma.

MOTHER   She look a little old for you, about thirty-five, forty years old?

MARTY   She's twenny-nine, Ma.

MOTHER   She's more than twenny-nine years old, Marty. That's what she tells you. She looks thirty-five, forty. She don't look Italian to me. I said, is she an Italian girl?

MARTY   I don't know. I don't think so.

MOTHER   She don't look like Italian to me. What kinda family she come from? There was something about her I don't like. It seems funny, the first time you meet her she comes to your empty house alone. These college girls, they all one step from the streets.

MARTY *turns, frowning, to his* MOTHER.

MARTY   What are you talkin' about? She's a nice girl.

MOTHER   I don't like her.

MARTY   You don't like her? You only met her for two minutes.

MOTHER   Don't bring her to the house no more.

MARTY   What didn't you like about her?

MOTHER   I don't know! She don't look like Italian to me, plenty nice Italian girls around.

MARTY   Well, let's not get into a fight about it, Ma. I just met the girl. I probably won't see her again.

MARTY *leaves frame.*

MOTHER   Eh, I'm no better than my sister Catherine.

Dissolve to: Interior, the bar . . . about an hour later. The after Mass crowd is there, about six men ranging from twenty to forty. A couple of women in the booths. One woman is holding a glass of beer in one hand and is gently rocking a baby carriage with the other. Sitting in the booth of Act One are ANGIE *and three other fellows, ages twenty, thirty-two, and forty. One of the fellows, aged thirty-two, is giving a critical résumé of a recent work of literature by Mickey Spillane.*

CRITIC . . . So the whole book winds up, Mike Hammer, he's inna room there with this doll. So he says: "You rat, you are the murderer." So she begins to con him, you know? She tells him how she loves him. And then, Bam! He shoots her in the stomach. So she's laying there, gasping for breath, and she says: "How could you do that?" And he says: "It was easy."

TWENTY-YEAR-OLD Boy, that Mickey Spillane. Boy, he can write.

ANGIE (*Leaning out of the booth and looking down the length of the bar, says, with some irritation*) What's keeping Marty?

CRITIC What I like about Mickey Spillane is he knows how to handle women. In one book, he picks up a tomato who gets hit with a car, and she throws a pass at him. And then he meets two beautiful twins, and they throw passes at him. And then he meets some beautiful society leader, and she throws a pass at him . . . and . . .

TWENTY-YEAR-OLD Boy, that Mickey Spillane, he sure can write . . .

ANGIE (*Looking out, down the bar again*) I don't know whatsa matter with Marty.

FORTY-YEAR-OLD Boy, Angie, what would you do if Marty ever died? You'd die right with him. A couple-a old bachelors hanging to each other like barnacles. There's Marty now.

ANGIE *leans out of the booth.*

ANGIE (*Calling out*) Hello, Marty, where you been?

Cut to: Front end of the bar. MARTY *has just come in. He waves back to* ANGIE, *acknowledges another hello from a man by the bar, goes over to the bar, and gets the* BARTENDER'S *attention.*

MARTY Hello, Lou, gimme change of a half and put a dime in it for a telephone call.

The BARTENDER *takes the half dollar, reaches into his apron pocket for the change.*

BARTENDER I hear you was at the Waverly Ballroom last night.

MARTY Yeah. Angie tell you?

BARTENDER (*Picking out change from palm full of silver*) Yeah, I hear you really got stuck with a dog.

MARTY She wasn't so bad.

BARTENDER (*Extending the change*) Angie says she was a real scrawny-looking thing. Well, you can't have good luck alla time. MARTY *takes the change slowly and frowns down at it. He moves down the bar and would make for the telephone booth, but* ANGIE *hails him from the booth.*

ANGIE   Who you gonna call, Marty?

MARTY   I was gonna call that girl from last night, take her to a movie tonight.

ANGIE   Are you kidding?

MARTY   She was a nice girl. I kinda liked her.

ANGIE   (*Indicating the spot in the booth vacated by the* FORTY-YEAR-OLD) Siddown. You can call her later.

> MARTY *pauses, frowning, and then shuffles to the booth where* ANGIE *and the other two sit. The* CRITIC *moves over for* MARTY. *There is an exchange of hellos as* MARTY *sits down.*

TWENTY-YEAR-OLD   I gotta girl, she's always asking me to marry her. So I look at that face, and I say to myself: "Could I stand looking at that face for the resta my life?"

CRITIC   Hey, Marty, you ever read a book called *I, the Jury,* by Mickey Spillane?

MARTY   No.

ANGIE   Listen, Marty, I gotta good place for us to go tonight. The kid here, he says, he was downna bazaar at Our Lady of Angels last night and . . .

MARTY   I don't feel like going to the bazaar, Angie. I thought I'd take this girl to a movie.

ANGIE   Boy, you really musta made out good last night.

MARTY   We just talked.

ANGIE   Boy, she must be some talker. She musta been about fifty years old.

CRITIC   I always figger a guy oughtta marry a girl who's twenny years younger than he is, so that when he's forty, his wife is a real nice-looking doll.

TWENTY-YEAR-OLD   That means he'd have to marry the girl when she was one year old.

CRITIC   I never thoughta that.

MARTY   I didn't think she was so bad-looking.

ANGIE   She musta kept you inna shadows all night.

CRITIC   Marty, you don't wanna hang around with dogs. It gives you a bad reputation.

ANGIE   Marty, let's go downna bazaar.

MARTY   I told this dog I was gonna call her today.

ANGIE   Brush her.

> MARTY *looks down at the dime he has been nervously turning between two fingers and then, frowning, he slips it into his jacket pocket. He lowers his face and looks down, scowling at his thoughts. Around him, the voices clip along.*

CRITIC   What's playing on Fordham Road? I think there's a good picture in the Loew's Paradise.

ANGIE   Let's go down to Forty-second Street and walk around. We're sure to wind up with something.

Slowly MARTY *begins to look up again. He looks from face to face as each speaks.*

CRITIC   I'll never forgive La Guardia for cutting burlesque outta New York City.

TWENTY-YEAR-OLD   There's burlesque over in Union City. Let's go to Union City. . . .

ANGIE   Ah, they're always crowded on Sunday night.

CRITIC   So wadda you figure on doing tonight, Angie?

ANGIE   I don't know. Wadda you figure on doing?

CRITIC   I don't know. (*Turns to the* TWENTY-YEAR-OLD.) Wadda you figure on doing? (*The* TWENTY-YEAR-OLD *shrugs.*)

Suddenly MARTY *brings his fist down on the booth table with a crash. The others turn, startled, toward him.* MARTY *rises.*

MARTY   "What are you doing tonight?" "I don't know, what are you doing?" Burlesque! Loew's Paradise! Miserable and lonely! Miserable and lonely and stupid! What am I, crazy or something? I got something good! What am I hanging around with you guys for?

He has said this in tones so loud that it attracts the attention of everyone in the bar. A little embarrassed, MARTY *turns and moves quickly to the phone booth, pausing outside the door to find his dime again.* ANGIE *is out of his seat immediately and hurries after him.*

ANGIE   (*A little shocked at* MARTY'S *outburst*) Whatsa matter with you?

MARTY   (*In a low, intense voice*) You don't like her. My mother don't like her. She's a dog, and I'm a fat, ugly, little man. All I know is I had a good time last night. I'm gonna have a good time tonight. If we have enough good times together, I'm going down on my knees and beg that girl to marry me. If we make a party again this New Year's, I gotta date for the party. You don't like her, that's too bad. (*He moves into the booth, sits, turns again to* ANGIE, *smiles.*) When you gonna get married, Angie? You're thirty-four years old. All your kid brothers are married. You oughtta be ashamed of yourself.

Still smiling at his private joke, he puts the dime into the slot and then—with a determined finger—he begins to dial.

FADE OUT

Further Suggestions for Study

1. Look carefully at Chayefsky's dialogue and try to find the secret of its realism.

2. If you were asked to re-write *Marty* as a typical soap-opera type of play, what changes would you make without altering the basic theme?

3. From the dialogue of the "so what do you feel like doing to-night" group, what did you learn of its attitudes?

4. Suggest the six most typical slice-of-life situations in the play.

5. If, after thinking about the play, you conclude that love should not be based purely on physical attraction, then on what should it be based?

6. Assuming that Marty and Clara do marry, what do you consider to be their chances, with conditions, for marital happiness?

7. If YOU were Marty's best friend, how would you talk him out of his defeatist attitude? Why was Marty a sad, little bachelor?

8. In what way is the Italian district of New York an ideal setting for the basic situation in the play?

9. How would you change the play if Marty were portrayed as a seventeen-year-old boy?

10. Assuming you were one of the judges who awarded *Marty* the Best Television Script Award, compose and deliver a three minute speech justifying your opinions.

Works of Paddy Chayefsky

Broadway Plays:
Middle of the Night
The Tenth Man
Gideon

Television Plays:
Marty (adapted from *Bachelor Party*)
The Goddess
Bachelor Party
Middle of the Night (adapted from the stage play)

A RAISIN IN THE SUN
BY LORRAINE HANSBERRY

Upper left: *WALTER: Ten thousand dollars . . .* (PHOTO: COLUMBIA PICTURES)

Upper right: *WALTER: Mama . . . you know what it means to climb up in the chariot?* (PHOTO: COLUMBIA PICTURES)

Lower: *MAMA: Oh, God . . . Look down here—and show me the strength.* (PHOTO: COLUMBIA PICTURES)

INTRODUCTION/*A Raisin in the Sun*

Audiences who left the theatre after seeing *A Raisin in the Sun* left silently. They left happily exhausted after an evening of laughter and tears. Not that this had been a "happy ending" play. The Younger family was left to face a new struggle as negroes settling in a white neighborhood. But at least there was the shining glow of Mama's optimism leading her pride-filled family into an unknown future.

Lorraine Hansberry, a young negro playwright, had set out to depict a negro family as "people." There had been enough plays and stories using negroes simply as stereotyped characters for yet another plot involving the color problem. But the Younger family is more than a proud, struggling, negro family. Each member symbolizes the eternal family unit in all its struggles and conflicting goals. Their crises transcend the injustices that face anyone born colored in a white world.

As we view or read the play we cannot help sharing the ulcer-producing crises of the Youngers: too many people living closely under one roof; the gnawing frustration of an insufficient weekly pay check; the need to preserve family pride in the face of sudden indignities; the fear of moving to a socially superior neighborhood with a minimum of money and a maximum of pride; the depressing realization that when poverty knocks at the door, love flies out through the window. Who cannot fail to share Walter's anguish as he cries out: "I'm thirty-five years old; I been married eleven years and I got a boy who sleeps in the living room—and all I got to give him is stories about how rich white people live . . ."?

The search for the "American Dream" of personal happiness through material success has been a constant theme threading its way through twentieth century literature. Theodore Dreiser wrestled with it in *An American Tragedy* (movie version: *A Place in the Sun*); John Braine portrayed it bitterly in his *Room at the Top;* Arthur Miller poignantly incorporated it in his modern tragedy, *The Death of a Salesman.* Lorraine Hansberry described the theme anew in *A Raisin in the Sun* by adding the frustrations of the negro trying to succeed in a white man's world.

What did Lorraine Hansberry do in her play to win the coveted New York Drama Critics' Award of Best American Play of 1958-1959? Could it be that she held the mirror up not only to the surface of life but to the secret, inner longings that every man and woman knows? Who has not felt the longing for self-realization, for a worthwhile purpose in life, for the dignity and joy that come with being accepted as oneself? Walter's cries for recognition echo in our minds long after we have left the theatre: "Nobody in this house is ever going to understand me . . . WILL SOMEBODY PLEASE LISTEN TO ME TODAY!"

A Raisin in the Sun was first presented in New York City, March 11, 1959, at the Ethel Barrymore Theatre with Ruby Dee as Ruth, Claudia McNeill as Mama, Diana Sands as Beneatha and Sidney Poitier as Walter Lee. The play was later made into a film starring members of the original stage cast.

As you read the play notice:

* The role of Mama as the anchor of the family.
* The fully rounded characterizations that reveal the good and the bad mosaic that makes up man.
* The conflicting goals of each member of the family.
* The sudden bursts of optimism and pessimism reflecting the moods of any real day in a man's life.

A RAISIN IN THE SUN

CHARACTERS

RUTH YOUNGER	JOSEPH ASAGAI
TRAVIS YOUNGER	GEORGE MURCHISON
WALTER LEE YOUNGER	KARL LINDER
BENEATHA YOUNGER	BOBO
LENA YOUNGER (MAMA)	MOVING MEN

ACT ONE

SCENE I

The YOUNGER *living room would be a comfortable and well-ordered room if it were not for a number of indestructible contradictions to this state of being. Its furnishings are typical and undistinguished and their primary feature now is that they have clearly had to accommodate the living of too many people for too many years—and they are tired. Still, we can see that at some time, a time probably no longer remembered by the family (except perhaps for* MAMA*) the furnishings of this room were actually selected with care and love and even hope—and brought to this apartment and arranged with taste and pride.*

That was a long time ago. Now the once loved pattern of the couch upholstery has to fight to show itself from under acres of crocheted doilies and couch covers which have themselves finally come to be more important than the upholstery. And here a table or a chair has been moved to disguise the worn places in the carpet; but the carpet has fought back by showing its weariness, with depressing uniformity, elsewhere on its surface.

Weariness has, in fact, won in this room. Everything has been polished, washed, sat on, used, scrubbed too often. All pretenses but living itself have long since vanished from the very atmosphere of this room.

Moreover, a section of this room, for it is not really a room unto itself, though the landlord's lease would make it seem so, slopes backward to provide a small kitchen area, where the family prepares the meals that are eaten in the living room proper, which must also serve as dining room. The single window that has been provided for these "two" rooms is located in this kitchen area. The sole natural light the family may enjoy in the course of a day is only that which fights its way through this little window.

At left, a door leads to a bedroom which is shared by MAMA *and her daughter,* BENEATHA. *At right, opposite, is a second room (which in the beginning of the life of this apartment was probably a breakfast room) which serves as a bedroom for* WALTER *and his wife,* RUTH.

Time: Sometime between World War II and the present.
Place: Chicago's Southside.

At Rise: It is morning dark in the living room. TRAVIS *is asleep on the make-down bed at center. An alarm clock sounds from within the bedroom at right, and presently* RUTH *enters from that room and closes the door behind her. She crosses sleepily toward the window. As she passes her sleeping son she reaches down and shakes him a little. At the window she raises the shade and a dusky Southside morning light comes in feebly. She fills a pot with water and puts it on to boil. She calls to the boy, between yawns, in a slightly muffled voice.*

RUTH *is about thirty. We can see that she was a pretty girl, even exceptionally so, but now it is apparent that life has been little that she expected, and disappointment has already begun to hang in her face. In a few years, before thirty-five even, she will be known among her people as a "settled woman."*

She crosses to her son and gives him a good, final, rousing shake.

RUTH   Come on now, boy, it's seven thirty! (*Her son sits up at last, in a stupor of sleepiness*) I say hurry up, Travis! You ain't the only person in the world got to use a bathroom! (*The child, a sturdy, handsome little boy of ten or eleven, drags himself out of the bed and almost blindly takes his towels and "today's clothes" from drawers and a closet and goes out to the bathroom, which is in an outside hall and which is shared by another family or families on the same floor.* RUTH *crosses to the bedroom door at right and opens it and calls in to her husband*) Walter Lee! . . . It's after seven thirty! Lemme see you do some waking up in there now! (*She waits*) You better get up from there, man! It's after seven thirty I tell you. (*She waits again*) All right, you just go ahead and lay there and next thing you know Travis be finished and Mr. Johnson'll be in there and you'll be fussing and cussing round here like a mad man! And be late too! (*She waits, at the end of patience*) Walter Lee—it's time for you to get up! *She waits another second and then starts to go into the bedroom, but is apparently satisfied that her husband has begun to get up. She stops, pulls the door to, and returns to the kitchen area. She wipes her face with a moist cloth and runs her fingers through her sleep-disheveled hair in a vain effort and ties an apron around her housecoat. The bedroom door at right opens and her husband stands in the doorway in his pajamas, which are rumpled and mismated. He is a lean, intense young man in his middle thirties, inclined to quick nervous movements and erratic speech habits—and always in his voice there is a quality of indictment.*

WALTER   Is he out yet?

RUTH   What you mean *out?* He ain't hardly got in there good yet.

WALTER   (*Wandering in, still more oriented to sleep than to a new day*) Well, what was you doing all that yelling for if I can't even get in there yet? (*Stopping and thinking*) Check coming today?

RUTH   They *said* Saturday and this is just Friday and I hopes to God you ain't going to get up here first thing this morning and start talking to me 'bout no money—'cause I 'bout don't want to hear it.

WALTER   Something the matter with you this morning?

RUTH   No—I'm just sleepy as the devil. What kind of eggs you want?

WALTER   Not scrambled. (RUTH *starts to scramble eggs*) Paper come? RUTH *points impatiently to the rolled up* Tribune *on the table, and he gets it and spreads it out and vaguely reads the front page*) Set off another bomb yesterday.

RUTH   (*Maximum indifference*) Did they?

WALTER   (*Looking up*) What's the matter with you?

RUTH   Ain't nothing the matter with me. And don't keep asking me that this morning.

WALTER   Ain't nobody bothering you. (*Reading the news of the day absently again*) Say Colonel McCormick is sick.

RUTH   (*Affecting tea-party interest*) Is he now? Poor thing.

WALTER   (*Sighing and looking at his watch*) Oh, me. (*He waits*) Now what is that boy doing in that bathroom all this time? He just going to have to start getting up earlier. I can't be being late to work on account of him fooling around in there.

RUTH   (*Turning on him*) Oh, no he ain't going to be getting up no earlier no such thing! It ain't his fault that he can't get to bed no

earlier nights 'cause he got a bunch of crazy good-for-nothing
clowns sitting up running their mouths in what is supposed to be
his bedroom after ten o'clock at night . . .

WALTER That's what you mad about, ain't it? The things I want to
talk about with my friends just couldn't be important in your
mind, could they?

*He rises and finds a cigarette in her handbag on the table and
crosses to the little window and looks out, smoking and deeply
enjoying this first one.*

RUTH (*Almost matter of factly, a complaint too automatic to deserve
emphasis*) Why you always got to smoke before you eat in the
morning?

WALTER (*At the window*) Just look at 'em down there . . . Running
and racing to work . . . (*He turns and faces his wife and watches
her a moment at the stove, and then, suddenly*) You look young
this morning, baby.

RUTH (*Indifferently*) Yeah?

WALTER Just for a second—stirring them eggs. It's gone now—just
for a second it was—you looked real young again. (*Then,
drily*) It's gone now—you look like yourself again.

RUTH Man, if you don't shut up and leave me alone.

WALTER (*Looking out to the street again*) First thing a man ought
to learn in life is not to make love to no colored woman first
thing in the morning. You all some evil people at eight o'clock
in the morning.

*TRAVIS appears in the hall doorway, almost fully dressed and
quite wide awake now, his towels and pajamas across his
shoulders. He opens the door and signals for his father to make
the bathroom in a hurry.*

TRAVIS (*Watching the bathroom*) Daddy, come on!

WALTER gets his bathroom utensils and flies out to the bathroom.

RUTH Sit down and have your breakfast, Travis.

TRAVIS Mama, this is Friday. (*Gleefully*) Check coming tomorrow,
huh?

RUTH You get your mind off money and eat your breakfast.

TRAVIS (*Eating*) This is the morning we supposed to bring the fifty
cents to school.

RUTH Well, I ain't got no fifty cents this morning.

TRAVIS Teacher say we have to.

RUTH   I don't care what teacher say. I ain't got it. Eat your breakfast, Travis.

TRAVIS   I *am* eating.

RUTH   Hush up now and just eat!

The boy gives her an exasperated look for her lack of understanding, and eats grudgingly.

TRAVIS   You think Grandmama would have it?

RUTH   No! And I want you to stop asking your grandmother for money, you hear me?

TRAVIS   (*Outraged*) Gaaaaleeee! I don't ask her, she just gimme it sometimes!

RUTH   Travis Willard Younger—I got too much on me this morning to be—

TRAVIS   Maybe Daddy—

RUTH   *Travis!*

The boy hushes abruptly. They are both quiet and tense for several seconds.

TRAVIS   (*Presently*) Could I maybe go carry some groceries in front of the supermarket for a little while after school then?

RUTH   Just hush, I said. (TRAVIS *jabs his spoon into his cereal bowl viciously, and rests his head in anger upon his fists*) If you through eating, you can get over there and make up your bed.
The boy obeys stiffly and crosses the room, almost mechanically, to the bed and more or less carefully folds the covering. He carries the bedding into his mother's room and returns with his books and cap.

TRAVIS   (*Sulking and standing apart from her unnaturally*) I'm gone.

RUTH   (*Looking up from the stove to inspect him automatically*) Come here. (*He crosses to her and she studies his head*) If you don't take this comb and fix this here head, you better! (TRAVIS *puts down his books with a great sigh of oppression, and crosses to the mirror. His mother mutters under her breath about his "slubbornness"*) 'Bout to march out of here with that head looking just like chickens slept in it! I just don't know where you get your slubborn ways . . . And get your jacket, too. Looks chilly out this morning.

TRAVIS   (*With conspicuously brushed hair and jacket*) I'm gone.

RUTH   Get carfare and milk money—(*Waving one finger*)—and not a single penny for no caps, you hear me?

TRAVIS (*With sullen politeness*) Yes'm.

> *He turns in outrage to leave. His mother watches after him as in his frustration he approaches the door almost comically. When she speaks to him, her voice has become a very gentle tease.*

RUTH (*Mocking; as she thinks he would say it*) Oh, Mama makes me so mad sometimes, I don't know what to do! (*She waits and continues to his back as he stands stock-still in front of the door*) I wouldn't kiss that woman good-bye for nothing in this world this morning! (*The boy finally turns around and rolls his eyes at her, knowing the mood has changed and he is vindicated; he does not, however, move toward her yet*) Not for nothing in this world! (*She finally laughs aloud at him and holds out her arms to him and we see that it is a way between them, very old and practiced. He crosses to her and allows her to embrace him warmly but keeps his face fixed with masculine rigidity. She holds him back from her presently and looks at him and runs her fingers over the features of his face. With utter gentleness—*) Now—whose little old angry man are you?

TRAVIS (*The masculinity and gruffness start to fade at last*) Aw gaalee —Mama . . .

RUTH (*Mimicking*) Aw—gaaaaalleeeee, Mama! (*She pushes him, with rough playfulness and finality, toward the door*) Get on out of here or you going to be late.

TRAVIS (*In the face of love, new aggressiveness*) Mama, could I *please* go carry groceries?

RUTH   Honey, it's starting to get so cold evenings.

WALTER (*Coming in from the bathroom and drawing a make-believe gun from a make-believe holster and shooting at his son*) What is it he wants to do?

RUTH   Go carry groceries after school at the supermarket.

WALTER   Well, let him go . . .

TRAVIS (*Quickly, to the ally*) I *have* to—she won't gimme the fifty cents . . .

WALTER (*To his wife only*) Why not?

RUTH (*Simply, and with flavour*) 'Cause we don't have it.

WALTER (*To RUTH only*) What you tell the boy things like that for? (*Reaching down into his pants with a rather important gesture*) Here, son—

He hands the boy the coin, but his eyes are directed to his wife's. TRAVIS *takes the money happily.*

TRAVIS   Thanks, Daddy.

He starts out. RUTH *watches both of them with murder in her eyes.* WALTER *stands and stares back at her with defiance, and suddenly reaches into his pocket again on an afterthought.*

WALTER   (*Without even looking at his son, still staring hard at his wife*) In fact, here's another fifty cents . . . Buy yourself some fruit today—or take a taxicab to school or something!

TRAVIS   Whoopee—

He leaps up and clasps his father around the middle with his legs, and they face each other in mutual appreciation; slowly WALTER LEE *peeks around the boy to catch the violent rays from his wife's eyes and draws his head back as if shot.*

WALTER   You better get down now—and get to school, man.

TRAVIS   (*At the door*) O.K. Good-bye.

(*He exits*)

WALTER   (*After him, pointing with pride*) That's *my* boy. (*She looks at him in disgust and turns back to her work*) You know what I was thinking 'bout in the bathroom this morning?

RUTH   No.

WALTER   How come you always try to be so pleasant!

RUTH   What is there to be pleasant 'bout!

WALTER   You want to know what I was thinking 'bout in the bathroom or not!

RUTH   I know what you thinking 'bout.

WALTER   (*Ignoring her*) 'Bout what me and Willy Harris was talking about last night.

RUTH   (*Immediately—a refrain*) Willy Harris is a good-for-nothing loud mouth.

WALTER   Anybody who talks to me has got to be a good-for-nothing loud mouth, ain't he? And what you know about who is just a good-for-nothing loud mouth? Charlie Atkins was just a "good-for-nothing loud mouth" too, wasn't he! When he wanted me to go in the dry-cleaning business with him. And now—he's grossing a hundred thousand a year. A hundred thousand dollars a year! You still can call *him* a loud mouth!

RUTH   (*Bitterly*) Oh, Walter Lee . . .

She folds her head on her arms over the table.

WALTER   (*Rising and coming to her and standing over her*) You tired, ain't you? Tired of everything. Me, the boy, the way we live—this beat-up hole—everything. Ain't you? (*She doesn't look up, doesn't answer*) So tired—moaning and groaning all the time, but you wouldn't do nothing to help, would you? You couldn't be on my side that long for nothing, could you?

RUTH   Walter, please leave me alone.

WALTER   A man needs for a woman to back him up . . .

RUTH   Walter—

WALTER   Mama would listen to you. You know she listen to you more than she do me and Bennie. She think more of you. All you have to do is just sit down with her when you drinking your coffee one morning and talking 'bout things like you do and— (*He sits down beside her and demonstrates graphically what he thinks her methods and tone should be*)—you just sip your coffee, see, and say easy like that you been thinking 'bout that deal Walter Lee is so interested in, 'bout the store and all, and sip some more coffee, like what you saying ain't really that important to you—And the next thing you know, she be listening good and asking you questions and when I come home—I can tell her the details. This ain't no fly-by-night proposition, baby. I mean we figured it out, me and Willy and Bobo.

RUTH   (*With a frown*) Bobo?

WALTER   Yeah. You see, this little liquor store we got in mind cost seventy-five thousand and we figured the initial investment on the place be 'bout thirty thousand, see. That be ten thousand each. Course, there's a couple of hundred you got to pay so's you don't spend your life just waiting for them clowns to let your license get approved—

RUTH   You mean graft?

WALTER   (*Frowning impatiently*) Don't call it that. See there, that just goes to show you what women understand about the world. Baby, don't *nothing* happen for you in this world 'less you pay *somebody* off!

RUTH   Walter, leave me alone! (*She raises her head and stares at him vigorously—then says, more quietly*) *Eat* your eggs, they gonna be cold.

WALTER   (*Straightening up from her and looking off*) That's it. There you are. Man say to his woman: I got me a dream. His woman say: Eat your eggs. (*Sadly, but gaining in power*) Man say: I got to take hold of this here world, baby! And a woman will say: Eat your eggs and go to work. (*Passionately now*) Man say: I got to change my life, I'm choking to death, baby! And his woman say—(*In utter anguish as he brings his fists down on his thighs*)—Your eggs is getting cold!

RUTH (*Softly*) Walter, that ain't none of our money.

WALTER (*Not listening at all or even looking at her*) This morning, I was lookin' in the mirror and thinking about it . . . I'm thirty-five years old; I been married eleven years and I got a boy who sleeps in the living room—(*Very, very quietly*)—and all I got to give him is stories about how rich white people live . . .

RUTH Eat your eggs, Walter.

WALTER *Damn my eggs . . . damn all the eggs that ever was!*

RUTH Then go to work.

WALTER (*Looking up at her*) See—I'm trying to talk to you 'bout myself—(*shaking his head with the repetition*)—and all you can say is eat them eggs and go to work.

RUTH (*Wearily*) Honey, you never say nothing new. I listen to you every day, every night and every morning, and you never say nothing new. (*Shrugging*) So you would rather *be* Mr. Arnold than be his chauffeur. So—I would *rather* be living in Buckingham Palace.

WALTER That is just what is wrong with the colored woman in this world . . . Don't understand about building their men up and making 'em feel like they somebody. Like they can do something.

RUTH (*Drily, but to hurt*) There *are* colored men who do things.

WALTER No thanks to the colored woman.

RUTH Well, being a colored woman, I guess I can't help myself none.

She rises and gets the ironing board and sets it up and attacks a huge pile of rough-dried clothes, sprinkling them in preparation for the ironing and then rolling them into tight fat balls.

WALTER (*Mumbling*) We one group of men tied to a race of women with small minds.

His sister BENEATHA enters. She is about twenty, as slim and intense as her brother. She is not as pretty as her sister-in-law, but her lean, almost intellectual face has a handsomeness of its own. She wears a bright-red flannel nightie, and her thick hair stands wildly about her head. Her speech is a mixture of many things; it is different from the rest of the family's insofar as education has permeated her sense of English—and perhaps the Midwest rather than the South has finally—at last—won out in her inflection; but not altogether, because over all of it is a soft slurring and transformed use of vowels which is the decided influence of the Southside. She passes through the room without looking at either RUTH *or* WALTER *and goes to the outside door and looks, a little blindly, out to the bathroom. She sees that it has been lost to the Johnsons. She closes the door with a sleepy vengeance and crosses to the table and sits down a little defeated.*

BENEATHA   I am going to start timing those people.

WALTER   You should get up earlier.

BENEATHA   (*Her face in her hands. She is still fighting the urge to go back to bed*)   Really—would you suggest dawn? Where's the paper?

WALTER   (*Pushing the paper across the table to her as he studies her almost clinically, as though he has never seen her before*)   You a horrible-looking chick at this hour.

BENEATHA   (*Drily*)   Good morning, everybody.

WALTER   (*Senselessly*)   How is school coming?

BENEATHA   (*In the same spirit*)   Lovely. Lovely. And you know, biology is the greatest. (*Looking up at him*) I dissected something that looked just like you yesterday.

WALTER   I just wondered if you've made up your mind and everything.

BENEATHA   (*Gaining in sharpness and impatience*)   And what did I answer yesterday morning—and the day before that?

RUTH   (*From the ironing board, like someone disinterested and old*)   Don't be so nasty, Bennie.

BENEATHA   (*Still to her brother*)   And the day before that and the day before that!

WALTER   (*Defensively*)   I'm interested in you. Something wrong with that? Ain't many girls who decide—

WALTER *and* BENEATHA   (*In unison*)   —"to be a doctor."
   (*Silence*)

WALTER   Have we figured out yet just exactly how much medical school is going to cost?

RUTH   Walter Lee, why don't you leave that girl alone and get out of here to work?

BENEATHA   (*Exits to the bathroom and bangs on the door*)   Come on out of there, please!

She comes back into the room.

WALTER   (*Looking at his sister intently*)   You know the check is coming tomorrow.

BENEATHA   (*Turning on him with a sharpness all her own*)   That money belongs to Mama, Walter, and it's for her to decide how she wants to use it. I don't care if she wants to buy a house or a rocket ship or just nail it up somewhere and look at it. It's hers. Not ours—*hers.*

WALTER   (*Bitterly*)   Now ain't that fine! You just got your mother's interest at heart, ain't you, girl? You such a nice girl—but if Mama got that money she can always take a few thousand and help you through school too—can't she?

BENEATHA   I have never asked anyone around here to do anything for me!

WALTER   No! And the line between asking and just accepting when the time comes is big and wide—ain't it!

BENEATHA   (*With fury*)   What do you want from me, Brother— that I quit school or just drop dead, which!

WALTER   I don't want nothing but for you to stop acting holy 'round here. Me and Ruth done made some sacrifices for you— why can't you do something for the family?

RUTH   Walter, don't be dragging me in it.

WALTER   You are in it—Don't you get up and go work in some-body's kitchen for the last three years to help put clothes on her back?

RUTH   Oh, Walter—that's not fair . . .

WALTER   It ain't that nobody expects you to get on your knees and say thank you, Brother; thank you, Ruth; thank you Mama— and thank you, Travis, for wearing the same pair of shoes for two semesters—

BENEATHA   (*Dropping to her knees*)   Well—I *do*—all right?—thank everybody . . . and forgive me for ever wanting to be anything at all . . . forgive me, forgive me!

RUTH   Please stop it! Your Mama'll hear you.

WALTER   Who the hell told you you had to be a doctor? If you so crazy 'bout messing 'round with sick people—then go be a nurse like other women—or just get married and be quiet . . .

BENEATHA   Well—you finally got it said . . . It took you three years but you finally got it said. Walter, give up; leave me alone—it's Mama's money.

WALTER   *He was my father, too!*

BENEATHA   So what? He was mine, too—and Travis' grandfather—but the insurance money belongs to Mama. Picking on me is not going to make her give it to you to invest in any liquor stores—(*Underbreath, dropping into a chair*)—and I for one say, God bless Mama for that!

WALTER   (*To* RUTH)   See—did you hear?

RUTH   Honey, please go to work.

WALTER   Nobody in this house is ever going to understand me.

BENEATHA   Because you're a nut.

WALTER   Who's a nut?

BENEATHA   You—you are a nut. Thee is mad, boy.

WALTER   (*Looking at his wife and his sister from the door, very sadly*)   The world's most backward race of people, and that's a fact.

BENEATHA   (*Turning slowly in her chair*)   And then there are all those prophets who would lead us out of the wilderness—(WALTER *slams out of the house*)—into the swamps!

RUTH   Bennie, why you always gotta be pickin' on your brother? Can't you be a little sweeter sometimes? (*Door opens.* WALTER *walks in*)

WALTER   (*To Ruth*)   I need some money for carfare.

RUTH (*Looks at him, then warms; teasing, but tenderly*)   Fifty cents? (*She goes to her bag and gets money*) Here, take a taxi.

WALTER *exits.* MAMA *enters. She is a woman in her early sixties, full-bodied and strong. She is one of those women of a certain grace and beauty who wear it so unobtrusively that it takes a while to notice. Her dark-brown face is surrounded by the total whiteness of her hair, and, being a woman who has adjusted to many things in life and overcome many more, her face is full of strength. She has, we can see, wit and faith of a kind that keep her eyes lit and full of interest and expectancy. She is, in a word, a beautiful woman. Her bearing is perhaps most like the noble bearing of the women of the Hereros of Southwest Africa—rather as if she imagines that as she walks she still bears a basket or a vessel upon her head. Her speech, on the other hand, is as careless as her carriage is precise—she is inclined to slur everything—but her voice is perhaps not so much quiet as simply soft.*

MAMA   What that 'round here slamming doors at this hour?

She crosses through the room, gets to the window, opens it, and brings in a feeble little plant growing doggedly in a small pot on the window sill. She feels the dirt and puts it back out.

RUTH   That was Walter Lee. He and Bennie was at it again.

MAMA   My children and they tempers. Lord, if this little old plant don't get more sun than it's been getting it ain't never going to see spring again. (*She turns from the window*) What's the matter with you this morning, Ruth? You looks right peaked. You aiming to iron all them things? Leave some for me. I'll get to 'em this afternoon. Bennie honey, it's too drafty for you to be sitting 'round half dressed. Where's your robe?

BENEATHA   In the cleaners.

MAMA   Well, go get mine and put it on.

BENEATHA   I'm not cold, Mama, honest.

MAMA   I know—but you so thin . . .

BENEATHA   (*Irritably*)   Mama, I'm not cold.

MAMA   (*Seeing the make-down bed as* TRAVIS *has left it*)   Lord have mercy, look at that poor bed. Bless his heart—he tries, don't he?

She moves to the bed TRAVIS *has sloppily made up.*

RUTH   No—he don't half try at all 'cause he knows you going to come along behind him and fix everything. That's just how come he don't know how to do nothing right now—you done spoiled that boy so.

MAMA   Well—he's a little boy. Ain't supposed to know 'bout house-keeping. My baby, that's what he is. What you fix for his breakfast this morning?

RUTH   (*Angrily*)   I feed my son, Lena!

MAMA   I ain't meddling—(*Underbreath; busy-bodyish*)   I just noticed all last week he had cold cereal, and when it starts getting this chilly in the fall a child ought to have some hot grits or something when he goes out in the cold—

RUTH   (*Furious*)   I gave him hot oats—is that all right!

MAMA   I ain't meddling. (*Pause*) Put a lot of nice butter on it? (RUTH *shoots her an angry look and does not reply*) He likes lots of butter.

RUTH (*Exasperated*) Lena—

MAMA (*To* BENEATHA. MAMA *is inclined to wander conversationally sometimes*) What was you and your brother fussing 'bout this morning?

BENEATHA It's not important, Mama.

She gets up and goes to look out at the bathroom, which is apparently free, and she picks up her towels and rushes out.

MAMA What was they fighting about?

RUTH Now you know as well as I do.

MAMA (*Shaking her head*) Brother still worrying hisself sick about that money?

RUTH You know he is.

MAMA You had breakfast?

RUTH Some coffee.

MAMA Girl, you better start eating and looking after yourself better. You almost thin as Travis.

RUTH Lena—

MAMA Un-hunh?

RUTH What are you going to do with it?

MAMA Now don't you start, child. It's too early in the morning to be talking about money. It ain't Christian.

RUTH It's just that he got his heart set on that store—

MAMA You mean that liquor store that Willy Harris want him to invest in?

RUTH Yes—

MAMA We ain't no business people, Ruth. We just plain working folks.

RUTH Ain't nobody business people till they go into business. Walter Lee say colored people ain't never going to start ahead till they start gambling on some different kinds of things in the world—investments and things.

MAMA What done got into you, girl? Walter Lee done finally sold you on investing.

RUTH No. Mama, something is happening between Walter and me. I don't know what it is—but he needs something—something I can't give him any more. He needs this chance, Lena.

MAMA (Frowning deeply) But liquor, honey—

RUTH Well—like Walter say—I spec people going to always be drinking themselves some liquor.

MAMA   Well—whether they drinks it or not ain't none of my business. But whether I go into business selling it to 'em *is,* and I don't want that on my ledger this late in life. (*Stopping suddenly and studying her daughter-in-law*) Ruth Younger, what's the matter with you today? You look like you could fall over right there.

RUTH   I'm tired.

MAMA   Then you better stay home from work today.

RUTH   I can't stay home. She'd be calling up the agency and screaming at them, "My girl didn't come in today—send me somebody! My girl didn't come in!" Oh, she just have a fit . . .

MAMA   Well, let her have it. I'll just call her up and say you got the flu—

RUTH   (*Laughing*)   Why the flu?

MAMA   'Cause it sounds respectable to 'em. Something white people get, too. They know 'bout the flu. Otherwise they think you been cut up or something when you tell 'em you sick.

RUTH   I got to go in. We need the money.

MAMA   Somebody would of thought my children done all but starved to death the way they talk about money here late. Child, we got a great big old check coming tomorrow.

RUTH   (*Sincerely, but also self-righteously*) · Now that's your money. It ain't got nothing to do with me. We all feel like that—Walter and Bennie and me—even Travis.

MAMA   (*Thoughtfully, and suddenly very far away*)   Ten thousand dollars—

RUTH   Sure is wonderful.

MAMA   Ten thousand dollars.

RUTH   You know what you should do, Miss Lena? You should take yourself a trip somewhere. To Europe or South America or someplace—

MAMA   (*Throwing up her hands at the thought*)   Oh, child!

RUTH   I'm serious. Just pack up and leave! Go on away and enjoy yourself some. Forget about the family and have yourself a ball for once in your life—

MAMA   (*Drily*)   You sound like I'm just about ready to die. Who'd go with me? What I look like wandering 'round Europe by myself?

RUTH   Shoot—these here rich white women do it all the time. They don't think nothing of packing up they suitcases and piling on one of them big steamships and—swoosh!—they gone, child.

MAMA   Something always told me I wasn't no rich white woman.

RUTH   Well—what are you going to do with it then?

MAMA   I ain't rightly decided. (*Thinking. She speaks now with emphasis*)   Some of it got to be put away for Beneatha and her schoolin'—and ain't nothing going to touch that part of it. Nothing. (*She waits several seconds, trying to make up her mind about something, and looks at* RUTH *a little tentatively before going on*)   Been thinking that we maybe could meet the notes on a little old two-story somewhere, with a yard where Travis could play in the summertime, if we use part of the insurance for a down payment and everybody kind of pitch in. I could maybe take on a little day work again, few days a week—

RUTH   (*Studying her mother-in-law furtively and concentrating on her ironing, anxious to encourage without seeming to*)   Well, Lord knows, we've put enough rent into this here rat trap to pay for four houses by now . . .

MAMA   (*Looking up at the words "rat trap" and then looking around and leaning back and sighing—in a suddenly reflective mood—*) "Rat trap"—yes, that's all it is. (*Smiling*)   I remember just as well the day me and Big Walter moved in here. Hadn't been married but two weeks and wasn't planning on living here no more than a year. (*She shakes her head at the dissolved dream*) We was going to set away, little by little, don't you know, and buy a little place out in Morgan Park. We had even picked out the house. (*Chuckling a little*)   Looks right dumpy today. But Lord, child, you should know all the dreams I had 'bout buying that house and fixing it up and making me a little garden in the back—(*She waits and stops smiling*)   And didn't none of it happen.

Dropping her hands in a futile gesture.

RUTH   (*Keeps her head down, ironing*)   Yes, life can be a barrel of disappointments, sometimes.

MAMA   Honey, Big Walter would come in here some nights back then and slump down on that couch there and just look at the rug, and look at me and look at the rug and then back to me —and I'd know he was down then . . . really down. (*After a second very long and thoughtful pause; she is seeing back to times that only she can see*) And then, Lord, when I lost that baby—little Claude—I almost thought I was going to lose Big Walter too. Oh, that man grieved hisself! He was one man to love his children.

RUTH   Ain't nothin' can tear at you like losin' your baby.

MAMA   I guess that's how come that man finally worked hisself to death like he done. Like he was fighting his own war with this here world that took his baby from him.

RUTH   He sure was a fine man, all right. I always liked Mr. Younger.

MAMA   Crazy 'bout his children! God knows there was plenty wrong with Walter Younger—hard-headed, mean, kind of wild with women—plenty wrong with him. But he sure loved his children. Always wanted them to have something—be something. That's where Brother gets all these notions, I reckon. Big Walter used to say, he'd get right wet in the eyes sometimes, lean his head back with the water standing in his eyes and say, "Seem like God didn't see fit to give the black man nothing but dreams—but He did give us children to make them dreams seem worth while."
(*She smiles*) He could talk like that, don't you know.

RUTH   Yes, he sure could. He was a good man, Mr. Younger.

MAMA   Yes, a fine man—just couldn't never catch up with his dreams, that's all.
    BENEATHA *comes in, brushing her hair and looking up to the ceiling, where the sound of a vacuum cleaner has started up.*

BENEATHA   What could be so dirty on that woman's rugs that she has to vacuum them every single day?

RUTH   I wish certain young women 'round here who I could name would take inspiration about certain rugs in a certain apartment I could also mention.

BENEATHA   (*Shrugging*) How much cleaning can a house need, for Christ's sakes.

MAMA   (*Not liking the Lord's name used thus*)   Bennie!

RUTH   Just listen to her—just listen!

BENEATHA   Oh, God!

MAMA   If you use the Lord's name just one more time—

BENEATHA   (*A bit of a whine*)   Oh, Mama—

RUTH   Fresh—just fresh as salt, this girl!

BENEATHA   (*Drily*)   Well—if the salt loses its savor—

MAMA   Now that will do. I just ain't going to have you 'round here reciting the scriptures in vain—you hear me?

BENEATHA   How did I manage to get on everybody's wrong side by just walking into a room?

RUTH   If you weren't so fresh—

BENEATHA   Ruth, I'm twenty years old.

MAMA   What time you be home from school today?

BENEATHA   Kind of late. (*With enthusiasm*) Madeleine is going to start my guitar lessons today.

MAMA *and* RUTH *look up with the same expression.*

MAMA   Your *what* kind of lessons?

BENEATHA   Guitar.

RUTH   Oh, Father!

MAMA   How come you done taken it in your mind to learn to play the guitar?

BENEATHA   I just want to, that's all.

MAMA (*Smiling*) Lord, child, don't you know what to do with yourself? How long it going to be before you get tired of this now—like you got tired of that little play-acting group you joined last year? (*Looking at Ruth*) And what was it the year before that?

RUTH   The horseback-riding club for which she bought that fifty-five-dollar riding habit that's been hanging in the closet ever since!

MAMA (*To* BENEATHA) Why you got to flit so from one thing to another, baby?

BENEATHA (*Sharply*) I just want to learn to play the guitar. Is there anything wrong with that?

MAMA   Ain't nobody trying to stop you. I just wonders sometimes why you has to flit so from one thing to another all the time. You ain't never done nothing with all that camera equipment you brought home—

BENEATHA   I don't flit! I—I experiment with different forms of expression—

RUTH   Like riding a horse?

BENEATHA   —People have to express themselves one way or another.

MAMA   What is it you want to express?

BENEATHA (*Angrily*) Me! (MAMA *and* RUTH *look at each other and burst into raucous laughter*) Don't worry—I don't expect you to understand.

MAMA (*To change the subject*) Who you going out with tomorrow night?

BENEATHA (*With displeasure*) George Murchison again.

MAMA (*Pleased*) Oh—you getting a little sweet on him?

RUTH You ask me, this child ain't sweet on nobody but herself —(*Underbreath*) Express herself!

They laugh.

BENEATHA Oh—I like George all right, Mama. I mean I like him enough to go out with him and stuff, but—

RUTH (*For devilment*) What does *and stuff* mean?

BENEATHA Mind your own business.

MAMA Stop picking at her now, Ruth. (*A thoughtful pause, and then a suspicious sudden look at her daughter as she turns in her chair for emphasis*) What *does* it mean?

BENEATHA (*Wearily*) Oh, I just mean I couldn't ever really be serious about George. He's—he's so shallow.

RUTH Shallow—what do you mean he's shallow? He's *Rich!*

MAMA Hush, Ruth.

BENEATHA I know he's rich. He knows he's rich, too.

RUTH Well—what other qualities a man got to have to satisfy you, little girl?

BENEATHA You wouldn't even begin to understand. Anybody who married Walter could not possibly understand.

MAMA (*Outraged*) What kind of way is that to talk about your brother?

BENEATHA Brother is a flip—let's face it.

MAMA (*To* RUTH, *helplessly*) What's a flip?

RUTH (*Glad to add kindling*) She's saying he's crazy.

BENEATHA Not crazy. Brother isn't really crazy yet—he—he's an elaborate neurotic.

MAMA Hush your mouth!

BENEATHA As for George. Well. George looks good—he's got a beautiful car and he takes me to nice places and, as my sister-in-law says, he is probably the richest boy I will ever get to know and I even like him sometimes—but if the Youngers are sitting around waiting to see if their little Bennie is going to tie up the family with the Murchisons, they are wasting their time.

RUTH You mean you wouldn't marry George Murchison if he asked you someday? That pretty, rich thing? Honey, I knew you was odd-—

BENEATHA   No I would not marry him if all I felt for him was what I feel now. Besides, George's family wouldn't really like it.

MAMA   Why not?

BENEATHA   Oh, Mama—The Murchisons are honest-to-God-real-*live*-rich colored people, and the only people in the world who are more snobbish than rich white people are rich colored people. I thought everybody knew that. I've met Mrs. Murchison. She's a scene!

MAMA   You must not dislike people 'cause they well off, honey.

BENEATHA   Why not? It makes just as much sense as disliking people 'cause they are poor, and lots of people do that.

RUTH   (*A wisdom-of-the-ages manner. To* MAMA) Well, she'll get over some of this—

BENEATHA   Get over it? What are you talking about, Ruth? Listen, I'm going to be a doctor. I'm not worried about who I'm going to marry yet—if I ever get married.

MAMA *and* RUTH   *If!*

MAMA   Now, Bennie—

BENEATHA   Oh, I probably will . . . but first I'm going to be a doctor, and George, for one, still thinks that's pretty funny. I couldn't be bothered with that. I am going to be a doctor and everybody around here better understand that!

MAMA (*Kindly*) 'Course you going to be a doctor, honey, God willing.

BENEATHA (*Drily*) God hasn't got a thing to do with it.

MAMA   Beneatha—that just wasn't necessary.

BENEATHA   Well—neither is God. I get sick of hearing about God.

MAMA   Beneatha!

BENEATHA   I mean it! I'm just tired of hearing about God all the time. What has He got to do with anything? Does he pay tuition?

MAMA   You 'bout to get your fresh little jaw slapped!

RUTH   That's just what she needs, all right!

BENEATHA   Why? Why can't I say what I want to around here, like everybody else?

MAMA   It don't sound nice for a young girl to say things like that— you wasn't brought up that way. Me and your father went to trouble to get you and Brother to church every Sunday.

BENEATHA   Mama, you don't understand. It's all a matter of ideas, and God is just one idea I don't accept. It's not important. I am not going out and be immoral or commit crimes because I don't believe in God. I don't even think about it. It's just that I get tired of Him getting credit for all the things the human race achieves through its own stubborn effort. There simply is no blasted God—there is only man and it is he who makes miracles!

MAMA *absorbs this speech, studies her daughter and rises slowly and crosses to* BENEATHA *and slaps her powerfully across the face. After, there is only silence and the daughter drops her eyes from her mother's face, and* MAMA *is very tall before her.*

MAMA   Now—you say after me, in my mother's house there is still God. (*There is a long pause and* BENEATHA *stares at the floor wordlessly.* MAMA *repeats the phrase with precision and cool emotion*) In my mother's house there is still God.

BENEATHA   In my mother's house there is still God.

A long pause.

MAMA (*Walking away from* BENEATHA, *too disturbed for triumphant posture. Stopping and turning back to her daughter*)   There are some ideas we ain't going to have in this house. Not long as I am at the head of this family.

BENEATHA   Yes, ma'am.

MAMA *walks out of the room.*

RUTH (*Almost gently, with profound understanding*)   You think you a woman, Bennie—but you still a little girl. What you did was childish—so you got treated like a child.

BENEATHA   I see. (*Quietly*) I also see that everybody thinks it's all right for Mama to be a tyrant. But all the tyranny in the world will never put a God in the heavens!

She picks up her books and goes out.

RUTH (*Goes to* MAMA's *door*)   She said she was sorry.

MAMA (*Coming out, going to her plant*)   They frightens me, Ruth. My children.

RUTH   You got good children, Lena. They just a little off sometimes —but they're good.

MAMA   No—there's something come down between me and them that don't let us understand each other and I don't know what it is. One done almost lost his mind thinking 'bout money all the time and the other done commence to talk about things I can't seem to understand in no form or fashion. What is it that's changing, Ruth?

RUTH (*Soothingly, older than her years*)   Now . . . you taking it all too seriously. You just got strong-willed children and it takes a strong woman like you to keep 'em in hand.

MAMA (*Looking at her plant and sprinkling a little water on it*) They spirited all right, my children. Got to admit they got spirit—Bennie and Walter. Like this little old plant that ain't never had enough sunshine or nothing—and look at it . . .

She has her back to RUTH, *who has had to stop ironing and lean against something and put the back of her hand to her forehead.*

RUTH (*Trying to keep* MAMA *from noticing*)   You . . . sure . . . loves that little old thing, don't you? . . .

MAMA   Well, I always wanted me a garden like I used to see sometimes at the back of the houses down home. This plant is close as I ever got to having one. (*She looks out of the window as she replaces the plant*) Lord, ain't nothing as dreary as the view from this window on a dreary day, is there? Why ain't you singing this morning, Ruth? Sing that "No Ways Tired." That song always lifts me up so—(*She turns at last to see that* RUTH *has slipped quietly into a chair, in a state of semiconsciousness*) Ruth! Ruth honey—what's the matter with you . . . Ruth!

Curtain

SCENE II

It is the following morning; a Saturday morning, and house cleaning is in progress at the YOUNGERS. *Furniture has been shoved hither and yon and* MAMA *is giving the kitchen-area walls a washing down.* BENEATHA, *in dungarees, with a handkerchief tied around her face, is spraying insecticide into the cracks in the walls. As they work, the radio is on and a Southside disk-jockey program is inappropriately filling the house with a rather exotic saxophone blues.* TRAVIS, *the sole idle one, is leaning on his arms, looking out of the window.*

TRAVIS   Grandmama, that stuff Bennie is using smells awful. Can I go downstairs, please?

MAMA   Did you get all them chores done already? I ain't seen you doing much.

TRAVIS   Yes'm—finished early. Where did Mama go this morning?

MAMA (*Looking at* BENEATHA)   She had to go on a little errand.

TRAVIS   **Where?**

MAMA   To tend to her business.

TRAVIS   Can I go outside then?

MAMA   Oh, I guess so. You better stay right in front of the house, though . . . and keep a good lookout for the postman.

TRAVIS   Yes'm. (*He starts out and decides to give his* AUNT BENEATHA *a good swat on the legs as he passes her*) Leave them poor little old cockroaches alone, they ain't bothering you none.

He runs as she swings the spray gun at him both viciously and playfully. WALTER *enters from the bedroom and goes to the phone.*

MAMA   Look out there, girl, before you be spilling some of that stuff on that child!

TRAVIS   (*Teasing*)   That's right—look out now!

He exits.

BENEATHA   (*Drily*)   I can't imagine that it would hurt him—it has never hurt the roaches.

MAMA   Well, little boys' hides ain't as tough as Southside roaches.

WALTER   (*Into phone*)   Hello—Let me talk to Willy Harris.

MAMA   You better get over there behind the bureau. I seen one marching out of there like Napoleon yesterday.

WALTER   Hello, Willy? It ain't come yet. It'll be here in a few minutes. Did the lawyer give you the papers?

BENEATHA   There's really only one way to get rid of them, Mama—

MAMA   How?

BENEATHA   Set fire to this building.

WALTER   Good. Good. I'll be right over.

BENEATHA   Where did Ruth go, Walter?

WALTER   I don't know.

He exits abruptly.

BENEATHA   Mama, where did Ruth go?

MAMA   (*Looking at her with meaning*)   To the doctor, I think.

BENEATHA   The doctor? What's the matter? (*They exchange glances*) You don't think—

MAMA   (*With her sense of drama*)   Now I ain't saying what I think. But I ain't never been wrong 'bout a woman neither.

The phone rings.

BENEATHA   (*At the phone*)   Hay-ho . . . (*Pause, and a moment of recognition*) Well—when did you get back! . . . And how was

it? . . . Of course I've missed you—in my way . . . This morning?
No . . . house cleaning and all that and Mama hates it if I let
people come over when the house is like this . . . You *have*?
Well, that's different . . . What is it—Oh, what the hell, come
on over . . . Right, see you then.

She hangs up.

MAMA (*Who has listened vigorously, as is her habit*) Who is that
you inviting over here with this house looking like this? You
ain't got the pride you was born with!

BENEATHA Asagai doesn't care how houses look, Mama—he's an
intellectual.

MAMA *Who?*

BENEATHA Asagai—Joseph Asagai. He's an African boy I met on
campus. He's been studying in Canada all summer.

MAMA What's his name?

BENEATHA Asagai, Joseph. Ah-sah-guy . . . He's from Nigeria.

MAMA Oh, that's the little country that was founded by slaves way
back . . .

BENEATHA No, Mama—that's Liberia.

MAMA I don't think I never met no African before.

BENEATHA Well, do me a favor and don't ask him a whole lot of
ignorant questions about Africans. I mean, do they wear clothes
and all that—

MAMA Well, now, I guess if you think we so ignorant 'round here
maybe you shouldn't bring your friends here—

BENEATHA It's just that people ask such crazy things. All anyone
seems to know about when it comes to Africa is Tarzan—

MAMA (*Indignantly*) Why should I know anything about Africa?

BENEATHA Why do you give money at church for the missionary
work?

MAMA Well, that's to help save people.

BENEATHA You mean save them from *heathenism*—

MAMA (*Innocently*) Yes.

BENEATHA I'm afraid they need more salvation from the British
and the French.

RUTH *comes in forlornly and pulls off her coat with dejection.
The both turn to look at her.*

RUTH (*Dispiritedly*) Well, I guess from all the happy faces—everybody knows.

BENEATHA You pregnant?

MAMA Lord have mercy, I sure hope it's a little old girl. Travis ought to have a sister.

BENEATHA *and* RUTH *give her a hopeless look for this grandmotherly enthusiasm.*

BENEATHA How far along are you?

RUTH Two months.

BENEATHA Did you mean to? I mean did you plan it or was it an accident?

MAMA What do you know about planning or not planning?

BENEATHA Oh, Mama.

RUTH (*Wearily*) She's twenty years old, Lena.

BENEATHA Did you plan it, Ruth?

RUTH Mind your own business.

BENEATHA It is my business—where is he going to live, on the *roof*? (*There is silence following the remark as the three women react to the sense of it*) Gee—I didn't mean that, Ruth, honest. Gee, I don't feel like that at all. I—I think it is wonderful.

RUTH (*Dully*) Wonderful.

BENEATHA Yes—really.

MAMA (*Looking at* RUTH, *worried*) Doctor say everything going to be all right?

RUTH (*Far away*) Yes—she says everything is going to be fine . . .

MAMA (*Immediately suspicious*) "She"—What doctor you went to?

RUTH *folds over, near hysteria.*

MAMA (*Worriedly hovering over* RUTH) Ruth honey—what's the matter with you—you sick?

RUTH *has her fists clenched on her thighs and is fighting hard to suppress a scream that seems to be rising in her.*

BENEATHA What's the matter with her, Mama?

MAMA (*Working her fingers in* RUTH's *shoulder to relax her*) She be all right. Women gets right depressed sometimes when they get her way. (*Speaking softly, expertly, rapidly*) Now you just relax. That's right . . . just lean back, don't think 'bout nothing at all . . . nothing at all—

RUTH I'm all right . . .

The glassy-eyed look melts and then she collapses into a fit of heavy sobbing. The bell rings.

BENEATHA Oh, my God—that must be Asagai.

MAMA (*To* RUTH) Come on now, honey. You need to lie down and rest awhile . . . then have some nice hot food.

They exit, RUTH's *weight on her mother-in-law.* BENEATHA, *herself profoundly disturbed, opens the door to admit a rather dramatic-looking young man with a large package.*

ASAGAI Hello, Alaiyo—

BENEATHA (*Holding the door open and regarding him with pleasure*) Hello . . . (*Long pause*) Well—come in. And please excuse everything. My mother was very upset about letting anyone come here with the place like this.

ASAGAI (*Coming into the room*) You look disturbed too . . . Is something wrong?

BENEATHA (*Still at the door, absently*) Yes . . . we've all got acute ghetto-itus. (*She smiles and comes toward him, finding a cigarette and sitting*) So—sit down! How was Canada?

ASAGAI (*A sophisticate*) Canadian.

BENEATHA (*Looking at him*) I'm very glad you are back.

ASAGAI (*Looking back at her in turn*) Are you really?

BENEATHA Yes—very.

ASAGAI Why—you were quite glad when I went away. What happened?

BENEATHA You went away.

ASAGAI Ahhhhhhhh.

BENEATHA Before—you wanted to be so serious before there was time.

ASAGAI How much time must there be before one knows what one feels.

BENEATHA (*Stalling this particular conversation. Her hands pressed together, in a deliberately childish gesture*) What did you bring me?

ASAGAI (*Handing her the package*) Open it and see.

BENEATHA (*Eagerly opening the package and drawing out some records and the colorful robes of a Nigerian woman*) Oh, Asagai! . . . You got them for me! . . . How beautiful . . . and the records too! (*She lifts out the robes and runs to the mirror with them and holds the drapery up in front of herself*)

ASAGAI (*Coming to her at the mirror*) I shall have to teach you how to drape it properly. (*He flings the material about her for the moment and stands back to look at her*) Ah—*Oh-pay-*

gay-day, oh-gbah-mu-shay. (*A Yoruba exclamation for admiration*) You wear it well . . . very well . . . mutilated hair and all.

BENEATHA (*Turning suddenly*)   My hair—what's wrong with my hair?

ASAGAI (*Shrugging*)   Were you born with it like that?

BENEATHA (*Reaching up to touch it*)   No . . . of course not.

She looks back to the mirror, disturbed.

ASAGAI (*Smiling*)   How then?

BENEATHA   You know perfectly well how . . . as crinkly as yours . . . that's how.

ASAGAI   And it is ugly to you that way?

BENEATHA (*Quickly*)   Oh, no—not ugly . . . (*More slowly, apologetically*) But it's so hard to manage when it's, well—raw.

ASAGAI   And so to accommodate that—you mutilate it every week?

BENEATHA   It's not mutilation!

ASAGAI (*Laughing aloud at her seriousness*)   Oh . . . please! I am only teasing you because you are so very serious about these things. (*He stands back from her and folds his arms across his chest as he watches her pulling at her hair and frowning in the mirror*) Do you remember the first time you met me at school? . . . (*He laughs*) You came up to me and said—and I thought you were the most serious little thing I had ever seen— you said: (*He imitates her*) "Mr. Asagai—I want very much to talk with you. About Africa. You see, Mr. Asagai, I am looking for my *identity!*"

He laughs.

BENEATHA (*Turning to him, not laughing*)   Yes—

Her face is quizzical, profoundly disturbed.

ASAGAI (*Still teasing and reaching out and taking her face in his hands and turning her profile to him*)   Well . . . it is true that this is not so much a profile of a Hollywood queen as perhaps a queen of the Nile—(*A mock dismissal of the importance of the question*) But what does it matter? Assimilationism is so popular in your country.

BENEATHA (*Wheeling, passionately, sharply*)   I am not an assimilationist!

ASAGAI (*The protest hangs in the room for a moment and* ASAGAI *studies her, his laughter fading*)   Such a serious one. (*There is a pause*) So—you like the robes? You must take excellent care of them—they are from my sister's personal wardrobe.

BENEATHA (*With incredulity*)   You—you sent all the way home—for me?

ASAGAI (*With charm*)   For you—I would do much more . . . Well, that is what I came for. I must go.

BENEATHA   Will you call me Monday?

ASAGAI   Yes . . . We have a great deal to talk about. I mean about identity and time and all that.

BENEATHA   Time?

ASAGAI   Yes. About how much time one needs to know what one feels.

BENEATHA   You never understood that there is more than one kind of feeling which can exist between a man and a woman—or, at least, there should be.

ASAGAI (*Shaking his head negatively but gently*)   No. Between a man and a woman there need be only one kind of feeling. I have that for you . . . Now even . . . right this moment . . .

BENEATHA   I know—and by itself—it won't do. I can find that anywhere.

ASAGAI   For a woman it should be enough.

BENEATHA   I know—because that's what it says in all the novels that men write. But it isn't. Go ahead and laugh—but I'm not interested in being someone's little episode in America or—(*With feminine vengeance*)—one of them! (ASAGAI *has burst into laughter again*) That's funny as hell, huh!

ASAGAI   It's just that every American girl I have known has said that to me. White—black—in this you are all the same. And the same speech, too!

BENEATHA (Angrily)   Yuk, yuk, yuk!

ASAGAI   It's how you can be sure that the world's most liberated women are not liberated at all. You all talk about it too much!
   MAMA *enters and is immediately all social charm because of the presence of a guest.*

BENEATHA   Oh—Mama—this is Mr. Asagai.

MAMA   How do you do?

ASAGAI (*Total politeness to an elder*)   How do you do, Mrs. Younger. Please forgive me for coming at such an outrageous hour on a Saturday.

MAMA Well, you are quite welcome. I just hope you understand that our house don't always look like this. (*Chatterish*) You must come again. I would love to hear all about—(*Not sure of the name*)—your country. I think it's so sad the way our American Negroes don't know nothing about Africa 'cept Tarzan and all that. And all that money they pour into these churches when they ought to be helping you people over there drive out them French and Englishmen done taken away your land.

The mother flashes a slightly superior look at her daughter upon completion of the recitation.

ASAGAI (*Taken aback by this sudden and acutely unrelated expression of sympathy*) Yes . . . yes . . .

MAMA (*Smiling at him suddenly and relaxing and looking him over*) How many miles is it from here to where you come from?

ASAGAI Many thousands.

MAMA (*Looking at him as she would* WALTER) I bet you don't half look after yourself, being away from your mama either. I spec you better come 'round here from time to time and get yourself some decent home-cooked meals . . .

ASAGAI (*Moved*) Thank you. Thank you very much. (*They are all quiet, then—*) Well . . . I must go. I will call you Monday, Alaiyo.

MAMA What's that he call you?

ASAGAI Oh—"Alaiyo." I hope you don't mind. It is what you would call a nickname, I think. It is a Yoruba word. I am a Yoruba.

MAMA (*Looking at* BENEATHA) I—I thought he was from—

ASAGAI (*Understanding*) Nigeria is my country. Yoruba is my tribal origin—

BENEATHA You didn't tell us what Alaiyo means . . . for all I know, you might be calling me Little Idiot or something . . .

ASAGAI Well . . . let me see . . . I do not know how just to explain it . . . The sense of a thing can be so different when it changes languages.

BENEATHA You're evading.

ASAGAI No—really it is difficult . . . (*Thinking*) It means . . . it means One for Whom Bread—Food—Is Not Enough. (*He looks at her*) Is that all right?

BENEATHA (*Understanding, softly*)   Thank you.

MAMA (*Looking from one to the other and not understanding any of it*)   Well . . . that's nice . . . You must come see us again —Mr.—

ASAGAI   Ah-sah-guy . . .

MAMA   Yes . . . Do come again.

ASAGAI   Good-bye.

He exits.

MAMA (*After him*)   Lord, that's a pretty thing just went out here! (*Insinuatingly, to her daughter*) Yes, I guess I see why we done commence to get so interested in Africa 'round here. Missionaries my Aunt Jenny!

She exits.

BENEATHA   Oh, Mama! . . .

She picks up the Nigerian dress and holds it up to her in front of the mirror again. She sets the headdress on haphazardly and then notices her hair again and clutches at it and then replaces the headdress and frowns at herself. Then she starts to wriggle in front of the mirror as she thinks a Nigerian woman might. TRAVIS *enters and regards her.*

TRAVIS   You cracking up?

BENEATHA   Shut up.

She pulls the headdress off and looks at herself in the mirror and clutches at her hair again and squinches her eyes as if trying to imagine something. Then, suddenly, she gets her raincoat and kerchief and hurriedly prepares for going out.

MAMA (*Coming back into the room*)   She's resting now. Travis, baby, run next door and ask Miss Johnson to please let me have a little kitchen cleanser. This here can is empty as Jacob's kettle.

TRAVIS   I just came in.

MAMA   Do as you told. (*He exits and she looks at her daughter*) Where you going?

BENEATHA (*Halting at the door*)   To become a queen of the Nile!

She exits in a breathless blaze of glory. RUTH *appears in the bedroom doorway.*

MAMA   Who told you to get up?

RUTH   Ain't nothing wrong with me to be lying in no bed for. Where did Bennie go?

MAMA (*Drumming her fingers*)   Far as I could make out—to Egypt. (RUTH *just looks at her*) What time is it getting to?

RUTH   Ten twenty. And the mailman going to ring that bell this morning just like he done every morning for the last umpteen years.

TRAVIS *comes in with the cleanser can.*

TRAVIS   She say to tell you that she don't have much.

MAMA (*Angrily*)   Lord, some people I could name sure is tight-fisted! (*Directing her grandson*) Mark two cans of cleanser down on the list there. If she that hard up for kitchen cleanser, I sure don't want to forget to get her none!

RUTH   Lena—maybe the woman is just short on cleanser—

MAMA (*Not listening*)   —Much baking powder as she done borrowed from me all these years, she could of done gone into the baking business!

The bell sounds suddenly and sharply and all three are stunned —serious and silent—mid-speech. In spite of all the other conversations and distractions of the morning, this is what they have been waiting for, even TRAVIS, *who looks helplessly from his mother to his grandmother.* RUTH *is the first to come to life again.*

RUTH (*To* TRAVIS) *Get down them steps, boy!*

TRAVIS *snaps to life and flies out to get the mail.*

MAMA (*Her eyes wide, her hand to her breast*)   You mean it done really come?

RUTH (*Excited*)   Oh, Miss Lena!

MAMA (*Collecting herself*)   Well . . . I don't know what we all so excited about 'round here for. We known it was coming for months.

RUTH   That's a whole lot different from having it come and being able to hold it in your hands . . . a piece of paper worth ten thousand dollars . . . (TRAVIS *bursts back into the room. He holds the envelope high above his head, like a little dancer, his face is radiant and he is breathless. He moves to his grandmother with sudden slow ceremony and puts the envelope into her hands. She accepts it, and then merely holds it and looks at it*) Come on! Open it . . . Lord have mercy, I wish Walter Lee was here!

TRAVIS   Open it, Grandmama!

MAMA (*Staring at it*) Now you all be quiet. It's just a check.

RUTH   Open it . . .

MAMA (*Still staring at it*) Now don't act silly . . . We ain't never been no people to act silly 'bout money—

RUTH (*Swiftly*) We ain't never had none before—*open it!*

MAMA *finally makes a good strong tear and pulls out the thin blue slice of paper and inspects it closely. The boy and his mother study it raptly over* MAMA's *shoulders.*

MAMA   Travis! (*She is counting off with doubt*) Is that the right number of zeros.

TRAVIS   Yes'm . . . ten thousand dollars. Gaalee, Grandmama, you rich.

MAMA (*She holds the check away from her, still looking at it. Slowly her face sobers into a mask of unhappiness*) Ten thousand dollars. (*She hands it to* RUTH) Put it away somewhere, Ruth. (*She does not look at* RUTH; *her eyes seem to be seeing something somewhere very far off*) Ten thousand dollars they give you. Ten thousand dollars.

TRAVIS (*To his mother, sincerely*) What's the matter with Grandmama—don't she want to be rich?

RUTH (*Distractedly*) You go on out and play now, baby. (TRAVIS *exits.* MAMA *starts wiping dishes absently, humming intently to herself.* RUTH *turns to her, with kind exasperation*) You've gone and got yourself upset.

MAMA (*Not looking at her*) I spec if it wasn't for you all . . . I would just put that money away or give it to the church or something.

RUTH   Now what kind of talk is that. Mr. Younger would just be plain mad if he could hear you talking foolish like that.

MAMA (*Stopping and staring off*) Yes . . . he sure would. (*Sighing*) We got enough to do with that money, all right. (*She halts then, and turns and looks at her daughter-in-law hard;* RUTH *avoids her eyes and* MAMA *wipes her hands with finality and starts to speak firmly to* RUTH) Where did you go today, girl?

RUTH   To the doctor.

MAMA (Impatiently) Now, Ruth . . . you know better than that. Old Doctor Jones is strange enough in his way but there ain't nothing 'bout him make somebody slip and call him "she"—like you done this morning.

RUTH   Well, that's what happened—my tongue slipped.

MAMA   You went to see that woman, didn't you?

RUTH (*Defensively, giving herself away*) What woman you talking about?

MAMA (*Angrily*) That woman who—

WALTER *enters in great excitement.*

WALTER   Did it come?

MAMA (*Quietly*) Can't you give people a Christian greeting before you start asking about money?

WALTER (*To* RUTH) Did it come? (RUTH *unfolds the check and lays it quietly before him, watching him intently with thoughts of her own.* WALTER *sits down and grasps it close and counts off the zeros*) Ten thousand dollars—(*He turns suddenly, frantically to his mother and draws some papers out of his breast pocket*) Mama—look. Old Willy Harris put everything on paper—

MAMA   Son—I think you ought to talk to your wife . . . I'll go on and leave you alone if you want—

WALTER   I can talk to her later—Mama, look—

MAMA   Son—

WALTER   WILL SOMEBODY PLEASE LISTEN TO ME TODAY!

MAMA (*Quietly*) I don't 'low no yellin' in this house, Walter Lee, and you know it—(WALTER *stares at them in frustration and starts to speak several times*) And there ain't going to be no investing in no liquor stores. I don't aim to have to speak on that again.

A long pause.

WALTER   Oh—so you don't aim to have to speak on that again? So *you* have decided . . . (*Crumpling his papers*) Well, *you* tell that to my boy tonight when you put him to sleep on the living-room couch . . . (*Turning to* MAMA *and speaking directly to her*) Yeah—and tell it to my wife, Mama, tomorrow when she has to go out of here to look after somebody else's kids. And tell it to *me*, Mama, every time we need a new pair of curtains and I have to watch *you* go out and work in somebody's kitchen. Yeah, you tell me then!

WALTER *starts out.*

RUTH   Where you going?

WALTER   I'm going out!

RUTH   Where?

WALTER   Just out of this house somewhere—

RUTH (*Getting her coat*) I'll come too.

WALTER   I don't want you to come!

RUTH   I got something to talk to you about, Walter.

WALTER   That's too bad.

MAMA   (*Still quietly*) Walter Lee—(*She waits and he finally turns and looks at her*) Sit down.

WALTER   I'm a grown man, Mama.

MAMA   Ain't nobody said you wasn't grown. But you still in my house and my presence. And as long as you are—you'll talk to your wife civil. Now sit down.

RUTH   (*Suddenly*) Oh, let him go on out and drink himself to death! He makes me sick to my stomach! (*She flings her coat against him*)

WALTER   (*Violently*) And you turn mine too, baby!
    RUTH *goes into their bedroom and slams the door behind her*) That was my greatest mistake—

MAMA   (*Still quietly*) Walter, what is the matter with you?

WALTER   Matter with me? Ain't nothing the matter with *me!*

MAMA   Yes there is. Something eating you up like a crazy man. Something more than me not giving you this money. The past few years I been watching it happen to you. You get all nervous acting and kind of wild in the eyes—(WALTER *jumps up impatiently at her words*) I said sit there now, I'm talking to you!

WALTER   Mama—I don't need no nagging at me today.

MAMA   Seem like you getting to a place where you always tied up in some kind of knot about something. But if anybody ask you 'bout it you just yell at 'em and bust out the house and go out and drink somewheres. Walter Lee, people can't live with that. Ruth's a good, patient girl in her way—but you getting to be too much. Boy, don't make the mistake of driving that girl away from you.

WALTER   Why—what she do for me?

MAMA   She loves you.

WALTER   Mama—I'm going out. I want to go off somewhere and be by myself for a while.

MAMA   I'm sorry 'bout your liquor store, son. It just wasn't the thing for us to do. That's what I want to tell you about—

WALTER   I got to go out, Mama—

He rises.

MAMA   It's dangerous, son.

WALTER   What's dangerous?

MAMA   When a man goes outside his home to look for peace.

WALTER   (*Beseechingly*) Then why can't there never be no peace in in this house then?

MAMA   You done found it in some other house?

WALTER   No—there ain't no woman! Why do women always think there's a woman somewhere when a man gets restless. (*Coming to her*) Mama—Mama—I want so many things . . .

MAMA   Yes, son—

WALTER   I want so many things that they are driving me kind of crazy . . . Mama—look at me.

MAMA   I'm looking at you. You a good-looking boy. You got a job, a nice wife, a fine boy and—

WALTER   A job (*Looks at her*) Mama, a job? I open and close car doors all day long. I drive a man around in his limousine and I say, "Yes, sir; no, sir; very good sir; shall I take the Drive, sir?" Mama, that ain't no kind of job . . . that ain't nothing at all. (*Very quietly*) Mama, I don't know if I can make you understand.

MAMA   Understand what, baby?

WALTER   (*Quietly*) Sometimes it's like I can see the future stretched out in front of me—just plain as day. The future, Mama. Hanging over there at the edge of my days. Just waiting for me—a big, looming blank space—full of *nothing*. Just waiting for *me*. (*Pause*) Mama—sometimes when I'm downtown and I pass them cool, quiet-looking restaurants where them white boys are sitting back and talking 'bout things . . . sitting there turning deals worth millions of dollars . . . sometimes I see guys don't look much older than me—

MAMA   Son—how come you talk so much 'bout money?

WALTER   (*With immense passion*) Because it is life, Mama!

MAMA   (*Quietly*) Oh—(*Very quietly*) So now it's life. Money is life. Once upon a time freedom used to be life—now it's money. I guess the world really do change . . .

WALTER   No—it was always money, Mama. We just didn't know about it.

MAMA   No . . . something has changed. (*She looks at him*) You something new, boy. In my time we was worried about not being lynched and getting to the North if we could and how to stay alive and still have a pinch of dignity too . . . Now here come you and Beneatha—talking 'bout things we ain't never even thought about hardly, me and your daddy. You ain't satisfied or proud of nothing we done. I mean that you had a home; that we kept you out of trouble till you was grown; that you don't have to ride to work on the back of nobody's streetcar— You my children—but how different we done become.

WALTER   You just don't understand, Mama, you just don't understand.

MAMA   Son—do you know your wife is expecting another baby? (WALTER *stands, stunned, and absorbs what his mother has said*) That's what she wanted to talk to you about. (WALTER *sinks down into a chair*) This ain't for me to be telling—but you ought to know. (*She waits*) I think Ruth is thinking 'bout getting rid of that child.

WALTER (*Slowly understanding*) No — no — Ruth wouldn't do that.

MAMA   When the world gets ugly enough—a woman will do anything for her family. *The part that's already living.*

WALTER   You don't know Ruth, Mama, if you think she would do that.

RUTH *opens the bedroom door and stands there a little limp.*

RUTH (*Beaten*) Yes I would too, Walter. (*Pause*) I gave her a five-dollar down payment.

There is total silence as the man stares at his wife and the mother stares at her son.

MAMA (*Presently*) Well—(*Tightly*) Well—son, I'm waiting to hear you say something . . . I'm waiting to hear how you be your father's son. Be the man he was . . . (*Pause*) Your wife say she going to destroy your child. And I'm waiting to hear you talk like him and say we a people who give children life, not who destroys them—(*she rises*) I'm waiting to see you stand up and look like your daddy and say we done give up one baby to poverty and that we ain't going to give up nary another one . . . I'm waiting.

WALTER   Ruth—

MAMA   If you a son of mine, tell her! (WALTER *turns, looks at her and can say nothing. She continues bitterly*) You . . . you are a disgrace to your father's memory. Somebody get me my hat.

Curtain

ACT TWO

SCENE I

Time: Later the same day.

At rise: RUTH *is ironing again. She has the radio going. Presently* BENEATHA'S *bedroom door opens and* RUTH'S *mouth falls and she puts down the iron in fascination.*

RUTH   What have we got on tonight!

BENEATHA   (*Emerging grandly from the doorway so that we can see her thoroughly robed in the costume Asagai brought*)   You are looking at what a well-dressed Nigerian woman wears—(*She parades for* RUTH, *her hair completely hidden by the headdress; she is coquettishly fanning herself with an ornate oriental fan, mistakenly more like Butterfly than any Nigerian that ever was*) Isn't it beautiful? (*She promenades to the radio and, with an arrogant flourish, turns off the good loud blues that is playing*) Enough of this assimilationist junk! (RUTH *follows her with her eyes as she goes to the phonograph and puts on a record and turns and waits ceremoniously for the music to come up. Then, with a shout—*) OCOMOGOSIAY!

   RUTH *jumps. The music comes up, a lovely Nigerian melody.* BENEATHA *listens, enraptured, her eyes far away—"back to the past." She begins to dance.* RUTH *is dumbfounded.*

RUTH   What kind of dance is that?

BENEATHA   A folk dance.

RUTH   (*Pearl Bailey*)   What kind of folks do that honey?

BENEATHA   It's from Nigeria. It's a dance of welcome.

RUTH   Who you welcoming?

BENEATHA   The men back to the village.

RUTH   Where they been?

BENEATHA   How should I know—out hunting or something. Anyway, they are coming back now . . .

BENEATHA   (*With the record*)

   Alundi, alundi
   Alundi, alunya
   Jop pu a jeepua
   Ang gu soooooooooooo
   Ai yai yae . . .
   Ayehaye—alundi . . .

WALTER *comes in during this performance; he has obviously been drinking. He leans against the door heavily and watches his sister, at first with distaste. Then his eyes look off—"back to the past"—as he lifts both his fists to the roof, screaming.*

WALTER   YEAH . . . AND ETHIOPIA STRETCH FORTH HER HANDS AGAIN! . . .

RUTH   (*Drily, looking at him*)   Yes—and Africa sure is claiming her own tonight. (*She gives them both up and starts ironing again*)

WALTER   (*All in a drunken, dramatic shout*)   Shut up! . . . I'm digging them drums . . . them drums move me! . . . (*He makes his weaving way to his wife's face and leans in close to her*) In my *heart of hearts*—(*He thumps his chest*)—I am much warrior!

RUTH   (*Without even looking up*)   In your heart of hearts you are much drunkard.

WALTER   (*Coming away from her and starting to wander around the room shouting*)   Me and Jomo . . . (*Intently, in his sister's face. She has stopped dancing to watch him in this unknown mood*) That's my man, Kenyatta. (*Shouting and thumping his chest*) FLAMING SPEAR! HOT DAMN! (*He is suddenly in possession of an imaginary spear and actively spearing enemies all over the room*) OCOMOGOSIAY . . . THE LION IS WAKING . . . OWIMOWEH! (*He pulls his shirt open and leaps up on a table and gestures with his spear. The bell rings.* RUTH *goes to answer*)

BENEATHA   (*To encourage* WALTER, *thoroughly caught up with this side of him*)   OCOMOGOSIAY, FLAMING SPEAR!

WALTER   (*On the table, very far gone, his eyes pure glass sheets. He sees what we cannot, that he is a leader of his people, a great chief, a descendant of Chaka, and that the hour to march has come*)   Listen, my black brothers—

BENEATHA   OCOMOGOSIAY!

WALTER   —Do you hear the waters rushing against the shores of the coastlands—

BENEATHA   OCOMOGOSIAY!

WALTER   —Do you hear the screeching of the cocks in yonder hills beyond where the chiefs meet in council for the coming of the mighty war—

BENEATHA   OCOMOGOSIAY!

WALTER   —Do you hear the beating of the wings of the birds flying low over the mountains and the low places of our land—
RUTH *opens the door.* GEORGE MURCHISON *enters.*

BENEATHA   OCOMOGOSIAY!

WALTER   —Do you hear the singing of the women, singing the war songs of our fathers to the babies in the great houses . . . singing the sweet war songs? OH, DO YOU HEAR, MY BLACK BROTHERS!

BENEATHA (*Completely gone*)   We hear you, Flaming Spear—

WALTER   Telling us to prepare for the greatness of the time—(*To* GEORGE) Black Brother!

He extends his hand for the fraternal clasp.

GEORGE   Black Brother, hell!

RUTH (*Having had enough, and embarrassed for the family*)   Beneatha, you got company—what's the matter with you? Walter Lee Younger, get down off that table and stop acting like a fool . . .

WALTER *comes down off the table suddenly and makes a quick Exit to the bathroom.*

RUTH   He's had a little to drink . . . I don't know what her excuse is.

GEORGE (*To* BENEATHA)   Look honey, we're going to the theatre— we're not going to be *in* it . . . so go change, huh?

RUTH   You expect this boy to go out with you looking like that?

BENEATHA (*Looking at* GEORGE)   That's up to George. If he's ashamed of his heritage—

GEORGE   Oh, don't be so proud of yourself, Bennie—just because you look eccentric.

BENEATHA   How can something that's natural be eccentric?

GEORGE   That's what being eccentric means—being natural. Get dressed.

BENEATHA   I don't like that George.

RUTH   Why must you and your brother make an argument out of everything people say?

BENEATHA   Because I hate assimilationist Negroes!

RUTH   Will somebody please tell me what assimila-who-ever means!

GEORGE   Oh, it's just a college girl's way of calling people Uncle Toms—but that isn't what it means at all.

RUTH   Well, what does it mean?

BENEATHA (*Cutting* GEORGE *off and staring at him as she replies to* RUTH) It means someone who is willing to give up his own culture and submerge himself completely in the dominant, and in this case, *oppressive* culture!

GEORGE   Oh, dear, dear, dear! Here we go! A lecture on the African past! On our Great West African Heritage! In one second we will hear all about the great Ashanti empires; the great Songhay civilizations; and the great sculpture of Bénin—and then some poetry in the Bantu—and the whole monologue will end with the word *heritage!* (*Nastily*) Let's face it, baby, your heritage is nothing but a bunch of raggedy-assed spirituals and some grass huts!

BENEATHA   *Grass huts!* (RUTH *crosses to her and forcibly pushes her toward the bedroom*) See there . . . you are standing there in your splendid ignorance talking about people who were the first to smelt iron on the face of the earth! (RUTH *is pushing her through the door*) The Ashanti were performing surgical operations when the English—(RUTH *pulls the door to, with* BENEATHA *on the other side, and smiles graciously at* GEORGE. BENEATHA *opens the door and shouts the end of the sentence defiantly at* GEORGE)—were still tattooing themselves with blue dragons . . . (*She goes back inside*)

RUTH   Have a seat, George. (*They both sit.* RUTH *folds her hands rather primly on her lap, determined to demonstrate the civilization of the family*) Warm, ain't it? I mean for September. (*Pause*) Just like they always say about Chicago weather: If it's too hot or cold for you, just wait a minute and it'll change. (*She smiles happily at this cliché of clichés*) Everybody say it's got to do with them bombs and things they keep setting off. (*Pause*) Would you like a nice cold beer?

GEORGE   No, thank you. I don't care for beer. (*He looks at his watch*) I hopes she hurries up.

RUTH   What time is the show?

GEORGE   It's an eight-thirty curtain. That's just Chicago though. In New York standard curtain time is eight forty.

He is rather proud of this knowledge.

RUTH (*Properly appreciating it*)   You get to New York a lot?

GEORGE (*Offhand*)   Few times a year.

RUTH   Oh—that's nice. I've never been to New York.

WALTER *enters. We feel he has relieved himself, but the edge of unreality is still with him.*

WALTER   New York ain't got nothing Chicago ain't. Just a bunch of hustling people all squeezed up together—being "Eastern."

He turns his face into a screw of displeasure.

GEORGE   Oh—you've been?

WALTER   *Plenty* of times.

RUTH (*Shocked at the lie*)   Walter Lee Younger!

WALTER (*Staring her down*)   Plenty! (*Pause*) What we got to drink in this house? Why don't you offer this man some refreshment. (*To* GEORGE) They don't know how to entertain people in this house, man.

GEORGE   Thank you—I don't really care for anything.

WALTER (*Feeling his head; sobriety coming*)   Where's Mama?

RUTH   She ain't come back yet.

WALTER (*Looking* MURCHISON *over from head to toe, scrutinizing his carefully casual tweed sports jacket over cashmere V-neck sweater over soft eyelet shirt and tie, and soft slacks, finished off with white buckskin shoes*)   Why all you college boys wear them fairyish-looking white shoes?

RUTH   Walter Lee!

GEORGE MURCHISON *ignores the remark.*

WALTER (*To* RUTH)   Well, they look crazy as hell—white shoes, cold as it is.

RUTH (*Crushed*)   You have to excuse him—

WALTER   No he don't! Excuse me for what? What you always excusing me for! I'll excuse myself when I needs to be excused! (*A pause*) They look as funny as them black knee socks Beneatha wears out of here all the time.

RUTH   It's the college *style*, Walter.

WALTER   Style, hell. She looks like she got burnt legs or something!

RUTH   Oh, Walter—

WALTER (*An irritable mimic*)   Oh, Walter! Oh, Walter! (*To* MURCHISON)   How's your old man making out? I understand you all going to buy that big hotel on the Drive? (*He finds a beer in the refrigerator, wanders over to* MURCHISON, *sipping and wiping his lips with the back of his hand, and straddling a chair backwards to talk to the other man*) Shrewd move. Your old man is all right, man. (*Tapping his head and half winking for emphasis*) I mean he knows how to operate. I mean he thinks *big,* you know what I mean, I mean for a *home,* you know? But I think he's kind of running out of ideas now. I'd like to talk to him. Listen, man, I got some plans that could turn this city upside down. I mean I think like he does. *Big.* Invest big, gamble big, hell, lose *big* if you have to, you know what I mean. It's hard to find a man on this whole Southside who understands my kind of thinking—you dig? (*He scrutinizes* MURCHISON *again, drinks his beer, squints his eyes and leans in close, confidential, man to man*) Me and you ought to sit down and talk sometimes, man. Man, I got me some ideas . . .

MURCHISON (*With boredom*) Yeah—sometimes we'll have to do that, Walter.

WALTER (*Understanding the indifference, and offended*)   Yeah— well, when you get the time, man. I know you a busy little boy.

RUTH   Walter, please—

WALTER (*Bitterly, hurt*)   I know ain't nothing in this world as busy as you colored college boys with your fraternity pins and white shoes . . .

RUTH (*Covering her face with humiliation*)   Oh, Walter Lee—

WALTER   I see you all the time—with the books tucked under your arms—going to your (*British A—a mimic*) "clahsses." And for what! What the hell you learning over there? Filling up your heads—(*Counting off on his fingers*)—with the sociology and the psychology—but they teaching you how to be a man? How to take over and run the world? They teaching you how to run a rubber plantation or a steel mill? Naw—just to talk proper and read books and wear white shoes . . .

GEORGE (*Looking at him with distaste, a little above it all*)   You're all wacked up with bitterness, man.

WALTER (*Intently, almost quietly, between the teeth, glaring at the boy*)   And you—ain't you bitter, man? Ain't you just about had it yet? Don't you see no stars gleaming that you can't reach out and grab? You happy?—You contented son-of-a-bitch— you happy? You got it made? Bitter? Man, I'm a volcano. Bitter? Here I am a giant—surrounded by ants! Ants who can't even understand what it is the giant is talking about.

RUTH (*Passionately and suddenly*)   Oh, Walter—ain't you with nobody!

WALTER (*Violently*)   No! 'Cause ain't nobody with me! Not even my own mother!

RUTH   Walter, that's a terrible thing to say!

BENEATHA *enters, dressed for the evening in a cocktail dress, with earrings.*

GEORGE   Well—hey, you look great.

BENEATHA   Let's go, George. See you all later.

RUTH   Have a nice time.

GEORGE   Thanks. Good night. (*To* WALTER, *sarcastically*) Good night, *Prometheus*.

BENEATHA *and* GEORGE *exit.*

WALTER (*To* RUTH)   Who is Prometheus?

RUTH   I don't know. Don't worry about it.

WALTER (*In fury, pointing after* GEORGE)   See there—they get to a point where they can't insult you man to man—they got to go talk about something ain't nobody never heard of!

RUTH   How do you know it was an insult? (*To humor him*) Maybe Prometheus is a nice fellow.

WALTER   Prometheus! I bet there ain't even no such thing! I bet that simple-minded clown—

RUTH   Walter—

She stops what she is doing and looks at him.

WALTER (*Yelling*)   Don't start!

RUTH   Start what?

WALTER   Your nagging! Where was I? Who was I with? How much money did I spend?

RUTH (*Plaintively*)   Walter Lee—why don't we just try to talk about it . . .

WALTER (*Not listening*)   I been out talking with people who understand me. People who care about the things I got on my mind.

RUTH (*Wearily*)   I guess that means people like Willy Harris.

WALTER   Yes, people like Willy Harris.

RUTH (*With a sudden flash of impatience*)   Why don't you all just hurry up and go into the banking business and stop talking about it!

WALTER   Why? You want to know why? 'Cause we all tied up in a race of people that don't know how to do nothing but moan, pray and have babies!

The line is too bitter even for him and he looks at her and sits down.

RUTH   Oh, Walter . . . (*Softly*) Honey, why can't you stop fighting me?

WALTER (*Without thinking*)   Who's fighting you? Who even cares about you?

This line begins the retardation of his mood.

RUTH   Well—(*She waits a long time, and then with resignation starts to put away her things*) I guess I might as well go on to bed . . . (*More or less to herself*) I don't know where we lost it . . . but we have . . . (*Then, to him*) I—I'm sorry about this new baby, Walter. I guess maybe I better go on and do what I started . . . I guess I just didn't realize how bad things was with us . . . I guess I just didn't realize—(*She starts out to the bedroom and stops*) You want some hot milk?

WALTER   Hot milk?

RUTH   Yes—hot milk.

WALTER   Why hot milk?

RUTH   'Cause after all that liquor you come home with you ought to have something hot in your stomach.

WALTER   I don't want no milk.

RUTH   You want some coffee then?

WALTER   No, I don't want no coffee. I don't want nothing hot to drink. (*Almost plaintively*) Why you always trying to give me something to eat?

RUTH (*Standing and looking at him helplessly*)   What else can I give you, Walter Lee Younger?

She stands and looks at him and presently turns to go out again. He lifts his head and watches her going away from him in a new mood which began to emerge when he asked her "Who cares about you?"

WALTER   It's been rough, ain't it, baby? (*She hears and stops but does not turn around and he continues to her back*) I guess between two people there ain't never as much understood as folks generally thinks there is. I mean like between me and you—(*She turns to face him*) How we gets to the place where we scared to talk softness to each other. (*He waits, thinking hard himself*) Why you think it got to be like that? (*He is thoughtful, almost as a child would be*) Ruth, what is it gets into people ought to be close?

RUTH   I don't know, honey. I think about it a lot.

WALTER   On account of you and me, you mean? The way things are with us. The way something done come down between us.

RUTH   There ain't so much between us, Walter . . . Not when you come to me and try to talk to me. Try to be with me . . . a little even.

WALTER (*Total honesty*)   Sometimes . . . sometimes . . . I don't even know how to try.

RUTH   Walter—

WALTER   Yes?

RUTH (*Coming to him, gently and with misgiving, but coming to him*)   Honey . . . life don't have to be like this. I mean sometimes people can do things so that things are better . . . You remember how we used to talk when Travis was born . . . about the way we were going to live . . . the kind of house . . . (*She is stroking his head*) Well, it's all starting to slip away from us . . .

MAMA *enters, and* WALTER *jumps up and shouts at her.*

WALTER   Mama, where have you been?

MAMA   My—them steps is longer than they used to be. Whew! (*She sits down and ignores him*) How you feeling this evening, Ruth?

RUTH *shrugs, disturbed some at having been prematurely interrupted and watching her husband knowingly.*

WALTER   Mama, where have you been all day?

MAMA (*Still ignoring him and leaning on the table and changing to more comfortable shoes*)   Where's Travis?

RUTH   I let him go out earlier and he ain't come back yet. Boy, is he going to get it!

WALTER   Mama!

MAMA (*As if she has heard him for the first time*)   Yes, son?

WALTER   Where did you go this afternoon?

MAMA   I went downtown to tend to some business that I had to tend to.

WALTER   What kind of business?

MAMA   You know better than to question me like a child, Brother.

WALTER (*Rising and bending over the table*)   Where were you, Mama? (*Bringing his fists down and shouting*) Mama, you didn't go do something with that insurance money, something crazy?

The front door opens slowly, interrupting him, and TRAVIS *peeks his head in, less than hopefully.*

TRAVIS (*To his mother*)   Mama, I—

RUTH   "Mama I" nothing! You're going to get it, boy! Get on in that bedroom and get yourself ready!

TRAVIS   But I—

MAMA   Why don't you all never let the child explain hisself.

RUTH   Keep out of it now, Lena.

MAMA *clamps her lips together, and* RUTH *advances toward her son menacingly.*

RUTH   A thousand times I have told you not to go off like that—

MAMA (*Holding out her arms to her grandson*)   Well at least let me tell him something. I want him to be the first one to hear . . . Come here, Travis. (*The boy obeys, gladly*) Travis—(*She takes him by the shoulder and looks into his face*)—you know that money we got in the mail this morning?

TRAVIS   Yes'm—

MAMA   Well—what you think your grandmama gone and done with that money?

TRAVIS   I don't know, Grandmama.

MAMA (*Putting her finger on his nose for emphasis*)   She went out and she bought you a house! (*The explosion comes from* WALTER *at the end of the revelation and he jumps up and turns away from all of them in a fury.* MAMA *continues,. to* TRAVIS) You glad about the house? It's going to be yours when you get to be a man.

TRAVIS   Yeah—I always wanted to live in a house.

MAMA   All right, gimme some sugar then—(TRAVIS *puts his arms around her neck as she watches her son over the boy's shoulder. Then, to* TRAVIS, *after the embrace*) Now when you say your prayers tonight, you thank God and your grandfather—'cause it was him who give you the house—in his way.

RUTH (*Taking the boy from* MAMA *and pushing him toward the bedroom*)   Now you get out of here and get ready for your beating.

TRAVIS   Aw, Mama—

RUTH   Get on in there—(*Closing the door behind him and turning radiantly to her mother-in-law*) So you went and did it!

MAMA (*Quietly, looking at her son with pain*)   Yes, I did.

RUTH (*Raising both arms classically*)   Praise God! (*Looks at* WALTER *a moment, who says nothing. She crosses rapidly to her husband*) Please, honey—let me be glad . . . you be glad too. (*She has laid her hands on his shoulders, but he shakes himself free of her roughly, without turning to face her)* Oh, Walter . . . a home . . . *a home. (She comes back to* MAMA*)* Well—where is it? How big is it? How much it going to cost?

MAMA Well—

RUTH When we moving?

MAMA *(Smiling at her)* First of the month.

RUTH *(Throwing back her head with jubilance)* *Praise God!*

MAMA *(Tentatively, still looking at her son's back turned against her and* RUTH*)* It's—it's a nice house too . . . *(She cannot help speaking directly to him. An imploring quality in her voice, her manner, makes her almost like a girl now)* Three bedrooms —nice big one for you and Ruth. . . . Me and Beneatha still have to share our room, but Travis have one of his own—and *(With difficulty)* I figure if the—new baby—is a boy, we could get one of them double-decker outfits . . . And there's a yard with a little patch of dirt where I could maybe get to grow me a few flowers . . . And a nice big basement . . .

RUTH Walter honey, be glad—

MAMA *(Still to his back, fingering things on the table)* 'Course I don't want to make it sound fancier than it is . . . It's just a plain little old house—but it's made good and solid—and it will be *ours.* Walter Lee—it makes a difference in a man when he can walk on floors that belong to *him* . . .

RUTH Where is it?

MAMA *(Frightened at this telling)* Well—well—it's out there in Clybourne Park—

RUTH'S *radiance fades abruptly, and* WALTER *finally turns slowly to face his mother with incredulity and hostility.*

RUTH Where?

MAMA *(Matter-of-factly)* Four o six Clybourne Street, Clybourne Park.

RUTH Clybourne Park? Mama, there ain't no colored people living in Clybourne Park.

MAMA *(Almost idiotically)* Well, I guess there's going to be some now.

WALTER *(Bitterly)* So that's the peace and comfort you went out and bought for us today!

MAMA *(Raising her eyes to meet his finally)* Son—I just tried to find the nicest place for the least amount of money for my **family.**

RUTH (*Trying to recover from the shock*)   Well—well—'course I ain't one never been 'fraid of no crackers, mind you—but—well, wasn't there no other houses nowhere?

MAMA   Them houses they put up for colored in them areas way out all seem to cost twice as much as other houses. I did the best I could.

RUTH (*Struck senseless with the news, in its various degrees of good-ness and trouble, she sits a moment, her fists propping her chin in thought, and then she starts to rise, bringing her fists down with vigor, the radiance spreading from cheek to cheek again*) Well—well!—All I can say is—if this is my time in life—*my time*—to say good-bye—(*And she builds with momentum as she starts to circle the room with an exuberant, almost tearfully happy release*)—to these Goddamned cracking walls!—(*She pounds the walls*)—and these marching roaches!—(*She wipes at an imaginary army of marching roaches*)—and this cramped little closet which ain't now or never was no kitchen! . . . then I say it loud and good, *Hallelujah! and goodbye misery . . . I don't never want to see your ugly face again!* (*She laughs joy-ously, having practically destroyed the apartment, and flings her arms up and lets them come down happily, slowly, reflec-tively, over her abdomen, aware for the first time perhaps that the life therein pulses with happiness and not despair*) Lena?

MAMA (*Moved, watching her happiness*)   Yes, honey?

RUTH (*Looking off*)   Is there—is there a whole lot of sunlight?

MAMA (*Understanding*)   Yes, child, there's a whole lot of sunlight.

Long pause.

RUTH (*Collecting herself and going to the door of the room* TRAVIS *is in*)   Well—I guess I better see 'bout Travis. (*To* MAMA) Lord, I sure don't feel like whipping nobody today!

She exits.

MAMA (*The mother and son are left alone now and the mother waits a long time, considering deeply, before she speaks*)   Son—you—you understand what I done, don't you? (WALTER *is silent and sullen*) I—I just seen my family falling apart today . . . just falling to pieces in front of my eyes . . . We couldn't of gone on like we was today. We was going backwards 'stead of forwards—talking 'bout killing babies and wishing each other was dead . . . When it gets like that in life—you just got to do something different, push on out and do something bigger . . . (*She waits*) I wish you say something, son . . . I wish you'd say how deep inside you you think I done the right thing—

WALTER (*Crossing slowly to his bedroom door and finally turning there and speaking measuredly*) What you need me to say you done right for? *You* the head of this family. You run our lives like you want to. It was your money and you did what you wanted with it. So what you need for me to say it was all right for? (*Bitterly, to hurt her as deeply as he knows is possible*) So you butchered up a dream of mine—you—who always talking 'bout your children's dreams . . .

MAMA   Walter Lee—

He just closes the door behind him, MAMA *sits alone, thinking heavily.*

Curtain

SCENE II

Time: Friday night. A few weeks later.

At rise: Packing crates mark the intention of the family to move.

BENEATHA *and* GEORGE *come in, presumably from an evening out again.*

GEORGE   O.K. . . . O.K., whatever you say . . . (*They both sit on the couch. He tries to kiss her. She moves away*) Look, we've had a nice evening; let's not spoil it, huh?

He again turns her head and tries to nuzzle in and she turns away from him, not with distaste but with momentary lack of interest; in a mood to pursue what they were talking about.

BENEATHA   I'm *trying* to talk to you.

GEORGE   We always talk.

BENEATHA   Yes—and I love to talk.

GEORGE (*Exasperated; rising*) I know it and I don't mind it sometimes . . . I want you to cut it out, see—The moody stuff, I mean. I don't like it. You're a nice-looking girl . . . all over. That's all you need, honey, forget the atmosphere. Guys aren't going to go for the atmosphere—they're going to go for what they see. Be glad for that. Drop the Garbo routine. It doesn't go with you. As for myself, I want a nice—(*Groping*)—simple (*Thoughtfully*)—sophisticated girl . . . not a poet—O.K.?

She rebuffs him again and he starts to leave.

BENEATHA   Why are you angry?

GEORGE   Because this is stupid! I don't go out with you to discuss the nature of "quiet desperation" or to hear all about your thoughts—because the world will go on thinking what it thinks regardless—

BENEATHA   Then why read books? Why go to school?

GEORGE   (*With artificial patience, counting on his fingers*)   It's simple. You read books—to learn facts—to get grades—to pass the course—to get a degree. That's all—it has nothing to do with thoughts.

A long pause.

BENEATHA   I see. (*A longer pause as she looks at him*) Good night, George.

GEORGE *looks at her a little oddly, and starts to exit. He meets* MAMA *coming in.*

GEORGE   Oh—hello, Mrs. Younger.

MAMA   Hello, George, how you feeling?

GEORGE   Fine—fine, how are you?

MAMA   Oh, a little tired. You know them steps can get you after a day's work. You all have a nice time tonight?

GEORGE   Yes—a fine time. Well, good night.

MAMA   Good night. (*He exists.* MAMA *closes the door behind her*) Hello, honey. What you sitting like that for?

BENEATHA   I'm just sitting.

MAMA   Didn't you have a nice time?

BENEATHA   No.

MAMA   No? What the matter?

BENEATHA   Mama, George is a fool—honest. (*She rises*)

MAMA (*Hustling around unloading the packages she has entered with. She stops*) Is he, baby?

BENEATHA   Yes.

MAMA   Well—I guess you better not waste your time with no fools.

BENEATHA *looks up at her mother, watching her put groceries in the refrigerator. Finally she gathers up her things and starts into the bedroom. At the door she stops and looks back at her mother.*

BENEATHA   Mama—

MAMA   Yes, baby—

BENEATHA   Thank you.

MAMA   For what?

BENEATHA   For understanding me this time.

She exits quickly and the mother stands, smiling a little, looking at the place where BENEATHA *just stood.* RUTH *enters.*

RUTH   Now don't you fool with any of this stuff, Lena—

MAMA   Oh, I just thought I'd sort a few things out.

The phone rings. RUTH *answers.*

RUTH   (*At the phone*)   Hello—just a minute. (*Goes to door*) Walter, it's Mrs. Arnold. (*Waits. Goes back to the phone. Tense*) Hello. Yes, this is his wife speaking . . . He's lying down now. Yes . . . well, he'll be in tomorrow. He's been very sick. Yes—I know we should have called, but we were so sure he'd be able to come in today. Yes—yes, I'm very sorry. Yes . . . Thank you very much. (*She hangs up.* WALTER *is standing in the doorway of the bedroom behind her*) That was Mrs. Arnold.

WALTER   (*Indifferently*)   Was it?

RUTH   She said if you don't come in tomorrow that they are getting a new man . . .

WALTER   Ain't that sad—ain't that crying sad.

RUTH   She said Mr. Arnold has had to take a cab for three days . . . Walter, you ain't been to work for three days! (*This is a revelation to her*) Where you been, Walter Lee Younger? (WALTER *looks at her and starts to laugh*) You're going to lose your job.

WALTER   That's right . . .

RUTH   Oh, Walter, and with your mother working like a dog every day—

WALTER   That's sad too— Everything is sad.

MAMA   What you been doing for these three days, son?

WALTER   Mama—you don't know all the things a man what got leisure can find to do in this city . . . What's this—Friday night? Well—Wednesday I borrowed Willy Harris' car and I went for a drive . . . just me and myself and I drove and drove . . . Way out . . . way past South Chicago, and I parked the car and I sat and looked at the steel mills all day long. I just sat in the car and looked at them big black chimneys for hours. Then I drove back and I went to the Green Hat. (*Pause*) And Thursday—Thursday I borrowed the car again and I got in it and I pointed it the other way and I drove the other way— for hours—way, way up to Wisconsin, and I looked at the farms. I just drove and looked at the farms. Then I drove back and I went to the Green Hat. (*Pause*) And today—today I didn't get the car. Today I just walked. All over the South-side. And I looked at the Negroes and they looked at me and finally I just sat down on the curb at Thirty-ninth and South Parkway and I just sat there and watched the Negroes go by. And then I went to the Green Hat. You all sad? You all depressed? And you know where I am going right now—

RUTH *goes out quietly.*

MAMA   Oh, Big Walter, is this the harvest of our days?

WALTER   You know what I like about the Green Hat? (*He turns the radio on and a steamy, deep blues pours into the room*) I like this little cat they got there who blows a sax . . . He blows. He talks to me. He ain't but 'bout five feet tall and he's got a conked head and his eyes is always closed and he's all music—

MAMA (*Rising and getting some papers out of her handbag*) Walter—

WALTER   And there's this other guy who plays the piano . . . and they got a sound. I mean they can work on some music . . . They got the best little combo in the world in the Green Hat . . . You can just sit there and drink and listen to them three men play and you realize that don't nothing matter worth a damn, but just being there—

MAMA   I've helped do it to you, haven't I, son? Walter, I been wrong.

WALTER   Naw—you ain't never been wrong about nothing, Mama.

MAMA   Listen to me, now. I say I been wrong, son. That I been doing to you what the rest of the world been doing to you. (*She stops and he looks up slowly at her and she meets his eyes pleadingly*) Walter—what you ain't never understood is that I ain't got nothing, don't own nothing, ain't never really wanted nothing that wasn't for you. There ain't nothing as precious to me . . . There ain't nothing worth holding on to, money, dreams, nothing else—if it means—if it means it's going to destroy my boy. (*She puts her papers in front of him and he watches her without speaking or moving*) I paid the man thirty-five hundred dollars down on the house. That leaves sixty-five hundred dollars. Monday morning I want you to take this money and take three thousand dollars and put it in a savings account for Beneatha's medical schooling. The rest, you put in a checking account—with your name on it. And from now on any penny that come out of it or that go in it is for you to look after. For you to decide. (*She drops her hands a little helplessly*) It ain't much, but it's all I got in the world and I'm putting it in your hands. I'm telling you to be the head of this family from now on like you supposed to be.

WALTER (*Stares at the money*) You trust me like that, Mama?

MAMA I ain't never stop trusting you. Like I ain't never stop loving you.

She goes out, and WALTER *sits looking at the money on the table as the music continues in its idiom, pulsing in the room. Finally, in a decisive gesture, he gets up, and, in mingled joy and desperation, picks up the money. At the same moment,* TRAVIS *enters for bed.*

TRAVIS What's the matter, Daddy? You drunk?

WALTER (*Sweetly, more sweetly than we have ever known him*) No, Daddy ain't drunk. Daddy ain't going to never be drunk again. . . .

TRAVIS Well, good night, Daddy.

(*The* FATHER *has come from behind the couch and leans over, embracing his son.*

WALTER Son, I feel like talking to you tonight.

TRAVIS About what?

WALTER Oh, about a lot of things. About you and what kind of man you going to be when you grow up. . . . Son—son, what do you want to be when you grow up?

TRAVIS A bus driver.

WALTER (*Laughing a little*) A what? Man, that ain't nothing to want to be!

TRAVIS Why not?

WALTER 'Cause, man—it ain't big enough—you know what I mean.

TRAVIS I don't know then. I can't make up my mind. Sometimes Mama ask me that too. And sometimes when I tell you I just want to be like you—she says she don't want me to be like that and sometimes she says she does. . . .

WALTER (*Gathering him up in his arms*) You know what, Travis? In seven years you going to be seventeen years old. And things is going to be very different with us in seven years, Travis. . . . One day when you are seventeen I'll come home—home from my office downtown somewhere—

TRAVIS You don't work in no office, Daddy.

WALTER   No—but after tonight. After what your daddy gonna do tonight, there's going to be offices—a whole lot of offices. . . .

TRAVIS   What you gonna do tonight, Daddy?

WALTER   You wouldn't understand yet, son, but your daddy's gonna make a transaction . . . a business transaction that's going to change our lives. . . . That's how come one day when you 'bout seventeen years old I'll come home and I'll be pretty tired, you know what I mean. after a day of conferences and secretaries getting things wrong the way they do . . . 'cause an executive's life is hell, man—(*The more he talks the farther away he gets*) And I'll pull the car up on the driveway . . . just a plain black Chrysler, I think, with white walls—no—black tires. More elegant. Rich people don't have to be flashy . . . though I'll have to get something a little sportier for Ruth—maybe a Cadillac convertible to do her shopping in. . . . And I'll come up the steps to the house and the gardener will be clipping away at the hedges and he'll say, "Good evening, Mr. Younger." And I'll say, "Hello, Jefferson, how are you this evening?" And I'll go inside and Ruth will come downstairs and meet me at the door and we'll kiss each other and she'll take my arm and we'll go up to your room to see you sitting on the floor with the catalogues of all the great schools in America around you. . . . All the great schools in the world! And—and I'll say, all right son —it's your seventeenth birthday, what is it you've decided? . . . Just tell me where you want to go to school and you'll *be* it. . . . Whatever you want to be—Yessir! (*He holds his arms open for* TRAVIS) You just name it, son . . . (TRAVIS *leaps into them*) and I hand you the world!

WALTER'S *voice has risen in pitch and hysterical promise and on the last line he lifts* TRAVIS *high.*

Blackout

SCENE III

Time: Saturday, moving day, one week later.

Before the curtain rises, RUTH'S *voice, a strident, dramatic church alto, cuts through the silence.*

It is, in the darkness, a triumphant surge, a penetrating statement of expectation: "Oh, Lord, I don't feel no ways tired! Children, oh, glory hallelujah!"

As the curtain rises we see that RUTH *is alone in the living room, finishing up the family's packing. It is moving day. She is nailing crates and tying cartons.* BENEATHA *enters, carrying a guitar case, and watches her exuberant sister-in-law.*

RUTH   Hey!

BENEATHA   (*Putting away the case*) Hi.

RUTH   (*Pointing at a package*) Honey—look in that package there and see what I found on sale this morning at the South Center. (RUTH *gets up and moves to the package and draws out some curtains*) Lookahere—hand-turned hems!

BENEATHA   How do you know the window size out there?

RUTH   (*Who hadn't thought of that*) Oh— Well, they bound to fit something in the whole house. Anyhow, they was too good a bargain to pass up. (RUTH *slaps her head, suddenly remembering something*) Oh, Bennie—I meant to put a special note on that carton over there. That's your mama's good china and she wants 'em to be very careful with it.

BENEATHA   I'll do it.

BENEATHA *finds a piece of paper and starts to draw large letters on it.*

RUTH   You know what I'm going to do soon as I get in that new house?

BENEATHA   What?

RUTH   Honey—I'm going to run me a tub of water up to here . . . (*With her fingers practically up to her nostrils*) And I'm going to get in it—and I am going to sit . . . and sit . . . and sit in that hot water and the first person who knocks to tell *me* to hurry up and come out—

BENEATHA   Gets shot at sunrise.

RUTH   (*Laughing happily*) You said it, sister! (*Noticing how large* BENEATHA *is absent-mindedly making the note*) Honey, they ain't going to read that from no airplane.

BENEATHA   (*Laughing herself*) I guess I always think things have more emphasis if they are big, somehow.

RUTH   (*Looking up at her and smiling*) You and your brother seem to have that as a philosophy of life. Lord, that man—done changed so 'round here. You know—you know what we did last night? Me and Walter Lee?

BENEATHA   What?

RUTH (*Smiling to herself*) We went to the movies. (*Looking at* BENEATHA *to see if she understands*) We went to the movies. You know the last time me and Walter went to the movies together?

BENEATHA   No.

RUTH   Me neither. That's how long it been. (*Smiling again*) But we went last night. The picture wasn't much good, but that didn't seem to matter. We went—and we held hands.

BENEATHA   Oh, Lord!

RUTH   We held hands—and you know what?

BENEATHA   What?

RUTH   When we came out of the show it was late and dark and all the stores and things was closed up . . . and it was kind of chilly and there wasn't many people on the streets . . . and we was still holding hands, me and Walter.

BENEATHA   You're killing me.

> WALTER *enters with a large package. His happiness is deep in him; he cannot keep still with his new-found exuberance. He is singing and wiggling and snapping his fingers. He puts his package in a corner and puts a phonograph record, which he has brought in with him, on the record prayer. As the music comes up he dances over to* RUTH *and tries to get her to dance with him. She gives in at last to his raunchiness and in a fit of giggling allows herself to be drawn into his mood and together they deliberately burlesque an old social dance of their youth.*

BENEATHA (*Regarding them a long time as they dance, then drawing in her breath for a deeply exaggerated comment which she does not particularly mean*) Talk about — olddddddddddd-fashion-eddddddd—Negroes!

WALTER (*Stopping momentarily*) What kind of Negroes?

> *He says this in fun. He is not angry with her today, nor with anyone. He starts to dance with his wife again.*

BENEATHA   Old-fashioned.

WALTER (*As he dances with* RUTH) You know, when these *New Negroes* have their convention—(*Pointing at his sister*)—that is going to be the chairman of the Committee on Unending Agitation. (*He goes on dancing, then stops*) Race, race, race! . . . Girl, I do believe you are the first person in the history of the entire human race to successfully brainwash yourself. (BENEATHA *breaks up and he goes on dancing. He stops again, enjoying his tease*) Damn, even the N double A C P takes a holiday sometimes! (BENEATHA *and* RUTH *laugh. He dances with* RUTH *some more and starts to laugh and stops and pantomimes someone over an operating table*) I can just see that chick someday looking down at some poor cat on an operating table before she starts to slice him, saying . . . (*Pulling his sleeves back maliciously*) "By the way, what are your views on civil rights down there? . . ."

He laughs at her again and starts to dance happily. The bell sounds.

BENEATHA Sticks and stones may break my bones but . . . words will never hurt me!

BENEATHA *goes to the door and opens it as* WALTER *and* RUTH *go on with the clowning.* BENEATHA *is somewhat surprised to see a quiet-looking middle-aged white man in a business suit holding his hat and a briefcase in his hand and consulting a small piece of paper.*

MAN Uh—how do you do, miss. I am looking for a Mrs.—(*He looks at the slip of paper*) Mrs. Lena Younger?

BENEATHA (*Smoothing her hair with slight embarrassment*) Oh—yes, that's my mother. Excuse me (*She closes the door and turns to quiet the other two*) Ruth! Brother! Somebody's here. (*Then she opens the door. The man casts a curious quick glance at all of them*) Uh—come in please.

MAN (*Coming in*) Thank you.

BENEATHA My mother isn't here just now. Is it business?

MAN Yes . . . well, of a sort.

WALTER (*Freely, the Man of the House*) Have a seat. I'm Mrs. Younger's son. I look after most of her business matters.

RUTH *and* BENEATHA *exchange amused glances.*

MAN (*Regarding* WALTER, *and sitting*) Well—My name is Karl Lindner . . .

WALTER (*Stretching out his hand*) Walter Younger. This is my wife —(RUTH *nods politely*)—and my sister.

LINDNER How do you do.

WALTER (*Amiably, as he sits himself easily on a chair, leaning with interest forward on his knees and looking expectantly into the newcomer's face*) What can we do for you, Mr. Lindner?

LINDNER (*Some minor shuffling of the hat and briefcase on his knees*) Well—I am a representative of the Clybourne Park Improvement Association—

WALTER (*Pointing*) Why don't you sit your things on the floor?

LINDER Oh—yes. Thank you. (*He slides the briefcase and hat under the chair*) And as I was saying—I am from the Clybourne Park Improvement Association and we have had it brought to our attention at the last meeting that you people—or at least your mother—has bought a piece of residential property at— (*He digs for the slip of paper again*)—four o six Clybourne Street . . .

WALTER That's right. Care for something to drink? Ruth, get Mr. Lindner a beer.

LINDNER (*Upset for some reason*) Oh—no, really. I mean thank you very much, but no thank you.

RUTH (*Innocently*) Some coffee?

LINDNER Thank you, nothing at all.
BENEATHA *is watching the man carefully.*

LINDNER Well, I don't know how much you folks know about our organization. (*He is a gentle man; thoughtful and somewhat labored in his manner*) It is one of these community organizations set up to look after—oh, you know, things like block upkeep and special projects and we also have what we call our New Neighbors Orientation Committee . . .

BENEATHA (*Drily*) Yes—and what do they do?

LINDNER (*Turning a little to her and then returning the main force to* WALTER) Well—it's what you might call a sort of welcoming committee, I guess. I mean they, we, I'm the chairman of the committee—go around and see the new people who move into the neighborhood and sort of give them the lowdown on the way we do things out in Clybourne Park.

BENEATHA (*With appreciation of the two meanings, which escape* RUTH *and* WALTER) Uh-huh.

LINDNER And we also have the category of what the association calls—(*He looks elsewhere*)—uh—special community problems . . .

BENEATHA Yes—and what are some of these?

WALTER Girl, let the man talk.

LINDNER (*With understated relief*) Thank you. I would sort of like to explain this thing in my own way. I mean I want to explain to you in a certain way.

WALTER   Go ahead.

LINDNER   Yes. Well. I'm going to try to get right to the point. I'm sure we'll all appreciate that in the long run.

BENEATHA   Yes.

WALTER   Be still now!

LINDNER   Well—

RUTH (*Still innocently*) Would you like another chair—you don't look comfortable.

LINDNER (*More frustrated than annoyed*) No, thank you very much. Please. Well—to get right to the point I—(*A great breath, and he is off at last*) I am sure you people must be aware of some of the incidents which have happened in various parts of the city when colored people have moved into certain areas—(BENEATHA *exhales heavily and starts tossing a piece of fruit up and down in the air*) Well— because we have what I think is going to be a unique type of organization in American community life—not only do we deplore that kind of thing—but we are trying to do something about it. (BENEATHA *stops tossing and turns with a new and quizzical interest to the man*) We feel—(*gaining confidence in his mission because of the interest in the faces of the people he is talking to*)—we feel that most of the trouble in this world, when you come right down to it—(*He hits his knee for emphasis*)—most of the trouble exists because people just don't sit down and talk to each other.

RUTH (*Nodding as she might in church, pleased with the remark*) You can say that again, mister.

LINDNER (*More encouraged by such affirmation*) That we don't try hard enough in this world to understand the other fellow's problem. The other guy's point of view.

RUTH   Now that's right.

BENEATHA *and* WALTER *merely watch and listen with genuine interest.*

LINDNER   Yes—that's the way we feel out in Clybourne Park. And that's why I was elected to come here this afternoon and talk to you people. Friendly like, you know, the way people should talk to each other and see if we couldn't find some way to work this thing out. As I say, the whole business is a matter of *caring* about the other fellow. Anybody can see that you are a nice family of folks, hard working and honest I'm sure. (BENEATHA *frowns slightly, quizzically, her head tilted regarding him*) Today everybody knows what it means to be on the outside of *something*. And of course, there is always somebody who is out to take the advantage of people who don't always understand.

WALTER   What do you mean?

LINDNER   Well—you see our community is made up of people who've worked hard as the dickens for years to build up that little community. They're not rich and fancy people; just hard-working honest people who don't really have much but those little homes and a dream of the kind of community they want to raise their children in. Now, I don't say we are perfect and there is a lot wrong in some of the things they want. But you've got to admit that a man, right or wrong, has the right to want to have the neighborhood he lives in a certain kind of way. And at the moment the overwhelming majority of our people out there feel that people get along better, take more of a common interest in the life of the community, when they share a common background. I want you to believe me when I tell you that race prejudice simply doesn't enter into it. It is a matter of the people of Clybourne Park believing, rightly or wrongly, as I say, that for the happiness of all concerned that our Negro families are happier when they live in their *own* communities.

BENEATHA (*With a grand and bitter gesture*) This, friends, is the Welcoming Committee!

WALTER (*Dumfounded, looking at* LINDNER) Is this what you came marching all the way over here to tell us?

LINDNER   Well, now we've been having a fine conversation. I hope you'll hear me all the way through.

WALTER (*Tightly*) Go ahead, man.

LINDNER   You see—in the face of all things I have said, we are prepared to make your family a very generous offer . . .

BENEATHA   Thirty pieces and not a coin less!

WALTER   Yeah?

LINDNER (*Putting on his glasses and drawing a form out of the brief-case*) Our association is prepared, through the collective effort of our people, to buy the house from you at a financial gain to your family.

RUTH   Lord have mercy, ain't this the living gall!

WALTER   All right, you through?

LINDNER   Well, I want to give you the exact terms of the financial arrangement—

WALTER   We don't want to hear no exact terms of no arrangements. I want to know if you got any more to tell us 'bout getting together?

LINDNER   (*Taking off his glasses*) Well—I don't suppose that you feel . . .

WALTER   Never mind how I feel—you got any more to say 'bout how people ought to sit down and talk to each other? . . . Get out of my house, man.

He turns his back and walks to the door.

LINDNER   (*Looking around at the hostile faces and reaching and assembling his hat and briefcase*) Well—I don't understand why you people are reacting this way. What do you think you are going to gain by moving into a neighborhood where you just aren't wanted and where some elements—well—people can get awful worked up when they feel that their whole way of life and everything they've worked for is threatened.

WALTER   Get out.

LINDNER   (*At the door, holding a small card*) Well—I'm sorry it went like this.

WALTER   Get out.

LINDNER   (*Almost sadly regarding* WALTER) You just can't force people to change their hearts, son.

He turns and puts his card on a table and exits. WALTER *pushes the door to with stinging hatred, and stands looking at it.* RUTH *just sits and* BENEATHA *just stands. They say nothing.* MAMA *and* TRAVIS *enter.*

MAMA   Well—this all the packing done got done since I left out of here this morning? I testify before God that my children got all the energy of the dead. What time the moving men due?

BENEATHA   Four o'clock. You had a caller, Mama.

She is smiling, teasingly.

MAMA   Sure enough—who?

BENEATHA   (*Her arms folded saucily*) The Welcoming Committee.

WALTER *and* RUTH *giggle.*

MAMA   (*Innocently*) Who?

BENEATHA   The Welcoming Committee. They said they're sure going to be glad to see you when you get there.

WALTER (*Devilishly*) Yeah, they said they can't hardly wait to see your face.

Laughter.

MAMA (*Sensing their facetiousness*) What's the matter with you all?

WALTER   Ain't nothing the matter with us. We just telling you 'bout the gentleman who came to see you this afternoon. From the Clybourne Park Improvement Association.

MAMA   What he want?

RUTH (*In the same mood as* BENEATHA *and* WALTER) To welcome you, honey.

WALTER   He said they can't hardly wait. He said the one thing they don't have, that they just *dying* to have out there is a fine family of colored people! (*To* RUTH *and* BENEATHA) Ain't that right?

RUTH *and* BENEATHA (*Mockingly*) Yea! He left his card in case—

They indicate the card, and MAMA *picks it up and throws it on the floor—understanding and looking off as she draws her chair up to the table on which she has put her plant and some sticks and some cord.*

MAMA   Father, give us strength (*Knowingly—and without fun*) Did he threaten us?

BENEATHA   Oh—Mama—they don't do it like that any more. He talked Brotherhood. He said everybody ought to learn how to sit down and hate each other with good Christian fellowship. *She and* WALTER *shake hands to ridicule the remark.*

MAMA (*Sadly*) Lord, protect us . . .

RUTH   You should hear the money those folks raised to buy the house from us. All we paid and then some.

BENEATHA   What they think we going to do—eat 'em?

RUTH   No, honey, marry 'em.

MAMA (*Shaking her head*) Lord, Lord, Lord . . .

RUTH   Well—that's the way the crackers crumble. Joke.

BENEATHA (*Laughingly noticing what her mother is doing*) Mama, what are you doing?

MAMA   Fixing my plant so it won't get hurt none on the way . . .

BENEATHA   Mama, you going to take *that* to the new house?

MAMA   Uh-huh—

BENEATHA   That raggedy-looking old thing?

MAMA (*Stopping and looking at her*) It expresses *me.*

RUTH (*With delight, to* BENEATHA) So there, Miss Thing!

Walter comes to MAMA *suddenly and bends down behind her and squeezes her in his arms with all his strength. She is overwhelmed by the suddenness of it and, though delighted, her manner is like that of* RUTH *with* TRAVIS.

MAMA   Look out now, boy! You make me mess up my thing here!

WALTER (*His face lit, he slips down on his knees beside her, his arms still about her*) Mama . . . you know what it means to climb up in the chariot?

MAMA (*Gruffly, very happy*) Get on away from me now . . .

RUTH (*Near the gift-wrapped package, trying to catch* WALTER's *eye*) Psst—

WALTER   What the old song say, Mama . . .

RUTH   Walter—Now?

She is pointing at the package.

WALTER (*Speaking the lines, sweetly, playfully, in his mother's face*)

I got wings . . . you got wings . . .
All God's Children got wings . . .

MAMA   Boy—get out of my face and do some work . . .

WALTER

When I get to heaven gonna put on my wings,
Gonna fly all over God's heaven . . .

BENEATHA (*Teasingly, from across the room*) Everybody talking 'bout heaven ain't going there!

WALTER (*To* RUTH, *who is carrying the box across to them*) I don't know, you think we ought to give her that . . . Seems to me she ain't been very appreciative around here.

MAMA (*Eying the box, which is obviously a gift*) What is that?

WALTER (*Taking it from* RUTH *and putting it on the table in front of* MAMA) Well—what you all think? Should we give it to her?

RUTH   Oh—she was pretty good today.

MAMA   I'll good you—

She turns her eyes to the box again.

BENEATHA   Open it, Mama.

She stands up, looks at it, turns and looks at all of them, and then presses her hands together and does not open the package.

WALTER (*Sweetly*) Open it, Mama. It's for you. (MAMA *looks in his eyes. It is the first present in her life without its being*

Christmas. Slowly she opens her package and lifts out, one by one, a brand-new sparkling set of gardening tools. WALTER *continues, prodding)* Ruth made up the note—read it . . .

MAMA *(picking up the card and adjusting her glasses)* "To our own Mrs. Miniver—Love from Brother, Ruth and Beneatha." Ain't that lovely . . .

TRAVIS *(Tugging at his father's sleeve)* Daddy, can I give her mine now?

WALTER   All right, son. (TRAVIS *flies to get his gift)* Travis didn't want to go in with the rest of us, Mama. He got his own. *(Somewhat amused)* We don't know what it is . . .

TRAVIS *(Racing back in the room with a large hatbox and putting it in front of his grandmother)* Here!

MAMA   Lord have mercy, baby. You done gone and bought your grandmother a hat?

TRAVIS *(Very proud)* Open it!

She does and lifts out an elaborate, but very elaborate, wide gardening hat, and all the adults break up at the sight of it.

RUTH   Travis, honey, what is that?

TRAVIS *(Who thinks it is beautiful and appropriate)* It's a gardening hat! Like the ladies always have on in the magazines when they work in their gardens.

BENEATHA *(giggling fiercely)* Travis—we were trying to make Mama Mrs. Miniver—not Scarlett O'Hara!

MAMA *(Indignantly)* What's the matter with you all! This here is a beautiful hat. *(Absurdly)* I always wanted me one just like it!

She pops it on her head to prove it to her grandson, and the hat is ludicrous and considerably oversized.

RUTH   Hot dog! Go, Mama!

WALTER *(Doubled over with laughter)* I'm sorry, Mama—but you look like you ready to go out and chop you some cotton sure enough!

They all laugh except MAMA, *out of deference to* TRAVIS' *feelings.*

MAMA *(Gathering the boy up to her)* Bless your heart—this is the prettiest hat I ever owned— (WALTER, RUTH *and* BENEATHA *chime in—noisily, festively and insincerely congratulating* TRAVIS *on his gift)* What are we all standing around here for? We ain't finished packin' yet. Bennie, you ain't packed one book.

The bell rings.

BENEATHA   That couldn't be the movers . . . It's not hardly two good yet—

BENEATHA *goes into her room.* MAMA *starts for door.*

WALTER   *(Turning, stiffening)* Wait—wait—I'll get it.

He stands and looks at the door.

MAMA   You expecting company, son?

WALTER   *(Just looking at the door)* Yeah—yeah . . .

MAMA *looks at* RUTH, *and they exchange innocent and unfrightened glances.*

MAMA   *(Not understanding)* Well, let them in, son.

BENEATHA   *(From her room)* We need some more string.

MAMA   Travis—you run to the hardware and get me some string cord.

MAMA *goes out and* WALTER *turns and looks at* RUTH. TRAVIS *goes to a dish for money.*

RUTH   Why don't you answer the door, man?

WALTER   *(Suddenly bounding across the floor to her)* 'Cause sometimes it hard to let the future begin! *(Stooping down in her face)*

> *I got wings! You got wings!*
> *All God's children got wings!*

He crosses to the door and throws it open. Standing there is a very slight little man in a not too prosperous business suit and with haunted frightened eyes and a hat pulled down tightly, brim up, around his forehead. TRAVIS *passes between the men and exits.* WALTER *leans deep in the man's face, still in his jubilance.*

> *When I get to heaven gonna put on my wings,*
> *Gonna fly all over God's heaven . . .*

The little man just stares at him.

> *Heaven—*

(Suddenly he stops and looks past the little man into the empty hallway) Where's Willy, man?

BOBO   He ain't with me.

WALTER   *(Not disturbed)* Oh—come on in. You know my wife.

BOBO   *(Dumbly, taking off his hat)* Yes—h'you, Miss Ruth.

RUTH (*Quietly, a mood apart from her husband already, seeing* BOBO)
Hello, Bobo.

WALTER   You right on time today . . . Right on time. That's the
way! (*He slaps* BOBO *on his back*) Sit down . . . lemme hear.

RUTH *stands stiffly and quietly in back of them, as though somehow she senses death, her eyes fixed on her husband.*

BOBO (*His frightened eyes on the floor, his hat in his hands*) Could
I please get a drink of water, before I tell you about it, Walter
Lee?

Walter does not take his eyes off the man. RUTH *goes blindly to
the tap and gets a glass of water and brings it to* BOBO.

WALTER   There ain't nothing wrong, is there?

BOBO   Lemme tell you—

WALTER   Man—didn't nothing go wrong?

BOBO   Lemme tell you—Walter Lee. (*Looking at* RUTH *and talking
to her more than to* WALTER) You know how it was. I got to
tell you how it was. I mean first I got to tell you how it was all
the way . . . I mean about the money I put in, Walter Lee . . .

WALTER (*With taut agitation now*) What about the money you put in?

BOBO   Well—it wasn't much as we told you—me and Will—(*He
stops*) I'm sorry, Walter. I got a bad feeling about it. I got a
real bad feeling about it . . .

WALTER   Man, what you telling me about all this for? . . . Tell me
what happened in Springfield . . .

BOBO   Springfield.

RUTH (*Like a dead woman*) What was supposed to happen in Springfield?

BOBO (*To her*) This deal that me and Walter went into with Willy
—Me and Willy was going to go down to Springfield and spread
some money 'round so's we wouldn't have to wait so long for the
liquor license . . . That's what we were going to do. Everybody
said that was the way you had to do, you understand, Miss Ruth?

WALTER   Man—what happened down there?

BOBO (*A pitiful man, near tears*) I'm trying to tell you, Walter.

WALTER (*Screaming at him suddenly*) THEN TELL ME, GOD-
DAMMIT . . . WHAT'S THE MATTER WITH YOU?

BOBO   Man . . . I didn't go to no Springfield, yesterday.

WALTER (*Halted, life hanging in the moment*) Why not?

BOBO (*The long way, the hard way to tell*) 'Cause I didn't have no
reasons to . . .

WALTER   Man, what are you talking about!

BOBO   I'm talking about the fact that when I got to the train station yesterday morning—eight o'clock like we planned . . . Man —*Willy didn't never show up.*

WALTER   Why . . . . where was he . . . where is he?

BOBO   That's what I'm trying to tell you . . . I don't know . . . I waited six hours . . . I called his house . . . and I waited . . . six hours . . . I waited in that train station six hours . . .(*Breaking into tears*) That was all the extra money I had in the world . . . (*Looking up at* WALTER *with the tears running down his face*) Man, *Willy is gone.*

WALTER   Gone, what you mean Willy is gone? Gone where? You mean he went by himself. You mean he went off to Springfield by himself—to take care of getting the license—(*Turns and looks anxiously at* RUTH) You mean maybe he didn't want too many people in on the business down there? (*Looks to* RUTH *again, as before*) You know Willy got his own ways. (*Looks back to* BOBO) Maybe you was late yesterday and he just went on down there without you. Maybe—maybe—he's been callin' you at home tryin' to tell you what happened or something. Maybe—maybe—he just got sick. He's somewhere—he's got to be somewhere. We just got to find him—me and you got to find him. (*Grabs* BOBO *senselessly by the collar and starts to shake him*) We got to!

BOBO   (*In sudden angry, frightened agony*) What's the matter with you, Walter! *When a cat take off with your money he don't leave you no maps!*

WALTER   (*Turning madly, as though he is looking for* WILLY *in the very room*) Willy! . . . Willy . . . don't do it . . . Please don't do it . . . Man, not with that money . . . Man, please, not with that money . . . Oh, God . . . Don't let it be true . . . (*He is wandering around, crying out for* WILLY *and looking for him or perhaps for help from God*) Man . . . I trusted you . . . Man, I put my life in your hands . . . (*He starts to crumple down on the floor as* RUTH *just covers her face in horror.* MAMA *opens the door and comes into the room, with* BENEATHA *behind her*) Man . . . (*He starts to pound the floor with his fists, sobbing wildly*) *That money is made out of my father's flesh . . .*

BOBO (*Standing over him helplessly*) I'm sorry, Walter . . . (*Only* WALTER'S *sobs reply.* BOBO *puts on his hat*) I had my life staked on this deal, too . . .

He exits.

MAMA (*To* WALTER) Son—(*She goes to him, bends down to him, talks to him, talks to his bent head*) Son . . . Is it gone? Son, I gave you sixty-five hundred dollars. Is it gone? All of it? Beneatha's money too?

WALTER (*Lifting his head slowly*) Mama . . . I never . . . went to the bank at all . . .

MAMA (*Not wanting to believe him*) You mean . . . your sister's school money . . . you used that too . . . Walter? . . .

WALTER Yessss! . . . All of it . . . It's all gone . . .

There is total silence, RUTH *stands with her face covered with hands;* BENEATHA *leans forlornly against a wall, fingering a piece of red ribbon from the mother's gift.* MAMA *stops and looks at her son without recognition and then, quite without thinking about it, starts to beat him senselessly in the face.* BENEATHA *goes to them and stops it.*

BENEATHA Mama!

MAMA *stops and looks at both of her children and rises slowly and wanders vaguely, aimlessly away from them.*

MAMA I seen . . . him . . . night after night . . . come in . . . and look at that rug . . . and then look at me . . . the red showing in his eyes . . . the veins moving in his head . . . I seen him grow thin and old before he was forty . . . working and working and working like somebody's old horse . . . killing himself—and you—you give it all away in a day . . .

BENEATHA Mama—

MAMA Oh, God . . . (*She looks up to Him*) Look down here—and show me the strength.

BENEATHA Mama—

MAMA (*Folding over*) Strength . . .

BENEATHA (*Plaintively*) Mama . . .

MAMA Strength!

Curtain

ACT THREE

An hour later.

At curtain, there is a sullen light of gloom in the living room, gray light not unlike that which began the first scene of Act One. At left we can see WALTER *within his room, alone with himself. He is stretched out on the bed, his shirt out and open, his arms under his head. He does not smoke, he does not cry out, he merely lies there, looking up at the ceiling, much as if he were alone in the world.*
In the living room BENEATHA *sits at the table, still surrounded by the now almost ominous packing crates. She sits looking off. We feel that this is a mood struck perhaps an hour before, and it lingers now, full of the empty sound of profound disappointment. We see on a line from her brother's bedroom the sameness of their attitudes. Presently the bell rings and* BENEATHA *rises without ambition or interest in answering. It is* ASAGAI, *smiling broadly, striding into the room with energy and happy expectation and conversation.*

ASAGAI   I came over . . . I had some free time. I thought I might help with the packing. Ah, I like the look of packing crates! A household in preparation for a journey! It depresses some people . . . but for me . . . it is another feeling. Something full of the flow of life, do you understand? Movement, progress . . . It makes me think of Africa.

BENEATHA   Africa!

ASAGAI   What kind of a mood is this? Have I told you how deeply you move me?

BENEATHA   He gave away the money, Asagai . . .

ASAGAI   Who gave away what money?

BENEATHA   The insurance money. My brother gave it away.

ASAGAI   Gave it away?

BENEATHA   He made an investment! With a man even Travis wouldn't have trusted.

ASAGAI   And it's gone?

BENEATHA   Gone!

ASAGAI   I'm very sorry . . . And you, now?

BENEATHA   Me? . . . Me? . . . Me I'm nothing . . . Me. When I was very small . . . we used to take our sleds out in the wintertime and the only hills we had were the ice-covered stone steps of some houses down the street. And we used to fill them in with snow and make them smooth and slide down them all day . . .

and it was very dangerous you know . . . far too steep . . . and sure enough one day a kid named Rufus came down too fast and hit the sidewalk . . . and we saw his face just split open right there in front of us . . . And I remember standing there looking at his bloody open face thinking that was the end of Rufus. But the ambulance came and they took him to the hospital and they fixed the broken bones and they sewed it all up . . . and the next time I saw Rufus he just had a little line down the middle of his face . . . I never got over that . . .

WALTER *sits up, listening on the bed. Throughout this scene it is important that we feel his reaction at all times, that he visibly respond to the words of his sister and* ASAGAI.

ASAGAI   What?

BENEATHA   That that was what one person could do for another, fix him up—sew up the problem, make him all right again. That was the most marvelous thing in the world . . . I wanted to do that. I always thought it was the one concrete thing in the world that a human being could do. Fix up the sick, you know—and make them whole again. This was truly being God . . .

ASAGAI   You wanted to be God?

BENEATHA   No—I wanted to cure. It used to be so important to me. I wanted to cure. It used to matter. I used to care. I mean about people and how their bodies hurt . . .

ASAGAI   And you've stopped caring?

BENEATHA   Yes—I think so.

ASAGAI   Why?

WALTER *rises, goes to the door of his room and is about to open it, then stops and stands listening, leaning on the door jamb.*

BENEATHA   Because it doesn't seem deep enough, close enough to what ails mankind—I mean this thing of sewing up bodies or administering drugs. Don't you understand? It was a child's reaction to the world. I thought that doctors had the secret to all the hurts . . . That's the way a child sees things—or an idealist.

ASAGAI   Children see things very well sometimes—and idealists even better.

BENEATHA   I know that's what you think. Because you are still where I left off—you still care. This is what you see for the world, for Africa. You with the dreams of the future will patch up all Africa—you are going to cure the Great Sore of colonialism with Independence—

ASAGAI Yes!

BENEATHA Yes—and you think that one word is the penicillin of the human spirit: "Independence!" But then what?

ASAGAI That will be the problem for another time. First we must get there.

BENEATHA And where does it end?

ASAGAI End? Who even spoke of an end? To life? To living?

BENEATHA An end to misery!

ASAGAI (*Smiling*) You sound like a French intellectual.

BENEATHA No! I sound like a human being who just had her future taken right out of her hands! While I was sleeping in my bed in there, things were happening in this world that directly concerned me—and nobody asked me, consulted me—they just went out and did things—and changed my life. Don't you see there isn't any real progress, Asagai, there is only one large circle that we march in, around and around, each of us with our own little picture—in front of us—our own little mirage that we think is the future.

ASAGAI That is the mistake.

BENEATHA What?

ASAGAI What you just said—about the circle. It isn't a circle—it is simply a long line—as in geometry, you know, one that reaches into infinity. And because we cannot see the end—we also cannot see how it changes. And it is very odd but those who see the changes are called "idealists"—and those who cannot, or refuse to think, they are the "realists." It is very strange, and amusing too, I think.

BENEATHA You—you are almost religious.

ASAGAI Yes . . . I think I have the religion of doing what is necessary in the world—and of worshipping man—because he is so marvelous, you see.

BENEATHA Man is foul! And the human race deserves its misery!

ASAGAI You see: *you* have become the religious one in the old sense. Already, and after such a small defeat, you are worshipping despair.

BENEATHA From now on, I worship the truth—and the truth is that people are puny, small and selfish. . . .

ASAGAI   Truth? Why is it that you despairing ones always think that only you have the truth? I never thought to see *you* like that. You! Your brother made a stupid, childish mistake—and you are grateful to him. So that now you can give up the ailing human race on account of it. You talk about what good is struggle; what good is anything? Where are we all going? And why are we bothering?

BENEATHA   *And you cannot answer it!* All your talk and dreams about Africa and Independence. Independence and then what? What about all the crooks and petty thieves and just plain idiots who will come into power to steal and plunder the same as before—only now they will be black and do it in the name of the new Independence—You cannot answer that.

ASAGAI   (*Shouting over her*) *I live the answer!* (*Pause*) In my village at home it is the exceptional man who can even read a newspaper . . . or who even *sees* a book at all. I will go home and much of what I will have to say will seem strange to the people of my village . . . But I will teach and work and things will happen, slowly and swiftly. At times it will seem that nothing changes at all . . . and then again . . . the sudden dramatic events which make history leap into the future. And then quiet again. Retrogression even. Guns, murder, revolution. And I even will have moments when I wonder if the quiet was not better than all that death and hatred. But I will look about my village at the illiteracy and disease and ignorance and I will not wonder long. And perhaps . . . perhaps I will be a great man . . . I mean perhaps I will hold on to the substance of truth and find my way always with the right course . . . and perhaps for it I will be butchered in my bed some night by the servants of empire . . .

BENEATHA   *The martyr!*

ASAGAI   . . . or perhaps I shall live to be a very old man, respected and esteemed in my new nation . . . And perhaps I shall hold office and this is what I'm trying to tell you, Alaiyo; perhaps the things I believe now for my country will be wrong and outmoded, and I will not understand and do terrible things to have things my way or merely to keep my power. Don't you see that there will be young men and women, not British soldiers then, but my own black countrymen . . . to step out of the shadows some evening and slit my then useless throat? Don't you see they have always been there . . . that they always will be. And that such a thing as my own death will be an advance? They who might kill me even . . . actually replenish me!

BENEATHA   Oh, Asagai, I know all that.

ASAGAI   Good! Then stop moaning and groaning and tell me what you plan to do.

BENEATHA   Do?

ASAGAI   I have a bit of a suggestion.

BENEATHA   What?

ASAGAI   (*Rather quietly for him*) That when it is all over—that you come home with me—

BENEATHA   (*Slapping herself on the forehead with exasperation born of misunderstanding*) Oh—Asagai—at this moment you decide to be romantic!

ASAGAI   (*Quickly understanding the misunderstanding*) My dear, young creature of the New World—I do not mean across the city—I mean across the ocean; home—to Africa.

BENEATHA   (*Slowly understanding and turning to him with murmured amazement*) To—to Nigeria?

ASAGAI   Yes! . . . (*Smiling and lifting his arms playfully*) Three hundred years later the African Prince rose up out of the seas and swept the maiden back across the middle passage over which her ancestors had come—

BENEATHA   (*Unable to play*) Nigeria?

ASAGAI   Nigeria. Home. (*Coming to her with genuine romantic flippancy*) I will show you our mountains and our stars; and give you cool drinks from gourds and teach you the old songs and the ways of our people—and, in time, we will pretend that —(*Very softly*)—you have only been away for a day—

She turns her back to him, thinking. He swings her around and takes her full in his arms in a long embrace which proceeds to passion.

BENEATHA   (*Pulling away*)   You're getting me all mixed up—

ASAGAI   Why?

BENEATHA   Too many things—too many things have happened today. I must sit down and think. I don't know what I feel about anything right this minute.

She promptly sits down and props her chin on her fist.

ASAGAI (*Charmed*)   All right, I shall leave you. No—don't get up.
(*Touching her, gently, sweetly*)   Just sit awhile and think . . .
Never be afraid to sit awhile and think. (*He goes to door and
looks at her*) How often I have looked at you and said, "Ah—
so this is what the New World hath finally wrought . . ."

He exits. BENEATHA *sits on alone. Presently* WALTER *enters
from his room and starts to rummage through things, feverishly
looking for something. She looks up and turns in her seat.*

BENEATHA (*Hissingly*)   Yes—just look at what the New World hath
wrought! . . . Just look! (*She gestures with bitter disgust*) There
he is! *Monsieur le petit bourgeois noir*—himself! There he is
—Symbol of a Rising Class! Entrepreneur! Titan of the system!
WALTER *ignores her completely and continues frantically and
destructively looking for something and hurling things to floor
and tearing things out of their place in his search.* BENEATHA
*ignores the eccentricity of his actions and goes on with the
monologue of insult*) Did you dream of yachts on Lake Michi-
gan, Brother? Did you see yourself on that Great Day sitting
down at the Conference Table, surrounded by all the mighty
·bald-headed men in America? All halted, waiting, breathless,
waiting for your pronouncements on industry? Waiting for you
—-Chairman of the Board? (WALTER *finds what he is looking
for—a small piece of white paper—and pushes it in his pocket
and puts on his coat and rushes out without ever having looked
at her. She shouts after him*) I look at you and I see the final
triumph of stupidity in the world!

The door slams and she returns to just sitting again. RUTH *comes
quickly out of* MAMA'S *room.*

RUTH   Who was that?

BENEATHA   Your husband.

RUTH   Where did he go?

BENEATHA   Who knows—maybe he has an appointment at U.S.
Steel.

RUTH (*Anxiously, with frightened eyes*)   You didn't say nothing
bad to him, did you?

BENEATHA   Bad? Say anything bad to him? No—I told him he was
a sweet boy and full of dreams and everything is strictly peachy
keen, as the ofay kids say!

MAMA *enters from her bedroom. She is lost, vague, trying to
catch hold, to make some sense of her former command of the*

world, but it still eludes her. A sense of waste overwhelms her gait; a measure of apology rides on her shoulders. She goes to her plant, which has remained on the table, looks at it, picks it up and takes it to the window sill and sits it outside, and she stands and looks at it a long moment. Then she closes the window, straightens her body with effort and turns around to her children.

MAMA   Well— ain't it a mess in here, though? (*A false cheerfulness, a beginning of something*) I guess we all better stop moping around and get some work done. All this unpacking and everything we got to do. (RUTH *raises her head slowly in response to the sense of the line; and* BENEATHA *in similar manner turns very slowly to look at her mother*) One of you all better call the moving people and tell 'em not to come.

RUTH   Tell 'em not to come?

MAMA   Of course, baby. Ain't no need in 'em coming all the way here and having to go back. They charges for that too. (*She sits down, fingers to her brow, thinking*) Lord, ever since I was a little girl, I always remembers people saying, "Lena—Lena Eggleston, you aims too high all the time. You needs to slow down and see life a little more like it is. Just slow down some." That's what they always used to say down home—"Lord, that Lena Eggleston is a high-minded thing. She'll get her due one day!"

RUTH   No. Lena . . .

MAMA   Me and Big Walter just didn't never learn right.

RUTH   Lena, no! We gotta go. Bennie—tell her . . . (*She rises and crosses to* BENEATHA *with her arms outstretched.* BENEATHA *doesn't respond*) Tell her we can still move . . . the notes ain't but a hundred and twenty-five a month. We got four grown people in this house—we can work.

MAMA (*To herself*) Just aimed too high all the time—

RUTH (*Turning and going to* MAMA *fast—the words pouring out with urgency and desperation*) Lena—I'll work . . . I'll work twenty hours a day in all the kitchens in Chicago . . . I'll strap my baby on my back if I have to and scrub all the floors in America and wash all the sheets in America if I have to—but we got to move . . . We got to get out of here . . .

MAMA *reaches out absently and pats* RUTH'S *hand.*

MAMA   No—I see things differently now. Been thinking 'bout some of the things we could do to fix this place up some. I seen a second-hand bureau over on Maxwell Street just the other day that could fit right there. (*She points to where the new furniture might go.* RUTH *wanders away from her*) Would need some new handles on it and then a little varnish and then it look like something brand-new. And—we can put up them new curtains in the kitchen . . . Why this place be looking fine. Cheer us all up so that we forget trouble ever came . . . (*To* RUTH) And you could get some nice screens to put up in your room round the baby's bassinet . . . (*She looks at both of them, pleadingly*) Sometimes you just got to know when to give up some things . . . and hold on to what you got.

WALTER *enters from the outside, looking spent and leaning against the door, his coat hanging from him.*

MAMA   Where you been, son?

WALTER   (*Breathing hard*) Made a call.

MAMA   To who, son?

WALTER   To The Man.

MAMA   What man, baby?

WALTER   The Man, Mama. Don't you know who The Man is?

RUTH   Walter Lee?

WALTER   *The Man.* Like the guys in the streets say—The Man, Captain Boss—Mistuh Charley . . . Old Captain Please Mr. Bossman . . .

BENEATHA   (*Suddenly*) Lindner!

WALTER   That's right! That's good. I told him to come right over.

BENEATHA   (*Fiercely, understanding*) For what? What do you want to see him for!

WALTER   (*Looking at his sister*) We going to do business with him.

MAMA   What you talking 'bout, son?

WALTER   Talking 'bout life, Mama. You all always telling me to see life like it is. Well—I laid in there on my back today . . . and I figured it out. Life just like it is. Who gets and who don't get. (*He sits down with his coat on and laughs*) Mama, you know it's all divided up. Life is. Sure enough. Between the takers and the "tooken." (*He laughs*) I've figured it out finally. (*He looks around at them*) Yeah. Some of us always getting "tooken." (*He laughs*) People like Willy Harris, they don't never get "tooken." And you know why the rest of us do? 'Cause we all mixed up. Mixed up bad. We get to looking 'round for the right and the wrong; and we worry about it and cry about it and stay up nights trying to figure out 'bout the wrong and the right of things all the time . . . And all the time, man, them takers is out there operating, just taking and taking. Willy Harris? Shoot— Willy Harris don't even count. He don't even count in the big scheme of things. But I'll say one thing for old Willy Harris . . . he's taught me something. He's taught me to keep my eye on what counts in this world. Yeah — (*Shouting out a little*) Thanks, Willy!

RUTH   What did you call that man for, Walter Lee?

WALTER   Called him to tell him to come on over to the show. Gonna put on a show for the man. Just what he wants to see. You see, Mama, the man came here today and he told us that them people out there where you want us to move—well they so upset they willing to pay us not to move out there. (*He laughs again*) And—and oh, Mama—you would of been proud of the way me and Ruth and Bennie acted. We told him to get out . . . Lord have mercy! We told the man to get out. Oh, we was some proud folks this afternoon, yeah. (*He lights a cigarette*) We were still full of that old-time stuff . . .

RUTH   (*Coming toward him slowly*) You talking 'bout taking them people's money to keep us from moving in that house?

WALTER   I ain't just talking 'bout it, baby—I'm telling you that's what's going to happen.

BENEATHA   Oh, God! Where is the bottom! Where is the real honest-to-God bottom so he can't go any farther!

WALTER   See—that's the old stuff. You and that boy that was here today. You all want everybody to carry a flag and a spear and sing some marching songs, huh? You wanna spend your life looking into things and trying to find the right and the wrong part, huh? Yeah. You know what's going to happen to that boy someday—he'll find himself sitting in a dungeon, locked in forever—and the takers will have the key! Forget it, baby! There ain't no causes—there ain't nothing but taking in this world, and he who takes most is smartest—and it don't make a damn bit of difference *how*.

MAMA   You making something inside me cry, son. Some awful pain inside me.

WALTER   Don't cry, Mama. Understand. That white man is going to walk in that door able to write checks for more money than we ever had. It's important to him and I'm going to help him . . . I'm going to put on the show, Mama.

MAMA   Son—I come from five generations of people who was slaves and sharecroppers—but ain't nobody in my family never let nobody pay 'em no money that was a way of telling us we wasn't fit to walk the earth. We ain't never been that poor. (*Raising her eyes and looking at him*) We ain't never been that dead inside.

BENEATHA   Well—we are dead now. All the talk about dreams and sunlight that goes on in this house. All dead.

WALTER   What's the matter with you all! I didn't make this world! It was give to me this way! Hell, yes, I want me some yachts someday! Yes, I want to hang some real pearls 'round my wife's neck. Ain't she supposed to wear no pearls? Somebody tell me —tell me, who decides which women is suppose to wear pearls in this world. I tell you I am a *man*—and I think my wife should wear some pearls in this world!

This last line hangs a good while and WALTER *begins to move about the room. The word "Man" has penetrated his consciousness; he mumbles it to himself repeatedly between strange agitated pauses as he moves about.*

MAMA   Baby, how you going to feel on the inside?

WALTER   Fine! . . . Going to feel fine . . . a man . . .

MAMA   You won't have nothing left then, Walter Lee.

WALTER   (*Coming to her*) I'm going to feel fine, Mama. I'm going to look that son-of-a-bitch in the eyes and say—(*He falters*)—and say, "All right, Mr. Lindner—(*He falters even more*)—that's your neighborhood out there. You got the right to keep it like you want. You got the right to have it like you want. Just write the check and—the house is yours." And, and I am going to say— (*His voice almost breaks*) And you—you people just put the money in my hand and you won't have to live next to this bunch of stinking niggers! . . . (*He straightens up and moves away from his mother, walking around the room*) Maybe—maybe I'll just get down on my black knees . . . (*He does so;* RUTH *and* BENNIE *and* MAMA *watch him in frozen horror*) Captain, Mistuh, Bossman. (*He starts crying*) A-hee-hee-hee! (*Wringing his hands in profoundly anguished imitat-*

tion) Yasssssuh! Great White Father, just gi' ussen de money, fo' God's sake, and we's ain't gwine come out deh and dirty up yo white folks neighborhood . . .

He breaks down completely, then gets up and goes into the bedroom.

BENEATHA   That is not a man. That is nothing but a toothless rat.

MAMA   Yes—death done come in this here house. (*She is nodding, slowly, reflectively*) Done come walking in my house. On the lips of my children. You what supposed to be my beginning again. You—what supposed to be my harvest. (*To* BENEATHA) You—you mourning your brother?

BENEATHA   He's no brother of mine.

MAMA   What you say?

BENEATHA   I said that that individual in that room is no brother of mine.

MAMA   That's what I thought you said. You feeling like you better than he is today? (BENEATHA *does not answer*) Yes? What you tell him a minute ago? That he wasn't a man? Yes? You give him up for me? You done wrote his epitaph too—like the rest of the world? Well, who give you the privilege?

BENEATHA   Be on my side for once! You saw what he just did, Mama! You saw him—down on his knees. Wasn't it you who taught me—to despise any man who would do that. Do what he's going to do.

MAMA   Yes—I taught you that. Me and your daddy. But I thought I taught you something else too . . . I thought I taught you to love him.

BENEATHA   Love him? There is nothing left to love.

MAMA   There is always something left to love. And if you ain't learned that, you ain't learned nothing. (*Looking at her*) Have you cried for that boy today? I don't mean for yourself and for the family 'cause we lost the money. I mean for him; what he been through and what it done to him. Child, when do you think is the time to love somebody the most; when they done good and made things easy for everybody? Well then, you ain't through learning—because that ain't the time at all. It's when he's at his lowest and can't believe in hisself 'cause the world done whipped him so. When you starts measuring somebody, measure him right, child, measure him right. Make sure you done taken into account what hills and valleys he come through before he got to wherever he is.

TRAVIS *bursts into the room at the end of the speech, leaving the door open.*

TRAVIS   Grandmama—the moving men are downstairs! The truck just pulled up.

MAMA   (*Turning and looking at him*) Are they, baby? They downstairs?

She sighs and sits. LINDNER *appears in the doorway. He peers in and knocks lightly, to gain attention, and comes in. All turn to look at him.*

LINDNER   (*Hat and briefcase in hand*) Uh—hello . . . (RUTH *crosses mechanically to the bedroom door and opens it and lets it swing open freely and slowly as the lights come up on* WALTER *within, still in his coat, sitting at the far corner of the room. He looks up and out through the room to* LINDNER.

RUTH   He's here.

A long minute passes and WALTER *slowly gets up.*

LINDNER   (*Coming to the table with efficiency, putting his briefcase on the table and starting to unfold papers and unscrew fountain pens*) Well, I certainly was glad to hear from you people. (WALTER *has begun the trek out of the room, slowly and awkwardly, rather like a small boy, passing the back of his sleeve across his mouth from time to time*) Life can really be so much simpler than people let it be most of the time. Well— with whom do I negotiate? You, Mrs. Younger, or your son here? (MAMA *sits with her hands folded on her lap and her eyes closed as* WALTER *advances.* TRAVIS *goes close to* LINDNER *and looks at the papers curiously*) Just some official papers, sonny.

RUTH   Travis, you go downstairs.

MAMA   (*Opening her eyes and looking into* WALTER'S) No. Travis, you stay right here. And you make him understand what you doing, Walter Lee. You teach him good. Like Willy Harris taught you. You show where our five generations done come to. Go ahead, son—

WALTER   (*Looks down into his boy's eyes.* TRAVIS *grins at him merrily and* WALTER *draws him beside him with his arm lightly around his shoulders*) Well, Mr. Lindner. (BENEATHA *turns away*) We called you—(*There is a profound, simple groping quality in his speech*)—because, well, me and my family (*He looks around and shifts from one foot to the other*) Well—we are very plain people . . .

LINDNER   Yes—

WALTER   I mean—I have worked as a chauffeur most of my life— and my wife here, she does domestic work in people's kitchens. So does my mother. I mean—we are plain people . . .

LINDNER   Yes, Mr. Younger—

WALTER (*Really like a small boy, looking down at his shoes and then up at the man*) And—uh—well, my father, well, he was a laborer most of his life.

LINDNER (*Absolutely confused*) Uh, yes—

WALTER (*Looking down at his toes once again*) My father almost beat a man to death once because this man called him a bad name or something, you know what I mean?

LINDNER   No, I'm afraid I don't.

WALTER (*Finally straightening up*) Well, what I mean is that we come from people who had a lot of pride. I mean—we are very proud people. And that's my sister over there and she's going to be a doctor—and we are very proud—

LINDNER   Well—I am sure that is very nice, but—

WALTER (*Starting to cry and facing the man eye to eye*) What I am telling you is that we called you over here to tell you that we are very proud and that this is—this is my son, who makes the sixth generation of our family in this country, and that we have all thought about your offer and we have decided to move into our house because my father—my father—he earned it. (MAMA *has her eyes closed and is rocking back and forth as though she were in church, with her head nodding the amen yes*) We don't want to make no trouble for nobody or fight no causes—but we will try to be good neighbors. That's all we got to say. (*He looks the man absolutely in the eyes*) We don't want your money. *He turns and walks away from the man.*

LINDNER (*Looking around at all of them*) I take it then that you have decided to occupy.

BENEATHA   That's what the man said.

LINDNER (*To* MAMA *in her reverie*) Then I would like to appeal to you, Mrs. Younger. You are older and wiser and understand things better I am sure . . .

MAMA (*Rising*) I am afraid you don't understand. My son said we was going to move and there ain't nothing left for me to say. (*Shaking her head with double meaning*) You know how these young folks is nowadays, mister. Can't do a thing with 'em. Good-bye.

LINDNER (*Folding up his materials*) Well—if you are that final about it . . . There is nothing left for me to say. (*He finishes. He is almost ignored by the family, who are concentrating on* WALTER LEE. *At the door* LINDNER *halts and looks around*) I sure hope you people know what you're doing.

He shakes his head and exits.

RUTH (*Looking around and coming to life*) Well, for God's sake—if the moving men are here—LET'S GET THE HELL OUT OF HERE!

MAMA (*Into action*) Ain't it the truth! Look at all this here mess. Ruth, put Travis' good jacket on him . . . Walter Lee, fix your tie and tuck your shirt in, you look just like somebody's hoodlum. Lord have mercy, where is my plant? (*She flies to get it amid the general bustling of the family, who are deliberately trying to ignore the nobility of the past moment*) You all start on down . . . Travis child, don't go empty-handed . . . Ruth, where did I put that box with my skillets in it? I want to be in charge of it myself . . . I'm going to make us the biggest dinner we ever ate tonight . . . Beneatha, what's the matter with them stockings? Pull them things up, girl . . .

The family starts to file out as two moving men appear and begin to carry out the heavier pieces of furniture, bumping into the family as they move about.

BENEATHA   Mama, Asagai—asked me to marry him today and go to Africa—

MAMA (*In the middle of her getting-ready activity*) He did? You ain't old enough to marry nobody—(*Seeing the moving men lifting one of her chairs precariously*) Darling, that ain't no bale of cotton, please handle it so we can sit in it again. I had that chair twenty-five years . . .

The movers sigh with exasperation and go on with their work.

BENEATHA (*Girlishly and unreasonably trying to pursue the conversation*) To go to Africa, Mama—be a doctor in Africa . . .

MAMA (*Distracted*) Yes, baby—

WALTER   Africa! What he want you to go to Africa for?

BENEATHA   To practice there . . .

WALTER   Girl, if you don't get all them silly ideas out your head! You better marry yourself a man with some loot . . .

BENEATHA (*Angrily, precisely as in the first scene of the play*) What have you got to do with who I marry!

WALTER   Plenty. Now I think George Murchison—

He and BENEATHA *go out yelling at each other vigorously;* BENEATHA *is heard saying that she would not marry* GEORGE MURCHISON *if he were Adam and she were Eve, etc. The anger is loud and real till their voices diminish.* RUTH *stands at the door and turns to* MAMA *and smiles knowingly.*

MAMA (*Fixing her hat at last*) Yeah—they something all right, my children . . .

RUTH   Yeah—they're something. Let's go, Lena.

MAMA (*Stalling, starting to look around at the house*) Yes—I'm coming. Ruth—

RUTH   Yes?

MAMA (*Quietly, woman to woman*) He finally come into his manhood today, didn't he? Kind of like a rainbow after the rain . . .

RUTH (*Biting her lip lest her own pride explode in front of* MAMA) Yes, Lena.

WALTER'S *voice calls for them raucously.*

MAMA (*Waving* RUTH *out vaguely*) All right, honey—go on down. I be down directly.

RUTH *hesitates, then exits.* MAMA *stands, at last alone in the living room, her plant on the table before her as the lights start to come down. She looks around at all the walls and ceilings and suddenly, despite herself, while the children call below, a great heaving thing rises in her and she puts her fist to her mouth, takes a final desperate look, pulls her coat about her, pats her hat and goes out. The lights dim down. The door opens and she comes back in, grabs her plant, and goes out for the last time.*

Curtain

Further Suggestions for Study

1. What traits make the characters in this play so believable?
2. How would YOU settle the three conflicting family goals?
   (a) Mama Younger wants to use the insurance money to provide a new home for her family, far away from the slum neighborhood.
   (b) Beneatha wants the family to finance her medical schooling.
   (c) Walter wants a business of his own.
3. Imagine the Younger family settled in the new home. What new struggles will have to be faced?
4. Exactly what constitutes Mama Younger's strength of character?
5. Why, at the end of the play, does Walter change his mind about accepting Lindner's money in return for an agreement not to move into the white neighborhood?
6. In what ways does the Younger home setting intensify the conflict?
7. Select any five *coups de théâtre* (highly dramatic crises or emotional scenes) and explain why these scenes achieve such an emotional impact.
8. What is the reason for Asagai, the Nigerian, being a part of the plot in *A Raisin in the Sun*? Why would the screen version omit the Asagai sequences? Would the play lose dramatically by the omission?
9. What would you consider to be the characteristics of the negro sense of humor?
10. Assuming you are the director of this play, how would you use setting, lighting, and background music to reflect the basic theme and mood?

INHERIT THE WIND

BY JEROME LAWRENCE AND ROBERT E. LEE

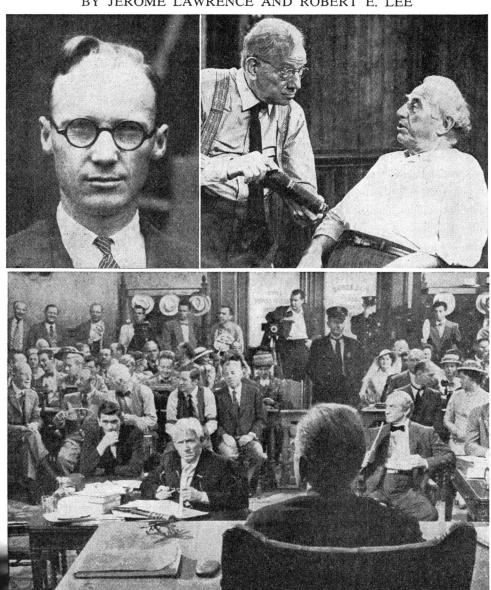

Upper left: *John T. Scopes in 1925 at the time of the trial.* (PHOTO: WORLD WIDE PHOTOS)

Upper right: *BRADY: Natural law was born in the mind of the Heavenly Father. He can change it, cancel it, use it as he pleases. It constantly amazes me that you apostles of science, for all your supposed wisdom, fail to grasp this simple fact.* (PHOTO: C.B.C.)

Lower: *The courtroom, Hillsboro Courthouse.* (PHOTO: UNITED ARTISTS)

INTRODUCTION/*Inherit the Wind*

When *Inherit the Wind* made its impact upon Broadway audiences in 1955, the theatre critics knew that a remarkable play had been written:

"One of the most stirring plays in recent years . . . Bursting with vitality . . . literature of the stage." (Atkinson, *New York Times.*)

"Magnificently written . . . one of the most exciting dramas of the last decade."   (Chapman, *New York Times.*)

"A tidal wave of drama. More than any other play in memory, based on history and aiming at a contemporary parallel, *Inherit the Wind* makes its points immediately applicable."

(Hawkins, *New York World Telegram and Sun.*)

What was it about this new play that produced such overwhelming praise wherever it was played? Drama critic John Rosenfield of the *Dallas Morning News* expressed it best when he wrote, after the world premiere at the Dallas Theatre, Texas, January 10, 1955: "A new play of power, humanity and universal truth. For an 'ideas' play, *Inherit the Wind* is argued in remarkably human terms . . . Messrs. Shaw and Ibsen often faltered at the same thing."

The secret of great theatre is the ability to lift the words of the script across the footlights and to hit the minds and hearts of the audience like an arrow of fire. The play's theme as expressed by Henry Drummond, "the right to think," is the stuff of which great, universal drama is made. As the play unfolds, the audience finds itself compelled to ask:

* How far can a law restrict our search for truth?
* Are we still assured the right to dissent?
* If all areas of knowledge were to be taught freely in schools, including religion, politics, ethics, what possible dangers would have to be guarded against considering the impressionable minds of young adults?
* Is Voltaire's dictum: "I disapprove of what you say but I will defend to the death your right to say it" still our guide?

Inherit the Wind is not a true, historical document. The authors deliberately chose to write the play as a piece of fiction based on the 1925 Scopes trial. Scopes, a young science teacher in his first year of teaching, taught a biology lesson while substituting for the regular teacher. The Butler Act of Tennessee prohibited the teaching of the theory of evolution in all universities and schools. In the play, William Jennings Bryan becomes Matthew Harrison Brady, Clarence Darrow becomes Henry Drummond, John Scopes becomes Bert Cates, H. L. Mencken becomes E. K. Hornbeck.

The play's historical background:

1. The Tennessee Legislature, January 28, 1925, passed the Butler Act prohibiting the teaching of Darwinism or the theory of evolution as it pertained to man.

2. The Civil Liberties Union in New York City asked John Thomas Scopes, a science teacher in Dayton, Tennessee to agree to be arrested, expenses paid, in a test case, on the grounds that he had taught evolution from the state approved biology textbook, *Civic Biology* by George William Hunter. Scopes agreed, in May, 1925, despite the fact that he had taught evolution only while substituting for the principal who was sick.

3. A few days later, William Jennings Bryan agreed to serve as special prosecutor. Bryan was a prominent lawyer, Democratic candidate for the Presidency of the United States of America in 1896, 1900, and in 1908, Secretary of State in the cabinet of Woodrow Wilson, 1913-15, a leader in the prohibition of alcohol movement, editor of the *Omaha World Herald,* and a world famous orator, remembered for his "Cross of Gold" speech at the Democratic National Convention, Chicago, 1896, when he advocated a double silver and gold monetary standard.

4. On hearing of Bryan's appointment, Clarence Darrow at once volunteered his free services as assistant defense counsel to Dudley Field Malone. Darrow was a famous criminal defense lawyer whose cases had included the recent (1925) Loeb and Leopold murder case. As a fervent humanitarian, Darrow was later (1932) to defend the Negroes in the famous Scottsboro case.

5. With the trial of Scopes convened for Dayton, Tennessee, the typical mountain town, population 1,800, became a summer fair in the days before the trial. Lemonade stands, popcorn vendors, side shows, travelling evangelists, and promoters of

every kind transformed the town into a circus. Hotel rates doubled as over three thousand photographers, newspapermen, cartoonists, radio newsmen, and the inevitable sensation seekers poured into the small town. Bryan himself travelled to the town in a loudspeaker truck extolling the virtues of Florida real estate.

6. The trial began on July 10th, 1925 and lasted eleven, broiling, summer heat days, ending in a verdict of guilty and a one hundred dollar fine.

7. Five days after the trial, Bryan died of (reportedly) apoplexy.

8. In the summer of 1926 the appeal to the Supreme Court of Tennessee was argued without the presence of Scopes. The verdict was a reversal of the Dayton judgement on a technicality: the one hundred dollar fine had been imposed by the judge instead of by the jury. The appeal court thus avoided the whole point of the trial by not expressing an opinion on whether or not Scopes had violated the law.

9. Scopes went on to complete a geology degree, on a scholarship grant, and was offered a university fellowship to study the origins of oil and gas formations. The president of the university administering the fellowship refused to accept Scopes' name for consideration on the grounds of his beliefs.

10. Scopes left the United States for a position with Gulf Oil of South America as a geologist, returned to the United States a married man and worked as a geologist until his retirement in 1964.

(Reference: *Centre of the Storm: Memoirs of John T. Scopes,* John Scopes and James Presley, Holt, Rinehart and Winston.)

Inherit the Wind was first presented at Theatre '55 on January 10, 1955 at Dallas, Texas. The first Broadway presentation was at the National Theatre, New York, April 21, 1955 with Paul Muni as Henry Drummond, Ed Begley as Matthew Harrison Brady, and Tony Randall as E. K. Hornbeck. The motion picture, 1960, featured Spencer Tracy as Henry Drummond and Frederick March as Matthew Harrison Brady. The television version of the play, 1965, featured Melvyn Douglas as Henry Drummond and Ed Begley as Matthew Harrison Brady.

As you read the play of *Inherit the Wind,* notice:

* The ways in which our system of trial by jury sometimes seems open to question.

* How the authors create character cameos within a mere few lines of dialogue, especially noticeable in the examination of the jurymen in ACT ONE, SCENE II.

* The ways in which the playwrights end each scene on a note of heightened suspense or emotion.

* The authors' direction that "the town is visible always, looming there, as much on trial as the individual defendant."

* The special position of Rachel within the plot. She seems to represent all of us who prefer not to suffer involvement in an unpopular cause.

* The difference between the hardbitten, cynical Hornbeck and the humanitarian Drummond in their reactions to the death of Brady.

INHERIT THE WIND

CHARACTERS

MELINDA	MRS. BLAIR
HOWARD	ELIJAH
RACHEL BROWN	E. K. HORNBECK
MEEKER	HURDY GURDY MAN
BERTRAM CATES	TIMMY
MR. GOODFELLOW	MAYOR
MRS. KREBS	MATTHEW HARRISON BRADY
REV. BROWN	MRS. BRADY
CORKIN	TOM DAVENPORT
BOLLINGER	HENRY DRUMMOND
PLATT	JUDGE
MR. BANNISTER	DUNLAP
MRS. LOOMIS	SILLERS
HOT DOG MAN	REUTERS MAN
MRS. McCLAIN	HARRY Y. ESTERBROOK

TOWNSPEOPLE, HAWKERS, REPORTERS, JURORS

ACT ONE

Scene I

In and around the Hillsboro Courthouse. The foreground is the actual courtroom, with jury box, judge's bench and a scattering of trial-scarred chairs and counsel tables. The back wall of the courtroom is non-existent. On a raked level above it is the courthouse square, the Main Street and the converging streets of the town. This is not so much a literal view of Hillsboro as it is an impression of a sleepy, obscure country town about to be vigorously awakened.

It is important to the concept of the play that the town is visible always, looming there, as much on trial as the individual defendant. The crowd is equally important throughout, so that the court becomes a cock-pit, an arena, with the active spectators on all sides of it.

It is an hour after dawn on a July day that promises to be a scorcher. HOWARD, *a boy of thirteen, wanders onto the courthouse lawn. He is barefoot, wearing a pair of his pa's cut-down overalls. He carries an improvised fishing pole and a tin can. He studies the ground carefully, searching for something. A young girl's voice calls from off-stage.*

MELINDA (*Calling sweetly*)   How-ard! (HOWARD, *annoyed, turns and looks toward the voice.* MELINDA, *a healthy, pigtailed girl of twelve, skips on*) Hello, Howard.

HOWARD *is disinterested, continues to search the ground.*

HOWARD   'Lo, Lindy.

MELINDA (*Making conversation*)   I think it's gonna be hotter'n yesterday. That rain last night didn't do much good.

HOWARD (*Professionally*)   It brought up the worms. (*Suddenly he spots one in the lawn. Swiftly he grabs for it, and holds it up proudly*) Lookit this fat one!

MELINDA (*Shivering*) How can you touch 'em? It makes me all goose bumpy!

HOWARD *dangles it in front of her face. She backs away, shuddering.*

HOWARD   What're yuh skeered of? *You* was a worm once!

MELINDA (*Shocked*) I wasn't neither!

HOWARD   You was so! When the whole world was covered with water, there was nuthin' but worms and blobs of jelly. And you and your whole family was worms!

MELINDA   We was not!

HOWARD   Blobs of jelly, then.

MELINDA   Howard Blair, that's sinful talk! I'm gonna tell my pa and he'll make you wash your mouth out with soap!

HOWARD   Ahhh, your old man's a monkey! (*Melinda gasps. She turns indignantly and runs off.* HOWARD *shrugs in the manner of a man-of-the-world*) 'Bye, Lindy. (*He deposits the worm in his tin can, and continues looking for more.* RACHEL *enters. She is twenty-two, pretty, but not beautiful. She wears a cotton summer dress. She carries a small composition-paper suitcase. There is a tense, distraught air about her. She may have been crying. She looks about nervously, as if she doesn't want to be seen. When she sees* HOWARD, *she hesitates; then she crosses quickly downstage into the courthouse area in the hope that the boy will not notice her. But he does see* RACHEL, *and watches her with puzzled curiosity. Then he spots another worm, tugs it out of the ground, and holds it up, wriggling.* HOWARD *addresses the worm*) What do you wanta be when you grow up?

RACHEL *stands uncertainly in the courthouse area. This is strange ground to her. Unsure, she looks about.*

RACHEL (*Tentatively, calling*) Mr. Meeker . . . ?

After a pause, a door at stage right opens. MR. MEEKER, *the bailiff, enters. There is no collar on his shirt; his hair is tousled, and there is shaving soap on his face, which he is wiping off with a towel as he enters.*

MEEKER (*A little irritably*) Who is it? (*Surprised*) Why, hello, Rachel. 'Scuse the way I look. (*He wipes the soap out of his ear. Then he notices her suitcase*) Not going' away, are you? Excitement's just startin'.

RACHEL (*Earnestly*) Mr. Meeker, don't let my father know I came here.

MEEKER (*Shrugs*) The Reverend don't tell me his business. Don't know why I should tell him mine.

RACHEL I want to see Bert Cates. Is he all right?

MEEKER Don't know why he shouldn't be. I always figured the safest place in the world is a jail.

RACHEL Can I go down and see him?

MEEKER Ain't a very proper place for a minister's daughter.

RACHEL I only want to see him for a minute.

MEEKER Sit down, Rachel. I'll bring him up. You can talk to him right here in the courtroom. (RACHEL *sits in one of the stiff wooden chairs.* MEEKER *starts out, then pauses*) Long as I've been bailiff here, we've never had nothin' but drunks, vagrants, couple of chicken thieves. (*A little dreamily*) Our best catch was that fella from Minnesota that chopped up his wife; we had to extradite him. (*Shakes his head*) Seems kinda queer havin' a school-teacher in our jail. (*Shrugs.*) Might improve the writin' on the walls.

MEEKER *goes out. Nervously,* RACHEL *looks around at the cold, official furnishings of the courtroom.* MEEKER *returns to the courtroom, followed by* BERT CATES. CATES *is a pale, thin young man of twenty-four. He is quiet, shy, well-mannered, not particularly good-looking.* RACHEL *and* CATES *face each other expressionlessly, without speaking.* MEEKER *pauses in the doorway.*

MEEKER I'll leave you two alone to talk. Don't run off, Bert.

MEEKER *goes out.* RACHEL *and* CATES *look at each other.*

RACHEL   Hello, Bert.

CATES   Rache, I told you not to come here.

RACHEL   I couldn't help it. Nobody saw me. Mr. Meeker won't tell
(*Troubled*) I keep thinking of you, locked up here—

CATES   (*Trying to cheer her up*) You know something funny? The
food's better than the boarding house. And you'd better not
tell anybody how cool it is down there, or we'll have a crime
wave every summer.

RACHEL   I stopped by your place and picked up some of your things.
A clean shirt, your best tie, some handkerchiefs.

CATES   Thanks.

RACHEL (*Rushing to him*) Bert, why don't you tell 'em it was all a
joke? Tell 'em you didn't mean to break a law, and you won't
do it again!

CATES   I suppose everybody's all steamed up about Brady coming.

RACHEL   He's coming in on a special train out of Chattanooga. Pa's
going to the station to meet him. Everybody is!

CATES   Strike up the band.

RACHEL   Bert, it's still not too late. Why can't you admit you're
wrong? If the biggest man in the country—next to the President,
maybe—if Matthew Harrison Brady comes here to tell the
whole world how wrong you are—

CATES   You still think I did wrong?

RACHEL   Why did you do it?

CATES   You know why I did it. I had the book in my hand, Hunter's
Civic Biology. I opened it up, and read my sophomore science
class Chapter 17, Darwin's *Origin of Species*. (RACHEL *starts
to protest*) All it says is that man wasn't just stuck here like
a geranium in a flower pot; that living comes from a *long*
miracle, it didn't just happen in seven days.

RACHEL   There's a law against it.

CATES   I know that.

RACHEL   Everybody says what you did is bad.

CATES   It isn't as simple as that. Good or bad, black or white, night
or day. Do you know, at the top of the world the twilight is
six months long?

RACHEL   But we don't live at the top of the world. We live in Hillsboro, and when the sun goes down, it's dark. And why do you
try to make it different? (RACHEL *gets the shirt, tie, and handkerchiefs from the suitcase*) Here,

CATES   Thanks, Rache.

RACHEL   Why can't you be on the right side of things?

CATES   Your father's side. (RACHEL *starts to leave.* CATES *runs after her*) Rache—love me!

They embrace. MEEKER *enters with a long-handled broom.*

MEEKER   (*Clears his throat*) I gotta sweep.

RACHEL *breaks away and hurries off.*

CATES   (*Calling*) Thanks for the shirt!

MEEKER, *who has been sweeping impassively now stops and leans on the broom.*

MEEKER   Imagine. Matthew Harrison Brady, comin' here. I voted for him for President. Twice. In nineteen hundred, and again in oh-eight. Wasn't old enough to vote for him the first time he ran. But my pa did. (*Turns proudly to* CATES) I *seen* him once. At a Chautauqua meeting in Chattanooga. (*Impressed, remembering*) The tent-poles shook! (CATES *moves nervously*) Who's gonna be your lawyer, son?

CATES   I don't know yet. I wrote to that newspaper in Baltimore. They're sending somebody.

MEEKER   (*Resumes sweeping*) He better be loud.

CATES   (*Picking up the shirt*) You want me to go back down?

MEEKER   No need. You can stay up here if you want.

CATES   (*Going toward the jail*) I'm supposed to be in jail; I'd better be in jail!

MEEKER *shrugs and follows* CATES *off. The lights fade in the courtroom area, and come up on the town: morning of a hot July day. The* STOREKEEPER *enters, unlocking his store.* MRS. KREBS *saunters across the square.*

STOREKEEPER   Warm enough for you, Mrs. Krebs?

MRS. KREBS   The Good Lord guv us the heat, and the Good Lord guv us the glands to sweat with.

STOREKEEPER   I bet the Devil ain't so obliging.

MRS. KREBS   Don't intend to find out.

The REVEREND JEREMIAH BROWN, *a gaunt, thin-lipped man, strides on. He looks around, scowling.*

STOREKEEPER   Good morning, Reverend.

BROWN   'Morning.

MRS. KREBS 'Morning Reverend.

BROWN   Mrs. Krebs. (*Shouting off*) Where's the banner? Why haven't you raised the banner?

CORKIN (*Entering, followed by another workman*) Paint didn't dry 'til jist now.

They are carrying a rolled-up canvas banner.

BROWN   See that you have it up before Mr. Brady arrives.

COOPER *enters, gestures "hello" to the others.*

CORKIN   Fast as we can do it, Reverend.

BROWN   We must show him at once what kind of a community this is.

CORKIN   Yes, Reverend. Come on, Phil. Hep.

They rig the banner to halyards between the buildings.

MRS. KREBS   Big day, Reverend.

CORKIN   Indeed it is. Picnic lunch ready, Mrs. Krebs?

MRS. KREBS   Fitt'n fer a king.

BANNISTER, PLATT *and other townspeople gather excitedly. They are colorful small-town citizens, but not caricatured rubes.*

BOLLINGER (*Running on, carrying his cornet*) Station master says old 94's on time out of Chattanooga. And Brady's on board all right!

COOPER   The minute Brady gets here, people gonna pour in. Town's gonna fill up like a rain barrel in a flood.

STOREKEEPER   That means business!

MELINDA *and her mother come on and set up a lemonade stand.*

BANNISTER   Where they gonna stay? Where we gonna sleep all them people?

MRS. KREBS   They got money, we'll sleep 'em.

PLATT   Looks like the biggest day for this town since we put up Coxey's army!

HOWARD (*Bolting on*) Hey! Ted Finney's got out his big bass drum. And y'oughta see what they done to the depot! Ribbons all over the rainspouts!

MELINDA   Lemonade! Lemonade!

The workmen hoist the banner above the heads of the crowd, where it hangs for the remainder of the action. The banner blares: "READ YOUR BIBLE."

CORKIN   It's all ready, Reverend.

The townspeople applaud, BOLLINGER *toots a ragged fanfare. A* HAWKER *in a white apron wheels on a hot-dog stand. The crowd mills about, in holiday spirit.*

HAWKER   Hot dogs! Get your red-hots! Hot dogs!

MRS. MCCLAIN *enters with a shopping bag full of frond fans.*

MRS. MCCLAIN   Get your fans. Compliments of Maley's Funeral Home. Thirty-five cents.

The stage is now full of eager and expectant people. MRS. BLAIR *shoves her way through the crowd, looking for her son.*

MRS. BLAIR   (*Calling*) Howard. Howard!

HOWARD   (*Racing to her*) Hey, Ma. This is just like the county fair.

MRS. BLAIR   Now you settle down and stop runnin' around and pay some attention when Mr. Brady gets here. Spit down your hair. (HOWARD *spits in her hand, and she pastes down a cowlick*) Hold still!

HOWARD *flashes off through the crowd.* ELIJAH, *a "holy man" from the hills, comes on with a wooden vegetable crate full of books. He is bearded, wild-haired, dressed in a tattered burlap smock. His feet are bare. He sets up shop between the hot dogs and the lemonade, with a placard reading:* "WHERE WILL YOU SPEND ETERNITY?".

ELIJAH   (*In a shrill, screeching voice*) Buy a Bible! Your guidebook to eternal life!

E. K. HORNBECK *wanders on, carrying a suitcase. He is a newspaperman in his middle thirties, who sneers politely at everything, including himself. His clothes—those of a sophisticated city-dweller—contrast sharply with the attire of the townspeople.*

HORNBECK *looks around, with wonderful contempt.*

MRS. MCCLAIN   (*To* HORNBECK) Want a fan? Compliments of Maley's Funeral Home—thirty-five cents!

HORNBECK   I'd die first.

MRS. KREBS   (*Unctuously, to* HORNBECK) You're a stranger, aren't you, mister? Want a nice clean place to stay?

HORNBECK   I had a nice clean place to stay, madame,
   And I left it to come here.

MRS. KREBS   (*Undaunted*) You're gonna need a room.

HORNBECK   I have a reservation at the Mansion House.

MRS. KREBS   Oh? (*She sniffs*) That's all right, I suppose, for them
as *likes* havin' a privy practically in the bedroom!

HORNBECK   The unplumbed and plumbing-less depths!

Ahhhh, Hillsboro—Heavenly Hillsboro.

The buckle on the Bible Belt.

The HAWKER *and* ELIJAH *converge on* HORNBECK *from opposite
sides.*

HAWKER   Hot dog?

ELIJAH   Bible?

HORNBECK *up-ends his suitcase and sits on it.*

HORNBECK   Now that poses a pretty problem!

Which is hungrier—my stomach or my soul?

HORNBECK *buys a hot dog.*

ELIJAH (*Miffed*) Are you an Evolutionist? An infidel? A sinner?

HORNBECK (*Munching the hot dog*) The worst kind. I write for a
newspaper. (HORNBECK *offers his hand*)

I'm E. K. Hornbeck, Baltimore *Herald.*

I don't believe I caught your name . . .?

ELIJAH (*Impressively*) They call me . . . Elijah.

HORNBECK (*Pleased*)

Elijah! Yes! Why, I had no idea you were still around.

I've read some of your stuff.

ELIJAH (*Haughtily*) I neither read nor write.

HORNBECK   Oh. Excuse me.

I must be thinking of another Elijah.

An ORGAN-GRINDER *enters, with a live monkey on a string.*
HORNBECK *spies the monkey gleefully; he greets the monk with
arms outstretched.*

Grandpa!

*Crosses to the monkey, bends down and shakes the monkey's
hand.*

Welcome to Hillsboro, sir!

Have you come to testify for the defense

Or for the prosecution?

The monkey, oddly enough, doesn't answer.

No comment?

That's fairly safe. But I warn you, sir,

You can't compete with all these monkeyshines.

MELINDA *hands the monkey a penny.*

MELINDA Look. He took my penny.

HORNBECK How could you ask for better proof than that?

There's the father of the human race!

TIMMY (*Running on, breathlessly*) Train's coming! I seen the smoke 'way up the track!

The train whistle sounds, off.

BROWN (*Taking command*) All the members of the Bible League, get ready! Let us show Mr. Brady the spirit in which we welcome him to Hillsboro.

MRS. BLAIR *blows her pitch pipe and the townspeople parade off singing "Marching to Zion." Even the* ORGAN-GRINDER *leaves his monkey tied to the hurdy-gurdy and joins the departing crowd. But* HORNBECK *stays behind.*

HORNBECK Amen. (*To the monkey*) Shield your eyes, monk!

You're about to meet the mightiest of your descendants.

A man who wears a cathedral for a cloak,

A church spire for a hat,

Whose tread has the thunder of the legions of the Lion-Hearted!

The STOREKEEPER *emerges from his establishment and looks in his own store window.* HORNBECK *turns to him.*

You're missing the show.

STOREKEEPER Somebody's got to mind the store.

HORNBECK May I ask your opinion, sir, on Evolution?

STOREKEEPER Don't have any opinions. They're bad for business.

Off-stage, a cheer. Then the thumping drum into "Gimme That Old-Time Religion" sung by the unseen townspeople.

HORNBECK (*To the monkey*) Sound the trumpet, beat the drum.

Everybody's come to town

To see your competition, monk.

Alive and breathing in the county cooler:

A high-school teacher—wild, untamed!

The crowd surges back, augmented, in a jubilant parade. Many are carrying banners, reading:

ARE YOU A MAN OR A MONKEY?

AMEND THE CONSTITUTION—PROHIBIT DARWIN

SAVE OUR SCHOOLS FROM SIN

MY ANCESTORS AIN'T APES!

WELCOME MATTHEW HARRISON BRADY

DOWN WITH DARWIN

BE A SWEET ANGEL

DON'T MONKEY WITH OUR SCHOOLS!

DARWIN IS WRONG!

DOWN WITH EVOLUTION

SWEETHEART, COME UNTO THE LORD

HORNBECK *goes to the background to watch the show.* MATTHEW HARRISON BRADY *comes on, a benign giant of a man, wearing a pith helmet. He basks in the cheers and the excitement, like a patriarch surrounded by his children. He is gray, balding, paunchy, an indeterminate sixty-five. He is followed by* MRS. BRADY; *the* MAYOR; REVEREND BROWN; TOM DAVENPORT, *the circuit district attorney; some newspapermen, and an army of the curious.*

ALL (*Singing*)

Gimme that old-time religion,
Gimme that old-time religion,
Gimme that old-time religion,
It's good enough for me!

It was good enough for father,
It was good enough for father,
It was good enough for father,
And it's good enough for me!

It was good for the Hebrew children,
It was good for the Hebrew children,
It was good for the Hebrew children,
And it's good enough for me!

Gimme that old-time religion,
Gimme that old-time religion,
Gimme that old-time religion,
It's good enough for me!

MAYOR (*Speaks*) Mr. Brady, if you please.

REVEREND (*Singing*) It is good enough for Brady.

CROWD

It is good enough for Brady,
It is good enough for Brady,
And it's good enough for me!

Cheers and applause. BRADY *seems to carry with him a built-in spotlight. So* MRS. BRADY—*pretty, fashionably dressed, a proper*

"Second Lady" to the nation's "Second Man"—seems always to be in his shadow. This does not annoy her. SARAH BRADY *is content that all her thoughts and emotions should gain the name of action through her husband.* BRADY *removes his hat and raises his hand. Obediently, the crowd falls to a hushed anticipatory silence.*

BRADY   Friends—and I can see most of you are my friends, from the way you have decked out your beautiful city of Hillsboro— (*There is a pleased reaction, and a spattering of applause. When* BRADY *speaks, there can be no doubt of his personal magnetism. Even* HORNBECK, *who slouches contemptuously at far left, is impressed with the speaker's power; for here is a man to be reckoned with*) Mrs. Brady and I are delighted to be among you! (BRADY *takes his wife's hand and draws her to his side*) I could only wish one thing: that you had not given us quite so warm a welcome! (BRADY *removes his alpaca coat. The crowd laughs.* BRADY *beams.* MRS. MCCLAIN *hands him a frond fan.* BRADY *takes it*) Bless you. (*He fans himself vigorously*) My friends of Hillsboro, you know why I have come here. I have not come merely to prosecute a lawbreaker, an arrogant youth who has spoken out against the Revealed Word. I have come because what has happened in a schoolroom of your town has unloosed a wicked attack from the big cities of the North!—an attack upon the law which you have so wisely placed among the statutes of this state. I am here to defend that which is most precious in the hearts of all of us: the Living Truth of the Scriptures!

Applause and emotional cheering.

PHOTOGRAPHER   Mr. Brady. Mr. Brady, a picture?

BRADY   I shall be happy to oblige! (*The townspeople, chanting "Go Tell It on the Mountain," move upstage.* BRADY *begins to organize a group photograph. To his wife*) Sarah . . .

MRS. BRADY (*Moving out of the camera range*) No, Matt. Just you and the dignitaries.

BRADY   You are the Mayor, are you not?

MAYOR (*Stepping forward, awkwardly*) I am, sir.

BRADY (*Extending his hand*) My name is Matthew Harrison Brady.

MAYOR   Oh, I know. Everybody knows that. I had a speech of welcome ready, but somehow it didn't seem necessary.

BRADY   I shall be honored to hear your greeting, sir.

The MAYOR *clears his throat and takes some notes from his pocket.*

MAYOR (*Sincerely*) Mr. Matthew Harrison Brady, this municipality is proud to have within its city limits the warrior who has always fought for us ordinary people. The lady folks of this town wouldn't have the vote if it wasn't for you, fightin' to give 'em all that suffrage. Mr. President Wilson wouldn't never have got to the White House and won the war if it wasn't for you supportin' him. And, in conclusion, the Governor of our state . . .

PHOTOGRAPHER   Hold it! (*The camera clicks*) Thank you.

MRS. BRADY is *disturbed by the informality of the pose.*

MRS. BRADY   Matt—you didn't have your coat on.

BRADY (*To the* PHOTOGRAPHER) Perhaps we should have a more formal pose. (*As* MRS. BRADY *helps him on with his coat*) Who is the spiritual leader of the community?

MAYOR   That would be the Reverend Jeremiah Brown.

REVEREND BROWN *steps forward.*

BROWN   Your servant and the Lord's.

BRADY *and* BROWN *shake hands.*

BRADY   The Reverend at my left, the Mayor at my right. (*Stiffly, they face the camera*) We must look grave, gentlemen, but not too serious. Hopeful, I think is the word. We must look hopeful.

BRADY *assumes the familiar oratorical pose. The camera clicks. Unnoticed, the barefoot* HOWARD *has stuck his head, mouth agape, into the picture. The* MAYOR *refers to the last page of his undelivered speech.*

MAYOR   In conclusion, the Governor of our state has vested in me the authority to confer upon you a commission as Honorary Colonel in the State Militia.

Applause.

BRADY (*Savouring it*) "Colonel Brady." I like the sound of that!

BROWN   We thought you might be hungry, Colonel Brady, after your train ride.

MAYOR   So the members of our Ladies' Aid have prepared a buffet lunch.

BRADY   Splendid, splendid—I could do with a little snack.

Some of the townspeople, at BROWN'S *direction, carry on a long picnic table, loaded with foodstuffs, potato salad, fried turkey,*

pickled fruits, cold meats and all the picnic paraphernalia.
RACHEL *comes on following the table, carrying a pitcher of
lemonade which she places on the table.*

BANNISTER (*An eager beaver*) You know, Mr. Brady—*Colonel*
Brady—all of us here voted for you three times.

BRADY   I trust it was in three separate elections!

There is laughter. TOM DAVENPORT, *a crisp business-like young
man, offers his hand to* BRADY.

DAVENPORT   Sir, I'm Tom Davenport.

BRADY (*Beaming*) Of course. Circuit district attorney. (*Putting his
arm around* DAVENPORT'S *shoulder*) We'll be a team, won't
we, young man! Quite a team! (*The picnic table is in place.
The sight of the food being uncovered is a magnetic attraction
to* BRADY. *He beams, and moistens his lips*) Ahhh, what a
handsome repast! (*Some of the women grin sheepishly at the
flattery.* BRADY *is a great eater, and he piles mountains of food
on his plate*) What a challenge it is, to fit on the old armour
again! To test the steel of our Truth against the blasphemies of
Science! To stand—

MRS. BRADY   Matthew, it's a warm day. Remember, the doctor told
you not to overeat.

BRADY   Don't worry, Mother. Just a bite or two. (*He hoists a huge
drumstick on his plate, then assails a mountain of potato salad*)
Who among you knows the defendant?—Cates, is that his
name?

DAVENPORT   Well, we *all* know him, sir.

MAYOR   Just about everybody in Hillsboro knows everybody else.

BRADY   Can someone tell me—is this fellow Cates a criminal by
nature?

RACHEL (*Almost involuntarily*) Bert isn't a criminal. He's good,
really. He's just—

RACHEL *seems to shrink from the attention that centres on her.
She takes an empty bowl and starts off with it.*

BRADY   Wait my child. Is Mr. Cates your friend?

RACHEL (*Looking down, trying to get away*) I can't tell you anything about him—

BROWN (*Fiercely*) Rachel! (*To* BRADY) My daughter will be pleased
to answer any questions about Bertram Cates.

BRADY   Your daughter, Reverend? You must be proud, indeed. (BROWN *nods.* BRADY *takes a mouthful of potato salad, turns to* RACHEL) Now. How did you come to be acquainted with Mr. Cates?

RACHEL   (*Suffering*) At school. I'm a schoolteacher, too.

BRADY   I'm sure you teach according to the precepts of the Lord.

RACHEL   I try. My pupils are only second-graders.

BRADY   Has Mr. Cates ever tried to pollute your mind with his heathen dogma?

RACHEL   Bert isn't a heathen!

BRADY   (*Sympathetically*) I understand your loyalty, my child. This man, the man in your jailhouse, is a fellow schoolteacher. Likeable, no doubt. And you are loath to speak out against him before all these people. (BRADY *takes her arm, still carrying his plate. He moves her easily away from the others. As they move*) Think of me as a friend, Rachel. And tell me what troubles you.

BRADY *moves her upstage and their conversation continues, inaudible to us.* BRADY *continues to eat,* RACHEL *speaks to him earnestly. The townspeople stand around the picnic table, munching the buffet lunch.*

BANNISTER   Who's gonna be the defense attorney?

DAVENPORT   We don't know yet. It hasn't been announced.

MAYOR   (*He hands a modest picnic plate to* MRS. BRADY) Whoever it is, he won't have much of a chance against your husband, will he, Mrs. Brady?

There are chortles of self-confident amusement. But HORNBECK *saunters toward the picnic table.*

HORNBECK   I disagree.

MAYOR   Who are you?

HORNBECK   Hornbeck. E. K. Hornbeck, of the Baltimore *Herald.*

BROWN   (*Can't quite place the name, but it has unpleasant connotations*) Hornbeck . . . Hornbeck . . .

HORNBECK   I am a newspaperman, bearing news.

When this sovereign state determined to indict
The sovereign mind of a less-than-sovereign schoolteacher,
My editors decided there was more than a headline here.
The Baltimore *Herald,* therefore, is happy to announce

That it is sending two representatives to "Heavenly Hillsboro":
The most brilliant reporter in America today,
Myself.
And the most agile legal mind of the Twentieth Century,
Henry Drummond.
This name is like a whip-crack.

MRS. BRADY (*Stunned*) Drummond!

BROWN   Henry Drummond, the agnostic?

BANNISTER   I heard about him. He got those two Chicago child murderers off just the other day.

BROWN   A vicious, godless man!

Blithely, HORNBECK *reaches across the picnic table and chooses a drumstick. He waves it jauntily toward the astonished party.*

HORNBECK   A Merry Christmas and a Jolly Fourth of July!

Munching the drumstick, HORNBECK *goes off. Unnoticed,* BRADY *and* RACHEL *have left the scene, missing this significant disclosure. There is a stunned pause.*

DAVENPORT   (*Genuinely impressed*) Henry Drummond for the defense. Well!

BROWN   Henry Drummond is an agent of darkness. (*With resolution*) We won't let him in the town!

DAVENPORT   I don't know by what law you could keep him out.

MAYOR   (*Rubbing his chin*) I'll look it up in the town ordinances.

BROWN   I saw Drummond once. In a courtroom in Ohio. A man was on trial for a most brutal crime. Although he knew—and admitted—the man was guilty, Drummond was perverting the evidence to cast the guilt away from the accused and onto you and me and all of society.

MRS. BRADY   Henry Drummond. Oh, dear me.

BROWN   I can still see him. A slouching hulk of a man, whose head juts out like an animal's (*He imitates* DRUMMOND'S *slouch.* MELINDA *watches, frightened*) You look into his face, and you wonder why God made such a man. And then you know that God didn't make him, that he is a creature of the Devil, perhaps even the Devil himself!

Little MELINDA *utters a frightened cry, and buries her head in the folds of her mother's skirt.* BRADY *re-enters with* RACHEL, *who has a confused and guilty look.* BRADY'S *plate has been scraped clean; only the fossil of the turkey leg remains. He looks at the ring of faces, which have been disturbed by* BROWN's *description of the heretic* DRUMMOND. MRS. BRADY *comes toward him.*

MRS. BRADY   Matt—they're bringing Henry Drummond for the defence.

BRADY (*Pale*) Drummond? (*The townspeople are impressed by the impact of his name on* BRADY) Henry Drummond!

BROWN   We won't allow him in the town!

MAYOR (*Lamely*) I think—maybe the Board of Health—

He trails off.

BRADY (*Crossing thoughtfully*) No. (*He turns*) I believe we should *welcome* Henry Drummond.

MAYOR (*Astonished*) Welcome him!

BRADY   If the enemy sends its Goliath into battle, it magnifies our cause. Henry Drummond has stalked the courtrooms of this land for forty years. When he fights, headlines follow. (*With growing fervor*) The whole world will be watching our victory over Drummond. (*Dramatically*) If St. George had slain a dragonfly, who would remember him?

Cheers and pleased reactions from the crowd.

MRS. BLAIR   Would you care to finish off the pickled apricots, Mr. Brady?

BRADY *takes them.*

BRADY   It would be a pity to see them go to waste.

MRS. BRADY   Matt, do you think—

BRADY   Have to build up my strength, Mother, for the battle ahead. (*Munching thoughtfully*) Now what will Drummond do? He'll try to make us forget the lawbreaker and put the law on trial. (*He turns to* RACHEL) But we'll have the *answer* for Mr. Drummond. Right here, in some of the things this sweet young lady has told me.

RACHEL   But Mr. Brady—

BRADY *turns to* BROWN.

BRADY   A fine girl, Reverend. Fine girl!

RACHEL *seems tormented, but helpless.*

BROWN   Rachel has always been taught to do the righteous thing.

RACHEL *moves off.*

BRADY   I'm sure she has.

MELINDA *hands him a glass of lemonade.*

BRADY   Thank you. A toast, then! A toast to tomorrow! To the beginning of the trial and the success of our cause. A toast, in good American lemonade!

He stands lifting his glass. Others rise and join the toast. BRADY *downs his drink.*

MRS. BRADY   Mr. Mayor, it's time now for Mr. Brady's nap. He always likes to nap after a meal.

MAYOR   We have a suite ready for you at the Mansion House. I think you'll find your bags already there.

BRADY   Very thoughtful, considerate of you.

MAYOR   If you'll come with me—it's only across the square.

BRADY   I want to thank all the members of the Ladies' Aid for preparing this nice little picnic repast.

MRS. KREBS *(Beaming)* Our pleasure, sir.

BRADY   And if I seemed to pick at my food, I don't want you to think I didn't enjoy it. *(Apologetically)* But you see, we had a box lunch on the train.

There is a good-humored reaction to this, and the BRADYS *move off accompanied by the throng of admirers, singing "It is good enough for Brady." Simultaneously the lights fade down on the courthouse lawn and fade up on the courtroom area.* HORNBECK *saunters on, chewing at an apple. He glances about the courtroom as if he were searching for something. When* RACHEL *hurries on,* HORNBECK *drops back into a shadow and she does not see him.*

RACHEL   *(Distressed)* Mr. Meeker. Mr. Meeker? *(She calls down toward the jail)* Bert, can you hear me? Bert, you've got to tell me what to do. I don't know what to do—

HORNBECK *takes a bite out of his apple.* RACHEL *turns sharply at the sound, surprised to find someone else in the courtroom.*

HORNBECK   *(Quietly)* I give advice, at remarkably low hourly rates. Ten percent off to unmarried young ladies, And special discounts to the clergy and their daughters.

RACHEL   What are you doing here?

HORNBECK   I'm inspecting the battlefield The night before the battle. Before it's cluttered With the debris of journalistic camp-followers.

Hiking himself up on a window ledge.
I'm scouting myself an observation post
To watch the fray.
RACHEL *starts to go off.*
Wait. Why do you want to see Bert Cates?
What's he to you, or you to him?
Can it be that both beauty and biology
Are on our side?
Again she starts to leave. But HORNBECK *jumps down from his ledge and crosses toward her.*
There's a newspaper here I'd like to have you see.
It just arrived
From that wicked modern Sodom and Gomorrah,
Baltimore.
RACHEL *looks at him quizzically as he fishes a tear sheet out of his pocket.*
Not the entire edition, of course.
No Happy Hooligan, Barney Google, Abe Kabibble.
Merely the part worth reading: E. K. Hornbeck's
Brilliant little symphony of words.
He offers her the sheet, but she doesn't take it.
You should read it.
Almost reluctantly, she starts to read.
                                My typewriter's been singing
A sweet, sad song about the Hillsboro heretic,
B. Cates: boy-Socrates, latter-day Dreyfus,
Romeo with a biology book.
He looks over her shoulder, admiring his own writing. He takes another bite out of the apple.
I may be rancid butter,
But I'm on your side of the bread.
RACHEL (*Looking up, surprised*) This sounds as if you're a friend of Bert's.
HORNBECK   As much as a critic can be a friend to anyone.
He sits backward on a chair, watching her head. He takes another bite out of his apple, then offers it to her.
Have a bite?
RACHEL, *busily reading, shakes her head.*
Don't worry. I'm not the serpent, Little Eva.
This isn't from the Tree of Knowledge.

You won't find one in the orchards of Heavenly Hillsboro.
Birches, beeches, butternuts. A few ignorance bushes.
No Tree of Knowldege.

RACHEL *has finished reading the copy; and she looks up at*
HORNBECK *with a new respect.*

RACHEL   Will this be published here, in the local paper?

HORNBECK   In the "Weekly Bugle"? Or whatever it is they call
The leaden stuff they blow through the local linotypes?
I doubt it.

RACHEL   It would help Bert if the people here could read this. It
would help them understand . . . ! (*She appraises* HORNBECK,
puzzled) I never would have expected you to write an article
like this. You seem so—

HORNBECK   Cynical? That's my fascination.
I do hateful things, for which people love me,
And lovable things for which they hate me.
I am a friend of enemies, the enemy of friends;
I am admired for my detestability.
I am both Poles and the Equator,
With no Temperate Zones between.

RACHEL   You make it sound as if Bert is a hero. I'd like to think
that, but I can't. A schoolteacher is a public servant: I think
he should do what the law and the school-board want him to.
If the superintendent says, "Miss Brown, you're to teach from
Whitley's *Second Reader*," I don't feel I have to give him an
argument.

HORNBECK   Ever give your pupils a snap-quiz on existence?

RACHEL   What?

HORNBECK   Where we came from, where we are, where we're going?

RACHEL   All the answers to those questions are in the Bible.

HORNBECK (*With a genuine incredulity*)
All?! You feed the youth of Hillsboro
From the little truck-garden of your mind?

RACHEL (*Offended, angry*) I think there must be something wrong
in what Bert believes, if a great man like Mr. Brady comes here
to speak out against him.

HORNBECK   Matthew Harrison Brady came here
To find himself a stump to shout from.
That's all.

RACHEL   You couldn't understand. Mr. Brady is the champion of ordinary people, like us.

HORNBECK   Wake up, Sleeping Beauty. The ordinary people
Played a dirty trick on Colonel Brady.
They ceased to exist.

RACHEL *looks puzzled.*

Time was
When Brady was the hero of the hinterland,
Water-boy for the great unwashed.
But they've got inside plumbing in their heads these days!
There's a highway through the backwoods now,
And the trees of the forest have reluctantly made room
For their leafless cousins the telephone poles.
Henry's Lizzie rattles into town
And leaves behind
The Yesterday-Messiah,
Standing in the road alone
In a cloud of flivver dust.
Emphatically, he brandishes the apple.
The boob has been de-boobed.
Colonel Brady's virginal small-towner
has been *had*—
By Marconi and Montgomery Ward.

HORNBECK *strolls out of the courtroom and onto the town square; the lights dissolve as before from one area to the other.* RACHEL *goes off in the darkness. The store fronts glow with sunset light. The* SHOPKEEPER *pulls the shade in his store window and locks the door.* MRS. MCCLAIN *crosses, fanning herself wearily.*

STOREKEEPER   Gonna be a hot night, Mrs. McClain.

MRS. MCCLAIN   I thought we'd get some relief when the sun went down.

HORNBECK *tosses away his apple core, then leans back and watches as the* SHOPKEEPER *and* MRS. MCCLAIN *go off. The* ORGAN-GRINDER *comes on, idly with his monkey.* MELINDA *enters attracted by the melody which tinkles in the twilight. She gives the monkey a penny. The* ORGAN-GRINDER *thanks her, and moves off.* MELINDA *is alone, back to the audience, in center stage.* HORNBECK, *silent and motionless, watches from*

*the side. The faces of the buildings are now red with the dying
moment of sunset.*

*A long, ominous shadow appears across the buildings, cast from
a figure approaching off stage.* MELINDA *awed, watches the
shadow grow.* HENRY DRUMMOND *enters, carrying a valise. He
is hunched over, head jutting forward, exactly as* BROWN
*described him. The red of the sun behind him hits his slouching
back, and his face is in the shadow.* MELINDA *turns and looks
at* DRUMMOND, *full in the face.*

MELINDA *(Terrified)* It's the Devil!

Screaming with fear MELINDA *runs off.* HORNBECK *crosses
slowly toward* DRUMMOND, *and offers his hand.*

HORNBECK   Hello, Devil. Welcome to Hell.

The lights fade

SCENE II

The courtroom. A few days later.

*The townspeople are packed into the sweltering courtroom. The
shapes of the buildings are dimly visible in the background, as if
Hillsboro itself were on trial. Court is in session, fans are pumping.
The humorless* JUDGE *sits at his bench; he has a nervous habit of
flashing an automatic smile after every ruling.* CATES *sits beside*
DRUMMOND *at a counsel table.* BRADY *sits grandly at another table,
fanning himself with benign self-assurance.* HORNBECK *is seated on
his window ledge.* RACHEL, *tense, is among the spectators. In the
jury box, ten of the twelve jurors are already seated.* BANNISTER *is
on the witness stand.* DAVENPORT *is examining him.*

DAVENPORT   Do you attend church regularly, Mr. Bannister?

BANNISTER   Only on Sundays.

DAVENPORT   That's good enough for the prosecution. Your Honor,
we will accept this man as a member of the jury.

Bannister starts toward the jury box.

JUDGE   One moment, Mr. Bannister. You're not excused.

BANNISTER   *(A little petulant)* I wanted that there front seat in the
jury box.

DRUMMOND   *(Rising)* Well, hold your horses, Bannister. You may get
it yet!

BANNISTER *returns to the witness chair.*

JUDGE   Mr. Drummond, you may examine the venireman.

DRUMMOND   Thank you, Your Honor. Mr. Bannister, how come you're so anxious to get that front seat over there?

BANNISTER   Everybody says this is going to be quite a show.

DRUMMOND   I hear the same thing. Ever read anything in a book about Evolution?

BANNISTER   Nope.

DRUMMOND   Or about a fella named Darwin?

BANNISTER   Can't say I have.

DRUMMOND   I'll bet you read your Bible.

BANNISTER   Nope.

DRUMMOND   How come?

BANNISTER   Can't read.

DRUMMOND   Well, you are fortunate. (*There are a few titters through the courtroom*) He'll do.

BANNISTER *turns toward the* JUDGE, *poised.*

JUDGE   Take your seat, Mr. Bannister. (BANNISTER *races to the jury box as if shot from a gun, and sits in the remaining front seat, beaming*) Mr. Meeker, will you call a venireman to fill the twelfth and last seat on the jury?

BRADY   (*Rising*) Your Honor, before we continue, will the court entertain a motion on a matter of procedure?

MEEKER   (*Calling toward the spectators*) Jesse H. Dunlap. You're next, Jesse.

JUDGE   Will the learned prosecutor state the motion?

BRADY   It has been called to my attention that the temperature in this courtroom is now 97 degrees Fahrenheit. (*He mops his forehead with a large handkerchief*) And it may get hotter! (*There is laughter.* BRADY *basks in the warmth of his popularity*) I do not feel the dignity of the court will suffer if we remove a few superfluous outer garments.

BRADY *indicates his alpaca coat.*

JUDGE   Does the defense have any objection to Colonel Brady's motion?

DRUMMOND   (*Askance*) I don't know if the dignity of the court can be upheld with these galluses I've got on.

JUDGE   We'll take that chance, Mr. Drummond. Those who wish to remove their coats may do so.

With relief, many of the spectators take off their coats and loosen their collar buttons. DRUMMOND *wears wide, bright purple suspenders. The spectators react.*

BRADY (*With affable sarcasm*) Is the counsel for the defense showing us the latest fashion in the great metropolitan city of Chicago?

DRUMMOND (*Pleased*) Glad you asked me that. I brought these along special. (*He cocks his thumbs in the suspenders*) Just so happens I bought these galluses at Peabody's General Store in *your* home town, Mr. Brady. Weeping Water, Nebraska.
DRUMMOND snaps the suspenders jauntily. There is amused reaction at this. BRADY *is nettled: this is his show, and he wants all the laughs. The* JUDGE *pounds for order.*

JUDGE   Let us proceed with the selection of the final juror.
MEEKER *brings* JESSE DUNLAP *to the stand. He is a rugged, righteous-looking man.*

MEEKER   State your name and occupation.

DUNLAP   Jesse H. Dunlap. Farmer and cabinetmaker.

DAVENPORT   Do you believe in the Bible, Mr. Dunlap?

DUNLAP (*Vigorously*) I believe in the Holy Word of God. And I believe in Matthew Harrison Brady!
There is some applause, and a few scattered "Amens." BRADY *waves acceptance.*

DAVENPORT   This man is acceptable to the prosecution.

JUDGE   Very well, Mr. Drummond?

DRUMMOND (*Quietly, without rising*) No questions. Not acceptable.

BRADY (*Annoyed*) Does Mr. Drummond refuse this man a place on the jury simply because he believes in the Bible?

DRUMMOND   If you find an Evolutionist in this town, you can refuse him.

BRADY (*Angrily*) I object to the defense attorney rejecting a worthy citizen without so much as asking him a question!

DRUMMOND (*Agreeably*) All right. I'll ask him a question. (*Saunters over to* DUNLAP) How are you?

DUNLAP (*A little surprised*) Kinda hot.

DRUMMOND   So am I. Excused.
DUNLAP *looks at the* JUDGE, *confused.*

JUDGE   You are excused from jury duty, Mr. Dunlap. You may step down.
DUNLAP *goes back and joins the spectators, a little miffed.*

BRADY (*Piously*) I object to the note of levity which the counsel for the defense is introducing into these proceedings.

JUDGE   The bench agrees with you in spirit, Colonel Brady.

DRUMMOND (*Rising angrily*) And I object to all this damned "Colonel" talk. I am not familiar with Mr. Brady's military record.

JUDGE   Well—he was made an Honorary Colonel in our State Militia. The day he arrived in Hillsboro.

DRUMMOND   The use of this title prejudices the case of my client: it calls up a picture of the prosecution, astride a white horse, ablaze in the uniform of a militia colonel, with all the forces of right and righteousness marshaled behind him.

JUDGE   What can we do?

DRUMMOND   Break him. Make him a private. I have no serious objection to the honorary title of "Private Brady."
There is a buzz of reaction. The JUDGE *gestures for the* MAYOR *to come over for a hurried, whispered conference.*

MAYOR (*After some whispering*) Well, we can't take it back—! (*There is another whispered exchange. Then the* MAYOR *steps gingerly toward* DRUMMOND) By—by authority of—well, I'm sure the Governor won't have any objection—I hereby appoint you, Mr. Drummond, a temporary Honorary Colonel in the State Militia.

DRUMMOND (*Shaking his head, amused*) Gentlemen, what can I say? It is not often in a man's life that he attains the exalted rank of "temporary Honorary Colonel."

MAYOR   It will be made permanent, of course, pending the arrival of the proper papers over the Governor's signature.

DRUMMOND (*Looking at the floor*) I thank you.

JUDGE   Colonel Brady. Colonel Drummond. You will examine the next venireman.
MEEKER *brings* GEORGE SILLERS *to the stand.*

MEEKER   State your name and occupation.

SILLERS   George Sillers. I work at the feed store.

DAVENPORT   Tell me, sir. Would you call yourself a religious man?

SILLERS   I guess I'm as religious as the next man.
BRADY *rises.* DAVENPORT *immediately steps back, deferring to his superior.*

BRADY   In Hillsboro, sir, that means a great deal. Do you have any children, Mr. Sillers?

SILLERS   Not as I know of.

BRADY   If you had a son, Mr. Sillers, or a daughter, what would you think if that sweet child came home from school and told you that a Godless teacher—

DRUMMOND   Objection! We're supposed to be choosing jury members! The prosecution's denouncing the defendant before the trial has even begun!

JUDGE   Objection sustained.

The JUDGE *and* BRADY *exchange meaningless smiles.*

BRADY   Mr. Sillers. Do you have any personal opinions with regard to the defendant that might prejudice you on his behalf?

SILLERS   Cates? I don't hardly know him. He bought some peat moss from me once, and paid his bill.

BRADY   Mr. Sillers impresses me as an honest, God-fearing man. I accept him.

JUDGE   Thank you, Colonel Brady. *Colonel* Drummond?

DRUMMOND   (*Strolling toward the witness chair*) Mr. Sillers you just said you were a religious man. Tell me something. Do you work at it very hard?

SILLERS   Well, I'm pretty busy down at the feed store. My wife tends to the religion for both of us.

DRUMMOND   In other words, you take care of this life, and your wife takes care of the next one?

DAVENPORT   Objection.

JUDGE   Objection sustained.

DRUMMOND   While your wife was tending to the religion, Mr. Sillers, did you ever happen to bump into a fella named Charles Darwin?

SILLERS   Not till recent.

DRUMMOND   From what you've heard about this Darwin, do you think your wife would want to have him over for Sunday dinner?

BRADY *rises magnificently.*

BRADY   Your Honor, my worthy opponent from Chicago is cluttering the issue with hypothetical questions—

DRUMMOND   (*Wheeling*) I'm doing *your* job, Colonel.

DAVENPORT   (*Leaping up*) The prosecution is perfectly able to handle its own arguments.

DRUMMOND   Look, I've established that Mr. Sillers isn't working very hard at religion. Now, for your sake, I want to make sure he isn't working at Evolution.

SILLERS (*Simply*) I'm just working at the feed store.

DRUMMOND (*To the* JUDGE) This man's all right. (*Turning*) Take a box seat, Mr. Sillers.

BRADY   I am not altogether satisfied that Mr. Sillers will render impartial—

DRUMMOND   Out of order. The prosecution has already accepted this man.

The following becomes a simultaneous wrangle among the attorneys.

BRADY   I want a fair trial.

DRUMMOND   So do I!

BRADY   Unless the state of mind of the members of the jury conforms to the laws and patterns of society—

DRUMMOND   Conform! Conform! What do you want to do—run the jury through a meat-grinder, so they all come out the same?

DAVENPORT   Your Honor!

BRADY   I've seen what you can do to a jury. Twist and tangle them. Nobody's forgotten the Endicott Publishing case—where you made the jury believe the obscenity was in their own minds, not on the printed page. It was immoral what you did to that jury. Tricking them. Judgment by confusion. Think you can get away with it here?

DRUMMOND   All I want is to prevent the clock-stoppers from dumping a load of medieval nonsense into the United States Constitution.

JUDGE   This is not a Federal court.

DRUMMOND (*Slapping his hand on the table*) Well, dammit, you've got to stop 'em somewhere.

The JUDGE *beats with his gavel.*

JUDGE   Gentlemen, you are *both* out of order. The bench holds that the jury has been selected. (BRADY *lets his arms fall, with a gesture of sweet charity*) Because of the lateness of the hour and the unusual heat, the court is recessed until ten o'clock tomorrow morning. (JUDGE *raps the gavel, and the court begins to break up. Then the* JUDGE *notices a slip of paper, and raps for order again*) Oh. The Reverend Brown has asked me to

make this announcement. There will be a prayer meeting tonight
on the courthouse lawn, to pray for justice and guidance. All
are invited.

DRUMMOND   Your Honor. I object to this commercial announcement.

JUDGE   Commercial announcement?

DRUMMOND   For Reverend Brown's product. Why don't you announce that there will be an Evolutionist meeting?

JUDGE   I have no knowledge of such a meeting.

DRUMMOND   That's understandable. It's bad enough that everybody
coming into this courtroom has to walk underneath a banner
that says: "Read Your Bible!" Your Honor, I want that sign
taken down! Or else I want another one put up—just as big,
just as big letters—saying "Read Your Darwin!"

JUDGE   That's preposterous!

DRUMMOND   It certainly is!

JUDGE   You are out of order, Colonel Drummond. The court stands
recessed.

*As the formality of the courtroom is relaxed, there is a general
feeling of relief. Spectators and jury members adjust their sticky
clothes, and start moving off. Many of the townspeople gather
around* BRADY, *to shake his hand, get his autograph, and to
stand for a moment in the great man's presence. They cluster
about him, and follow* BRADY *as he goes off, the shepherd leading his flock. In marked contrast,* DRUMMOND *packs away his
brief in a tattered leather case; but no one comes near him.*
RACHEL *moves toward* BERT. *They stand face-to-face, wordlessly. Both seem to wish the whole painful turmoil were over.
Suddenly,* RACHEL *darts to* DRUMMOND's *side.* CATES *opens his
mouth to stop her, but she speaks rapidly, with pent-up tension.*

RACHEL   Mr. Drummond. You've got to call the whole thing off.
It's not too late. Bert knows he did wrong. He didn't mean to.
And he's sorry. Now why can't he just stand up and say to everybody: "I did wrong. I broke a law. I admit it. I won't do it
again." Then they'd stop all this fuss, and—everything would be
like it was.

DRUMMOND *looks at* RACHEL, *not unkindly.*

DRUMMOND   Who are you?

RACHEL   I'm—a friend of Bert's.

DRUMMOND *turns to* CATES.

DRUMMOND   How about it, boy? Getting cold feet?

CATES   I never thought it would be like this. Like Barnum and Bailey coming to town.

DRUMMOND (*Easily*) We can call it off. You want to quit?

RACHEL (*Coming to* BERT'S *side*) Yes!

CATES   People look at me as if I was a murderer. Worse than a murderer! That fella from Minnesota who killed his wife— remember, Rachel—half the town turned out to see 'em put him on the train. They just looked at him as if he was a curiosity— not like they *hated* him! Not like he'd done anything really wrong! Just different!

DRUMMOND (*Laughs a little to himself*) There's nothing very original about murdering your wife.

CATES   People I thought were my friends look at me now as if I had horns growing out of my head.

DRUMMOND   You murder a wife; it isn't nearly as bad as murdering an old wives' tale. Kill one of their fairy-tale notions, and they call down the wrath of God, Brady, and the state legislature.

RACHEL   You make a joke out of everything. You seem to think it's so funny!

DRUMMOND   Lady, when you lose your power to laugh, you lose your power to think straight.

CATES   Mr. Drummond, I can't laugh. I'm scared.

DRUMMOND   Good. You'd be a damned fool if you weren't.

RACHEL (*Bitterly*) You're supposed to help Bert; but every time you swear you make it worse for him.

DRUMMOND (*Honestly*) I'm sorry if I offend you. (*He smiles*) But I don't swear just for the hell of it. (*He fingers his galluses*) You see, I figure language is a poor enough means of communication as it is. So we ought to use all the words we've got. Besides, there are damned few words that everybody understands.

RACHEL   You don't care anything about Bert! You just want a chance to make speeches against the Bible!

DRUMMOND   I care a great deal about Bert. I care a great deal about what Bert thinks.

RACHEL   Well, I care about what people in this town think of *him.*

DRUMMOND (*Quietly*) Can you buy back his respectability by making him a coward? (*He spades his hands in his hip pockets*) I understand what Bert's going through. It's the loneliest feeling in the world—to find yourself standing up when everybody else is sitting down. To have everybody look at you and say, "What's the matter with him?" I know. I know what it feels like. Walking down an empty street, listening to the sound of your own footsteps. Shutters closed, blinds drawn, doors locked against you. And you aren't sure whether you're walking toward something, or if you're just walking away. (*He takes a deep breath, then turns abruptly*) Cates, I'll change your plea and we'll call off the whole business—on one condition. If you honestly believe you committed a criminal act against the citizens of this state and the minds of their children. If you honestly believe that you're wrong and the law's right. Then the hell with it. I'll pack my grip and go back to Chicago, where it's a cool hundred in the shade.

RACHEL (*Eagerly*) Bert knows he's wrong. Don't you, Bert?

DRUMMOND   Don't prompt the witness.

CATES (*Indecisive*) What do you think, Mr. Drummond?

DRUMMOND   I'm here. That tells you what I think. (*He looks squarely at* CATES) Well, what's the verdict, Bert? You want to find yourself guilty before the jury does?

CATES (*Quietly, with determination*) No, sir. I'm not gonna quit.

RACHEL (*Protesting*) Bert!

CATES   It wouldn't do any good now, anyhow. (*He turns to* RACHEL) If you'll stick by me, Rache—well, we can fight it out.
He smiles at her wanly. All the others have gone now, except MEEKER *and* DRUMMOND. RACHEL *shakes her head, bewildered, tears forming in her eyes.*

RACHEL   I don't know what to do; I don't know what to do.

CATES (*Frowning*) What's the matter, Rache?

RACHEL   I don't want to do it, Bert; but Mr. Brady says—

DRUMMOND   What does Brady say?

RACHEL (*Looking down*) They want me to testify against Bert.

CATES (*Stunned*) You can't!

MEEKER   I don't mean to rush you, Bert; but we gotta close up the shop.

CATES *is genuinely panicked.*

CATES   Rache, some of the things I've talked to you about are things you just say to your own heart. (*He starts to go with* MEEKER, *then turns back*) If you get up on the stand and say those things out loud—(*He shakes his head*) Don't you understand? The words I've said to you—softly, in the dark—just trying to figure out what the stars are for, or what might be on the back side of the moon—

MEEKER   Bert—

CATES   They were questions, Rache. I was just asking questions. If you repeat those things on the witness stand, Brady'll make 'em sound like answers. And they'll crucify me!

CATES *and* MEEKER *go off. The lights are slowly dimming.* DRUMMOND *puts on his coat, sizing up* RACHEL *as he does so.* RACHER, *torn, is almost unconscious of his presence or of her surroundings.*

DRUMMOND (*Kindly, quietly*)   What's your name? Rachel what?

RACHEL   Rachel Brown. Can they make me testify?

DRUMMOND   I'm afraid so. It would be nice if nobody ever had to make anybody do anything. But—(*He takes his brief case*) Don't let Brady scare you. He only *seems* to be bigger than the law.

RACHEL   It's not Mr. Brady. It's my father.

DRUMMOND   Who's your father?

RACHEL   The Reverend Jeremiah Brown. (DRUMMOND *whistles softly through his teeth*) I remember feeling this way when I was a little girl. I would wake up at night, terrified of the dark. I'd think sometimes that my bed was on the ceiling, and the whole house was upside down; and if I didn't hang onto the mattress, I might fall outward into the stars. (*She shivers a little, remembering*) I wanted to run to my father, and have him tell me I was safe, that everything was all right. But I was always more frightened of him than I was of falling. It's the same way now.

DRUMMOND (*Softly*)   Is your mother dead?

RACHEL   I never knew my mother. (*Distraught*) Is it true? Is Bert wicked?

DRUMMOND (*With simple conviction*) Bert Cates is a good man. Maybe even a great one. And it takes strength for a woman to love such a man. Especially when he's a pariah in the community.

RACHEL I'm only confusing Bert. And he's confused enough as it is.

DRUMMOND The man who has everything figured out is probably a fool. College examinations notwithstanding, it takes a very smart fella to say "I don't know the answer!"

DRUMMOND *puts on his hat, touches the brim of it as a gesture of good-bye and goes slowly off.*

Curtain

ACT TWO

SCENE I

The courthouse lawn. The same night. The oppressive heat of the day has softened into a pleasant summer evening. Two lampposts spread a glow over the town square, and TWO WORKMEN *are assembling the platform for the prayer meeting. One of the* WORKMEN *glances up at the* READ YOUR BIBLE *banner.*

FIRST WORKMAN   What're we gonna do about this sign?

SECOND WORKMAN   The Devil don't run this town. Leave it up.

> BRADY *enters, followed by a knot of reporters.* HORNBECK *brings up the rear; he alone is not bothering to take notes. Apparently this informal press conference has been in progress for some time, and* BRADY *is now bringing it to a climax.*

BRADY   —and I hope that you will tell the readers of your newspapers that here in Hillsboro we are fighting the fight of the Faithful throughout the world!

All write. BRADY *eyes* HORNBECK, *leaning lazily, not writing.*

REPORTER   (*British accent*) A question, Mr. Brady.

BRADY   Certainly. Where are you from, young man?

REPORTER   London, sir. Reuters News Agency.

BRADY   Excellent. I have many friends in the United Kingdom.

REPORTER   What is your personal opinion of Henry Drummond?

BRADY   I'm glad you asked me that. I want people everywhere to know I bear no personal animosity toward Henry Drummond. There was a time when we were on the same side of the fence. He gave me active support in my campaign of 1908—and I welcomed it. (*Almost impassioned, speaking at writing tempo, so all the reporters can get it down*) But I say that if my own *brother* challenged the faith of millions, as Mr. Drummond is doing, I would oppose him still! (*The* WORKMEN *pound; the townspeople begin to gather*) I think that's all for this evening, gentlemen. (*The reporters scatter.* BRADY *turns to* HORNBECK) Mr. Hornbeck, my clipping service has sent me some of your dispatches.

HORNBECK   How flattering to know I'm being clipped.

BRADY   It grieves me to read reporting that is so—biased.

HORNBECK   I'm no reporter, Colonel. I'm a critic.

BRADY   I hope you will stay for Reverend Brown's prayer meeting. It may bring you some enlightenment.

HORNBECK   It may. I'm here on a press pass, and I don't intend To miss any part of the show.

REVEREND BROWN enters with MRS. BRADY *on his arm.* HORNBECK *passes them jauntily, and crosses downstage.*

BRADY   Good evening, Reverend. How are you, Mother?

MRS. BRADY   The Reverend Brown was good enough to escort me.

BRADY   Reverend, I'm looking forward to your prayer meeting.

BROWN   You will find our people are fervent in their belief.

MRS. BRADY crosses to her husband.

MRS. BRADY   I know it's warm, Matt; but these night breezes can be treacherous. And you know how you perspire.

She takes a small kerchief out of her handbag and tucks it around his neck. He laughs a little.

BRADY   Mother is always so worried about my throat.

BROWN   (*Consulting his watch*) I always like to begin my meetings at the time announced.

BRADY   Most commendable. Proceed, Reverend. After you.

BROWN *mounts the few steps to the platform.* BRADY *follows him, loving the feel of the board beneath his feet. This is the squared circle where he had fought so many bouts with the English language, and won. The prayer meeting is motion picture, radio, and tent-show to these people. To them, the* REVEREND BROWN *is a combination Milton Sills and Douglas Fairbanks. He grasps the podium and stares down at them sternly.* BRADY *is benign. He sits with his legs crossed, an arm crooked over one corner of his chair.* BROWN *is milking the expectant pause. Just as he is ready to speak,* DRUMMOND *comes in and stands at the fringe of the crowd.* BROWN *glowers at* DRUMMOND. *The crowd chants.*

BROWN   Brothers and sisters, I come to you on the Wings of the Word. The Wings of the Word are beating loud in the tree-tops! The Lord's Word is howling in the Wind, and flashing in the belly of the Cloud!

WOMAN   I hear it!

MAN   I see it, Reverend!

BROWN   And we *believe* the Word!

ALL   We believe!

BROWN   We believe the Glory of the Word!

ALL   Glory, Glory! Amen, amen!

RACHEL *comes on, but remains at the fringes of the crowd.*

BROWN   Hearken to the Word! (*He lowers his voice*) The Word tells us that the World was created in Seven Days. In the beginning, the earth was without form, and void. And the Lord said, "Let there be light!"

VOICES   Ahhhh . . !

BROWN   And there *was* light! And the Lord saw the Light and the Light saw the Lord, and the Light said, "Am I good, Lord?" And the Lord said, "Thou art good!"

MAN   (*Deep-voiced, singing*) And the evening and the morning were the first day!

VOICES   Amen, amen!

BROWN   (*Calling out*) The Lord said, "Let there be Firmament!" And even as He spoke, it was so! And the Firmament bowed down before Him and said, "Am I good, Lord?" And the Lord said, "Thou art good!"

MAN   (*Singing*) And the evening and the morning were the second day!

VOICES   Amen, amen!

BROWN   On the Third Day brought He forth the Dry Land, and the Grass, and the Fruit Tree! And on the Fourth Day made He the Sun, the Moon, and the Stars—and He pronounced them Good!

VOICES   Amen.

BROWN   On the Fifth Day He peopled the sea with fish. And the air with fowl. And made He great whales. And he blessed them all. But on the morning of the Sixth Day, the Lord rose, and His eye was dark, and a scowl lay across His face. (*Shouts*) Why? Why was the Lord troubled?

ALL   Why? Tell us why! Tell the troubles of the Lord!

BROWN   (*Dropping his voice almost to a whisper*) He looked about Him, did the Lord; at all His handiwork, bowed down before Him. And He said, "It is not good, it is not enough, it is not finished. I . . . shall . . . make . . . Me . . . a . . . *Man!*"
The crowd bursts out into an orgy of hosannahs and waving arms.

ALL   Glory, Hosannah! Bless the Lord who created us!

WOMAN (*Shouting out*) Bow down! Bow down before the Lord!

MAN   Are we good, Lord? Tell us! Are we good?

BROWN (*Answering*) The Lord said, "Yea, thou are good! For I have created ye in My Image, after My Likeness! Be fruitful, and multiply, and replenish the Earth, and subdue it!"

MAN (*Deep-voiced, singing*) The Lord made Man master of the Earth . . . !

ALL   Glory, glory! Bless the Lord!

BROWN (*Whipping 'em up*) Do we believe?

ALL (*In chorus*) Yes!

BROWN   Do we believe the Word?

ALL (*Coming back like a whip-crack*) Yes!

BROWN   Do we believe the Truth of the Word?

ALL   Yes!

BROWN (*Pointing a finger toward the jail*) Do we curse the man who denies the Word?

ALL (*Crescendo, each answer mightier than the one before*) Yes!

BROWN   Do we cast out this sinner in our midst?

ALL   Yes!

> *Each crash of sound from the crowd seems to strike* RACHEL *physically, and shake her.*

BROWN   Do we call down hellfire on the man who has sinned against the Word?

ALL (*Roaring*) Yes!

BROWN (*Deliberately shattering the rhythm, to go into a frenzied prayer, hands clasped together and lifted heavenward*) O Lord of the Tempest and the Thunder! O Lord of Righteousness and Wrath! We pray that Thou wilt make a sign unto us! Strike down this sinner, as Thou didst Thine enemies of old, in the days of the Pharaohs! (*All lean forward, almost expecting the heavens to open with a thunderbolt.* RACHEL *is white.* BRADY *shifts uncomfortably in his chair; this is pretty strong stuff, even for him*) Let him feel the terror of Thy sword! For all eternity, let his soul writhe in anguish and damnation—

RACHEL   *No!* (*She rushes to the platform*) No, Father. Don't pray to destroy Bert!

BROWN   Lord, we call down the same curse on those who ask grace for this sinner—though they be blood of my blood, and flesh of my flesh!

BRADY (*Rising, grasping* BROWN's *arm*) Reverend Brown, I know it is the great zeal of your faith which makes you utter this prayer! But it is possible to be overzealous, to destroy that which you hope to save—so that nothing is left but emptiness. (BROWN *turns*) Remember the Wisdom of Solomon in the Book of Proverbs—(*Softly*) "He that troubleth his own house . . . shall inherit the wind." (BRADY *leads* BROWN *to a chair, then turns to the townspeople*) The Bible also tells us that God forgives His children. And we, the Children of God, should forgive each other. (RACHEL *slips off*) My good friends, return to your homes. The blessings of the Lord be with you all. (*Slowly the townspeople move off, singing and humming "Go, Tell It on the Mountain."* BRADY *is left alone on stage with* DRUMMOND, *who still watches him impassively.* BRADY *crosses to* DRUMMOND) We were good friends once. I was always glad of your support. What happened between us? There used to be a mutuality of understanding and admiration. Why is it, my old friend, that you have moved so far away from me?

A pause. They study each other.

DRUMMOND (*Slowly*) All motion is relative. Perhaps is it *you* who have moved away—by standing still.

The words have a sharp impact on BRADY. *For a moment, he stands still, his mouth open, staring at* DRUMMOND. *Then he takes two faltering steps backward, looks at* DRUMMOND *again, then moves off the stage.* DRUMMOND *stands alone. Slowly the lights fade on the silent man. The curtain falls momentarily.*

Scene II

The courtroom, two days later. It is bright midday, and the trial is in full swing. The JUDGE *is on the bench; the jury, lawyers, officials and spectators crowd the courtroom.* HOWARD, *the thirteen-year-old boy, is on the witness stand. He is wretched in a starched collar and Sunday suit. The weather is as relentlessly hot as before* BRADY *is examining the boy, who is a witness for the prosecution.*

BRADY   Go on, Howard. Tell them what else Mr. Cates told you in the classroom.

HOWARD   Well, he said at first the earth was too hot for any life. Then it cooled off a mite, and cells and things begun to live.

BRADY   Cells?

HOWARD   Little bugs like, in the water. After that, the little bugs got to be bigger bugs, and sprouted legs and crawled up on the land.

BRADY   How long did this take, according to Mr. Cates?

HOWARD   Couple million years. Maybe longer. Then comes the fishes and the reptiles and the mammals. Man's a mammal.

BRADY   Along with the dogs and the cattle in the field: did he say that?

HOWARD   Yes, sir.

DRUMMOND *is about to protest against prompting the witness; then he decides it isn't worth the trouble.*

BRADY   Now, Howard, how did *man* come out of this slimy mess of bugs and serpents, according to your—"Professor"?

HOWARD   Man was sort of evoluted. From the "Old World Monkeys."

BRADY *slaps his thigh.*

BRADY   Did you hear that, my friends? "Old World Monkeys"! According to Mr. Cates, you and I aren't even descended from good American monkeys! (*There is laughter*) Howard, listen carefully. In all this talk of bugs and "Evil-ution," of slime and ooze, did Mr. Cates ever make any reference to God?

HOWARD   Not as I remember.

BRADY   Or the miracle He achieved in seven days as described in the beautiful Book of Genesis?

HOWARD   No, sir.

BRADY *stretches out his arms in an all-embracing gesture.*

BRADY   Ladies and gentlemen—

DRUMMOND   Objection! I ask that the court remind the learned counsel that this not a Chautauqua tent. He is supposed to be submitting evidence to a jury. There are no ladies on the jury.

BRADY   Your Honor, I have no intention of making a speech. There is no need. I am sure that everyone on the jury, everyone within the sound of this boy's voice, is moved by his tragic confusion. He has been taught that he wriggled up like an animal from the filth and the muck below! (*Continuing fervently, the spirit is upon him*) I say that these Bible-haters, these "Evil-utionists," are brewers of poison. And the legislature of this sovereign state has had the wisdom to demand that the peddlers of poison—in bottles or in books—clearly label the products they attempt to sell! (*There is applause.* HOWARD *gulps.* BRADY *points at the boy*)

I tell you, if this law is not upheld, this boy will become one of a generation, shorn of its faith by the teachings of Godless science! But if the full penalty of the law is meted out to Bertram Cates, the faithful the whole world over, who are watching us here, and listening to our every word, will call this courtroom blessed!

Applause. Dramatically, BRADY *moves to his chair. Condescendingly, he waves to* DRUMMOND.

BRADY   Your witness, sir.

BRADY *sits.* DRUMMOND *rises, slouches toward the witness stand.*

DRUMMOND   Well, I sure am glad Colonel Brady didn't make a speech! (*Nobody laughs. The courtroom seems to resent* DRUMMOND'S *gentle ridicule of the orator. To many, there is an effrontery in* DRUMMOND'S *very voice--folksy and relaxed. It's rather like a harmonica following a symphony concert*) Howard, I heard you say that the world used to be pretty hot.

HOWARD   That's what Mr. Cates said.

DRUMMOND   You figure it was any hotter then than it is right now?

HOWARD   Guess it musta been. Mr. Cates read it to us from a book.

DRUMMOND   Do you know what book?

HOWARD   I guess that Mr. Darwin thought it up.

DRUMMOND   (*Leaning on the arm of the boy's chair*) You figure anything's wrong about that, Howard?

HOWARD   Well, I dunno—

DAVENPORT   (*Leaping up, crisply*) Objection, Your Honor. The defense is asking that a thirteen-year-old boy hand down an opinion on a question of morality!

DRUMMOND   (*To the* JUDGE) I am trying to establish, Your Honor, that Howard—or Colonel Brady—or Charles Darwin—or anyone in this courtroom—or *you,* sir—has the right to *think!*

JUDGE   Colonel Drummond, the right to think is not on trial here.

DRUMMOND   (*Energetically*) With all respect to the bench, I hold that the right to think is very much on trial! It is fearfully in danger in the proceedings of this court!

BRADY   (*Rises*) A *man* is on trial!

DRUMMOND   A thinking man! And he is threatened with fine and imprisonment because he chooses to speak what he thinks.

JUDGE   Colonel Drummond, would you please rephrase your question?

DRUMMOND (*To* HOWARD) Let's put it this way, Howard. All this fuss and feathers about Evolution, do you think it hurt you any?

HOWARD   Sir?

DRUMMOND   Did it do you any harm? You still feel reasonably fit? What Mr. Cates told you, did it hurt your baseball game any? Affect your pitching arm?

He punches HOWARD'S *right arm playfully.*

HOWARD   No, sir. I'm a leftie.

DRUMMOND   A southpaw, eh? Still honor your father and mother?

HOWARD   Sure.

DRUMMOND   Haven't murdered anybody since breakfast?

DAVENPORT   Objection.

JUDGE   Objection sustained.

DRUMMOND *shrugs.*

BRADY   Ask him if his Holy Faith in the scriptures has been shattered—

DRUMMOND   When I need your valuable help, Colonel, you may rest assured I shall humbly ask for it. (*Turning*) Howard, do you believe everything Mr. Cates told you?

HOWARD   (*Frowning*) I'm not sure. I gotta think it over.

DRUMMOND   Good for you. Your pa's a farmer, isn't he?

HOWARD   Yes, sir.

DRUMMOND   Got a tractor?

HOWARD   Brand new one.

DRUMMOND   You figure a tractor's sinful, because it isn't mentioned in the Bible?

HOWARD   (*Thinking*) Don't know.

DRUMMOND   Moses never made a phone call. Suppose that makes the telephone an instrument of the Devil?

HOWARD   I never thought of it that way.

BRADY   (*Rising, booming*) Neither did anybody else! Your Honor, the defense makes the same old error of all Godless men! They confuse material things with the great spiritual realities of the Revealed Word! (*Turning to* DRUMMOND) Why do you bewilder this child? Does Right have no meaning to you, sir?

BRADY'S *hands are outstretched, palms upward, pleading.*

DRUMMOND *stares at* BRADY *long and thoughtfully.*

DRUMMOND   (*In a low voice*) Realizing that I may prejudice the case of my client, I must say that "Right" has no meaning to me whatsoever! (*There is a buzz of reaction in the courtroom*) *Truth* has meaning—as a direction. But one of the peculiar imbecilities of our time is the grid of morality we have placed on human behavior: so that every act of man must be measured against an arbitrary latitude of right and longitude of wrong— in exact minutes, seconds, and degrees! (*He turns to* HOWARD) Do you have any idea what I'm talking about, Howard?

HOWARD   No, sir.

DRUMMOND   Well, maybe you will. Someday. Thank you, son. That's all.

JUDGE   The witness is excused. (*He raps his gavel, but* HOWARD *remains in the chair, staring goop-eyed at his newly found idol*) We won't need you any more, Howard: you can go back to your pa now. (HOWARD *gets up, and joins the spectators*) Next witness.

DAVENPORT   Will Miss Rachel Brown come forward, please?

RACHEL *emerges from among the spectators. She comes forward quickly, as if wanting to get the whole thing over with. She looks at no one.* CATES *watches her with a hopeless expression:* Et tu, Brute. MEEKER *swears her in perfunctorily.*

BRADY   Miss Brown. You are a teacher at the Hillsboro Consolidated School?

RACHEL   (*Flat*) Yes.

BRADY   So you have had ample opportunity to know the defendant, Mr. Cates, professionally?

RACHEL   Yes.

BRADY   (*With exaggerated gentleness*) Is Mr. Cates a member of the spiritual community to which you belong?

DRUMMOND   (*Rises*) Objection! I don't understand this chatter about "spiritual communities." If the prosecution wants to know if they go to the same church, why doesn't he ask that?

JUDGE   Uh-objection overruled. (DRUMMOND *slouches, disgruntled.* CATES *stares at* RACHEL *disbelievingly, while her eyes remain on the floor. The exchange between* DRUMMOND *and the* JUDGE *seems to have unnerved her, however*) You will answer the question, please.

RACHEL   I did answer it, didn't I? What was the question?

BRADY   Do you and Mr. Cates attend the same church?

RACHEL   Not any more. Bert dropped out two summers ago.

BRADY   **Why?**

RACHEL It was what happened with the little Stebbins boy.

BRADY Would you tell us about that, please?

RACHEL The boy was eleven years old, and he went swimming in the river, and got a cramp, and drowned. Bert felt awful about it. He lived right next door, and Tommy Stebbins used to come over to the boarding house and look through Bert's microscope. Bert said the boy had a quick mind, and he might even be a scientist when he grew up. At the funeral, Pa preached that Tommy didn't die in a state of grace, because his folks had never had him baptized—

CATES, *who has been smoldering through this recitation, suddenly leaps angrily to his feet.*

CATES Tell 'em what your father really said! That Tommy's soul was damned, writhing in hellfire!

DUNLAP (*Shaking his fist at* CATES) Cates, you sinner!

The JUDGE *raps for order. There is confusion in the courtroom.*

CATES Religion's supposed to comfort people, isn't it? Not frighten them to death!

JUDGE We will have order, please!

DRUMMOND *tugs* CATES *back to his seat.*

DRUMMOND Your Honor, I request that the defendant's remarks be stricken from the record.

The JUDGE *nods.*

BRADY But how can we strike this young man's bigoted opinions from the memory of this community? (BRADY *turns, about to play his trump card*) Now, my dear. Will you tell the jury some more of Mr. Cates' opinions on the subject of religion?

DRUMMOND Objection! Objection! Objection! Hearsay testimony is not admissible.

JUDGE The court sees no objection to this line of question. Proceed, Colonel Brady.

BRADY Will you merely repeat in your own words some of the conversations you had with the defendant?

RACHEL'S *eyes meet* BERT'S. *She hesitates.*

RACHEL I don't remember exactly—

BRADY (*Helpfully*) What you told me the other day. That presumably "humorous" remark Mr. Cates made about the Heavenly Father.

RACHEL Bert said—

She stops.

BRADY Go ahead, my dear.

RACHEL (Pathetically) I can't—

JUDGE May I remind you, Miss Brown, that you are testifying under oath, and it is unlawful to withhold pertinent information.

RACHEL —Bert was just talking about some of the things he'd read. He—He—

BRADY Were you shocked when he told you these things? (RACHEL *looks down*) Describe to the court your innermost feelings when Bertram Cates said to you: "God did not create Man! Man created God!"

There is a flurry of reaction.

DRUMMOND (*Leaping to his feet*) Objection!

RACHEL (*Blurting*) Bert didn't say that! He was just joking. What he said was: "God created Man in His own image—and Man, being a gentleman, returned the compliment."

HORNBECK *guffaws and pointedly scribbles this down.* BRADY *is pleased.* RACHEL *seems hopelessly torn.*

BRADY Go on, my dear. Tell us some more. What did he say about the holy state of matrimony? Did he compare it with the breeding of animals?

RACHEL No, he didn't say that—He didn't *mean* that. That's not what I told you. All he said was—

She opens her mouth to speak, but nothing comes out. An emotional block makes her unable to utter a sound. Her lips move wordlessly.

JUDGE Are you ill, Miss Brown? Would you care for a glass of water?

The fatuity of this suggestion makes RACHEL *crumble into a near breakdown.*

BRADY Under the circumstances, I believe the witness should be dismissed.

DRUMMOND And will the defense have no chance to challenge some of these statements the prosecutor has put in the mouth of the witness?

CATES *is moved by* RACHEL'S *obvious distress.*

CATES (*To* DRUMMOND) Don't plague her. Let her go.

DRUMMOND (*Pauses, then sighs*) No questions.

JUDGE   For the time being, the witness is excused. (REVEREND BROWN *comes forward to help his daughter from the stand. His demeanor is unsympathetic as he escorts her from the courtroom. There is a hushed babble of excitement*) Does the prosecution wish to call any further witnesses?

DAVENPORT   Not at the present time, Your Honor.

JUDGE   We shall proceed with the case for the defense. Colonel Drummond.

DRUMMOND (*Rising*) Your Honor, I wish to call Dr. Amos D. Keller, head of the Department of Zoology at the University of Chicago.

BRADY   Objection.

DRUMMOND *turns, startled.*

DRUMMOND   On what grounds?

BRADY   I wish to inquire what possible relevance the testimony of a *Zoo*-ology professor can have in this trial.

DRUMMOND (*Reasonably*) It has every relevance! My client is on trial for teaching Evolution. Any testimony relating to his alleged infringement of the law must be admitted!

BRADY   Irrelevant, immaterial, inadmissible.

DRUMMOND (*Sharply*) Why? If Bertram Cates were accused of murder, would it be irrelevant to call expert witnesses to examine the weapon? Would you rule out testimony that the so-called murder weapon was incapable of firing a bullet?

JUDGE   I fail to grasp the learned counsel's meaning.

DRUMMOND   Oh. (*With exaggerated gestures, as if explaining things to a small child*) Your Honor, the defense wishes to place Dr. Keller on the stand to explain to the gentlemen of the jury exactly what the evolutionary theory is. How can they pass judgment on it if they don't know what it's all about?

BRADY   I hold that the very law we are here to enforce excludes such testimony! The people of this state have made it very clear that they do not want this *zoo*-ological hogwash slobbered around the schoolrooms! And I refuse to allow these agnostic scientists to employ this courtroom as a sounding board, as a platform from which they can shout their heresies into the headlines!

JUDGE (*After some thoughtful hesitation*) Colonel Drummond, the court rules that zoology is irrelevant to the case.

The JUDGE flashes his customary mechanical and humorless grin.

DRUMMOND   Agnostic scientists! Then I call Dr. Allen Page— (*Staring straight at* BRADY) Deacon of the Congregational Church—and professor of geology and archeology at Oberlin College.

BRADY (*Drily*) Objection!

JUDGE   Objection sustained.

Again, the meaningless grin.

DRUMMOND (*Astonished*) In one breath, does the court deny the existence of zoology, geology and archeology?

JUDGE   We do not deny the existence of these sciences: but they do not relate to this point of law.

DRUMMOND (*Fiery*) I call Walter Aaronson, philosopher, anthropologist, author! One of the most brilliant minds in the world today! Objection, Colonel Brady?

BRADY (*Nodding, smugly*) Objection.

DRUMMOND   Your Honor! The Defense has brought to Hillsboro— at great expense and inconvenience—fifteen noted scientists! The great thinkers of our time! Their testimony is basic to the defense of my client. For it is my intent to show this court that what Bertram Cates spoke quietly one spring afternoon in the Hillsboro High School is no crime! It is incontrovertible as geometry in every enlightened community of minds!

JUDGE   In *this* community, Colonel Drummond—and in this sovereign state—exactly the opposite is the case. The language of the law is clear; we do not need experts to question the validity of a law that is already on the books.

DRUMMOND, *for once in his life, has hit a legal roadblock.*

DRUMMOND (*Scowling*) In other words, the court rules out any expert testimony on Charles Darwin's *Origin of Species* or *Descent of Man*?

JUDGE   The court so rules.

DRUMMOND *is flabbergasted. His case is cooked and he knows it. He looks around helplessly.*

DRUMMOND (*There's the glint of an idea in his eye*) Would the court admit expert testimony regarding a book known as the Holy Bible?

JUDGE (*Hesitates, turns to* BRADY) Any objection, Colonel Brady?

BRADY   If the counsel can advance the case of the defendant through the use of the Holy Scriptures, the prosecution will take no exception!

DRUMMOND   Good (*With relish*) I call to the stand one of the world's foremost experts on the Bible and its teachings— Matthew Harrison Brady!

There is an uproar in the courtroom. The JUDGE *raps for order.*

DAVENPORT   Your Honor, this is preposterous!

JUDGE (*Confused*) I—well, it's highly unorthodox. I've never known an instance where the defense called the prosecuting attorney as a witness.

BRADY *rises. Waits for the crowd's reaction to subside.*

BRADY   Your Honor, this entire trial is unorthodox. If the interests of Right and Justice will be served, I will take the stand.

DAVENPORT (*Helplessly*) But Colonel Brady—

Buzz of awed reaction. The giants are about to meet head-on. The JUDGE *raps the gavel again, nervously.*

JUDGE (*To* BRADY) The court will support you if you wish to decline to testify—as a witness against your own case. . . .

BRADY (*With conviction*) Your Honor, I shall not testify *against* anything I shall speak out, as I have all my life—on behalf of the Living Truth of the Holy Scriptures!

DAVENPORT *sits, resigned but nervous.*

JUDGE (*To* MEEKER, *in a nervous whisper*) Uh—Mr. Meeker, you'd better swear in the witness, please . . .

DRUMMOND *moistens his lips in anticipation.* BRADY *moves to the witness stand in grandiose style.* MEEKER *holds out a Bible.* BRADY *puts his left hand on the book, and raises his right hand.*

MEEKER   Do you solemnly swear to tell the truth, the whole truth, and nothing but the truth, so help you God?

BRADY (*Booming*) I do.

MRS. KREBS   And he will!

BRADY *sits, confident and assured. His air is that of a benign and learned mathematician about to be quizzed by a schoolboy on matters of short division.*

DRUMMOND   Am I correct, sir, in calling on you as an authority on the Bible?

BRADY   I believe it is not boastful to say that I have studied the Bible as much as any layman. And I have tried to live according to its precepts.

DRUMMOND   Bully for you. Now, I suppose you can quote me chapter and verse right straight through the King James Version, can't you?

BRADY   There are many portions of the Holy Bible that I have committed to memory.

DRUMMOND *crosses to counsel table and picks up a copy of Darwin.*

DRUMMOND   I don't suppose you've memorized many passages from the *Origin of Species?*

BRADY   I am not in the least interested in the pagan hypotheses of that book.

DRUMMOND   Never read it?

BRADY   And I never will.

DRUMMOND   Then how in perdition do you have the gall to whoop up this holy war against something you don't know anything about? How can you be so cocksure that the body of scientific knowledge systematized in the writings of Charles Darwin is, in any way, irreconcilable with the spirit of the Book of Genesis?

BRADY   Would you state that question again, please?

DRUMMOND   Let me put it this way. (*He flips several pages in the book*) On page nineteen of *Origin of Species,* Darwin states—

DAVENPORT *leaps up.*

DAVENPORT   I object to this, Your Honor. Colonel Brady has been called as an authority on the Bible. Now the "gentleman from Chicago" is using this opportunity to read into the record scientific testimony which you, Your Honor, have previously ruled is irrelevant. If he's going to examine Colonel Brady on the Bible, let him stick to the Bible, the Holy Bible, and only the Bible!

DRUMMOND *cocks an eye at the bench.*

JUDGE   (*Clears his throat*) You will confine your questions to the Bible.

DRUMMOND *slaps shut the volume of Darwin.*

DRUMMOND   (*Not angrily*) All right. I get the scent in the wind. (*He tosses the volume of Darwin on the counsel table*) We'll play in *your* ball park, Colonel. (*He searches for a copy of the Bible, finally gets* MEEKER'S. *Without opening it,* DRUMMOND *scrutinizes the binding from several angles)* Now let's get this straight. Let's get it clear. This *is* the book that you're an expert on?

BRADY *is annoyed at* DRUMMOND's *elementary attitude and condescension.*

BRADY   That is correct.

DRUMMOND   Now tell me. Do you feel that every word that's written in this book should be taken literally?

BRADY   Everything in the Bible should be accepted, exactly as it is given there.

DRUMMOND *(Leafing through the Bible)* Now take this place where the whale swallows Jonah. Do you figure that actually happened?

BRADY   The Bible does not say "a whale," it says "a big fish."

DRUMMOND   Matter of fact, it says "a great fish"—but it's pretty much the same thing. What's your feeling about that?

BRADY   I believe in a God who can make a whale and who can make a man and make both do what He pleases!

VOICES   Amen, amen!

DRUMMOND *(Turning sharply to the clerk)* I want those "Amens" in the record! *(He wheels back to* BRADY*)* I recollect a story about Joshua, making the sun stand still. Now as an expert, you tell me that's as true as the Jonah business. Right? (BRADY *nods, blandly)* That's a pretty neat trick. You suppose Houdini could do it?

BRADY   I do not question or scoff at the miracles of the Lord—as do ye of little faith.

DRUMMOND   Have you ever pondered just what would naturally happen to the earth if the sun stood still?

BRADY   You can testify to that if I get you on the stand.

There is laughter.

DRUMMOND   If they say that the sun stood still, they must've had a notion that the sun moves around the earth. Think that's the way of things? Or don't you believe the earth moves around the sun?

BRADY   I have faith in the Bible!

DRUMMOND   You don't have faith in the solar system.

BRADY *(Doggedly)* The sun stopped.

DRUMMOND   Good. *(Level and direct)* Now if what you say factually happened—if Joshua halted the sun in the sky—that means the earth stopped spinning on its axis; continents toppled over each other, mountains flew out into space. And the earth, arrested in its orbit, shriveled to a cinder and crashed into the sun. (*Turning*) How come they miss *this* tidbit of news.

BRADY   They missed it because it didn't happen.

DRUMMOND   It must've happened! According to natural law. Or don't you believe in natural law, Colonel? Would you like to ban Copernicus from the classroom, along with Charles Darwin? Pass a law to wipe out all the scientific development since Joshua. Revelations—period!

BRADY (*Calmly, as if instructing a child*) Natural law was born in the mind of the Heavenly Father. He can change it, cancel it, use it as He pleases. It constantly amazes me that you apostles of science, for all your supposed wisdom, fail to grasp this simple fact.

DRUMMOND *flips a few pages in the Bible.*

DRUMMOND   Listen to this: Genesis 4—16. "And Cain went out from the presence of the Lord, and dwelt in the land of Nod, on the East of Eden. And Cain *knew his wife*!" Where the hell did *she* come from?

BRADY   Who?

DRUMMOND   Mrs. Cain. Cain's wife. If, "In the beginning" there were only Adam and Eve, and Cain and Abel, where'd this extra woman spring from? Ever figure that out?

BRADY (*Cool*) No, sir. I will leave the agnostics to hunt for her.

Laughter.

DRUMMOND   Never bothered you?

BRADY   Never bothered me.

DRUMMOND   Never tried to find out?

BRADY   No.

DRUMMOND   Figure somebody pulled off another creation, over in the next county?

BRADY   The Bible satisfies me, it is enough.

DRUMMOND   It frightens me to imagine the state of learning in this world if everyone had your driving curiosity.

DRUMMOND *is still probing for a weakness in Goliath's armor. He thumbs a few pages further in the Bible.*

DRUMMOND   This book now goes into a lot of "begats." (*He reads*) "And Aphraxad begat Salah; and Salah begat Eber" and so on and so on. These pretty important folks?

BRADY   They are the generations of the holy men and women of the Bible.

DRUMMOND   How did they go about all this "begatting"?

BRADY   What do you mean?

DRUMMOND   I mean, did people "begat" in those days about the same way they get themselves "begat" today?

BRADY   The process is about the same. I don't think your scientists have improved it any.

Laughter.

DRUMMOND   In other words, these folks were conceived and brought forth through the normal biological function known as *sex.* (*There is hush-hush reaction through the court.* HOWARD'S *mother clamps her hands over the boy's ears, but he wriggles free*) What do you think of sex, Colonel Brady?

BRADY   In what spirit is this question asked?

DRUMMOND   I'm not asking what you think of sex as a father, or as a husband. Or a Presidential candidate. You're up here as an expert on the Bible. What's the Biblical evaluation of sex?

BRADY   It is considered "Original Sin."

DRUMMOND   (*With mock amazement*) And all these holy people got themselves "begat" through "Original Sin"? (BRADY *does not answer. He scowls, and shifts his weight in his chair*) All this sinning make 'em any less holy?

DAVENPORT   Your Honor, where is this leading us? What does it have to do with the State versus Bertram Cates?

JUDGE   Colonel Drummond, the court must be satisfied that this line of questioning has some bearing on the case.

DRUMMOND   (*Fiery*) You've ruled out all my witnesses. I must be allowed to examine the one witness you've left me in my own way!

BRADY   (*With dignity*) Your Honor, I am willing to sit here and endure Mr. Drummond's sneering and his disrespect. For he is pleading the case of the prosecution by his contempt for all that is holy.

DRUMMOND   I object, I object, I object.

BRADY   On what grounds? Is it possible that something *is* holy to the celebrated agnostic?

DRUMMOND   (*His voice drops, intensively*) The individual human mind. In a child's power to master the multiplication table there is more sanctity than in all your shouted "Amens!", "Holy, Holies!" and "Hosannahs!" An idea is a greater monument than a cathedral. And the advance of man's knowledge is more of a miracle than any sticks turned to snakes, or the parting of waters! But we are now to halt the march of progress because Mr. Brady frightens us with a fable? (*Turning to the jury, reasonably*) Gentlemen, progress has never been a bargain. You've got to pay for it. Sometimes I think there's a man behind a counter who says, "All right, you can have a telephone; but you'll have to give up privacy, the charm of distance. Madam, you may vote; but at a price; you lose the right to retreat behind a powder-puff or a petticoat. Mister, you may conquer the air; but the birds will lose their wonder, and the clouds will smell of gasoline!" (*Thoughtfully, seeming to look beyond the courtroom*) Darwin moved us forward to a hilltop, where we could look back and see the way from which we came. But for this view, this insight, this knowledge, we must abandon our faith in the pleasant poetry of Genesis.

BRADY   We must *not* abandon faith! Faith is the important thing!

DRUMMOND   Then why did God plague us with the power to think? Mr. Brady, why do you deny the *one* faculty which lifts man above all other creatures on the earth: the power of his brain to reason? What other merit have we? The elephant is larger, the horse is stronger and swifter, the butterfly more beautiful, the mosquito more prolific, even the simple sponge is more durable! (*Wheeling on* BRADY) Or does a *sponge* think?

BRADY   I don't know. I'm a man, not a sponge.

There are a few snickers at this; the crowd seems to be slipping away from BRADY *and aligning itself more and more with* DRUMMOND.

DRUMMOND   Do you think a sponge thinks?

BRADY   If the Lord wishes a sponge to think, it thinks.

DRUMMOND   Does a man have the same privileges that a sponge does?

BRADY   Of course.

DRUMMOND (*Roaring, for the first time: stretching his arm toward* CATES) This man wishes to be accorded the same privilege as a sponge! *He wishes to think!*

There is some applause. The sound of it strikes BRADY *exactly as if he had been slapped in the face.*

BRADY But your client is wrong! He is deluded! He has lost his way!

DRUMMOND It's sad that we aren't all gifted with your positive knowledge of Right and Wrong, Mr. Brady. (DRUMMOND *strides to one of the uncalled witnesses seated behind him, and takes from him a rock, about the size of a tennis ball.* DRUMMOND *weighs the rock in his hand as he saunters back toward* BRADY) How old do you think this rock is?

BRADY (*Intoning*) I am more interested in the Rock of Ages, than I am in the Age of Rocks.

A couple of die-hard "Amens." DRUMMOND *ignores this glib gag.*

DRUMMOND Dr. Page of Oberlin College tells me that this rock is at least ten million years old.

BRADY (*Sarcastically*) Well, well, Colonel Drummond! You managed to sneak in some of that scientific testimony after all.

DRUMMOND *opens up the rock, which splits into two halves. He shows it to* BRADY.

DRUMMOND Look, Mr. Brady. These are the fossil remains of a pre-historic marine creature, which was found in this very county—and which lived here millions of years ago, when these very mountain ranges were submerged in water.

BRADY I know. The Bible gives a fine account of the flood. But your professor is a little mixed up on his dates. That rock is not more than six thousand years old.

DRUMMOND How do you know?

BRADY A fine Biblical scholar, Bishop Usher, has determined for us the exact date and hour of the Creation. It occurred in the Year 4,004, B.C.

DRUMMOND That's Bishop Usher's opinion.

BRADY It is not an opinion. It is literal fact, which the good Bishop arrived at through careful computation of the ages of the prophets as set down in the Old Testament. In fact, he determined that the Lord began the Creation on the 23rd of October in the Year 4,004 B.C.—at uh, at 9 A.M.!

DRUMMOND   That Eastern Standard Time? (*Laughter*) or Rocky
Mountain Time? (*More laughter*) It wasn't daylight-saving
time, was it? Because the Lord didn't make the sun until the
fourth day!

BRADY   (*Fidgeting*) That is correct.

DRUMMOND   (*Sharply*) The first day. Was it a twenty-four-hour day?

BRADY   The Bible says it was a day.

DRUMMOND   There wasn't any sun. How do you know how long
it was?

BRADY   (*Determined*) The Bible says it was a day.

DRUMMOND   A normal day, a literal day, a twenty-four-hour day?
Pause. BRADY *is unsure.*

BRADY   I do not know.

DRUMMOND   What do you think?

BRADY   (*Floundering*) I do not think about things that . . . I do not
think about!

DRUMMOND   Do you ever think about things that you *do* think
about? (*There is some laughter. But it is dampened by the
knowledge and awareness throughout the courtroom, that the
trap is about to be sprung*) Isn't it possible that first day was
twenty-*five* hours long? There was no way to measure it, no way
to tell! *Could* it have been twenty-five hours?
Pause. The entire courtroom seems to lean forward.

BRADY   (*Hesitates—then*) It is . . . possible . . .

DRUMMOND's *got him. And he knows it! This is the turning
point. From here on, the tempo mounts.* DRUMMOND *is now
fully in the driver's seat. He pounds his questions faster and
faster.*

DRUMMOND   Oh. You interpret that the first day recorded in the
Book of Genesis could be of indeterminate length.

BRADY   (*Wriggling*) I mean to state that the day referred to is not
necessarily a twenty-four-hour day.

DRUMMOND   It could have been thirty hours! Or a month! Or a
year! Or a hundred years! (*He brandishes the rock underneath*
BRADY'S *nose*) *Or ten million years!*

DAVENPORT *is able to restrain himself no longer. He realizes
that* DRUMMOND *has* BRADY *in his pocket. Red-faced, he leaps
up to protest.*

DAVENPORT   I protest! This is not only irrelevant, immaterial—it is
illegal! (*There is excited reaction in the courtroom. The* JUDGE

pounds for order, but the emotional tension will not subside)
I demand to know the purpose of Mr. Drummond's examination! What is he trying to do?

Both BRADY *and* DRUMMOND *crane forward, hurling their answers not at the court, but at each other.*

BRADY   I'll tell you what he's trying to do! He wants to destroy everybody's belief in the Bible, and in God!

DRUMMOND   You know that's not true. I'm trying to stop you bigots and ignoramuses from controlling the education of the United States! And you know it!

Arms out, DAVENPORT *pleads to the court, but is unheard. The* JUDGE *hammers for order.*

JUDGE   (*Shouting*) I shall ask the bailiff to clear the court, unless there is order here.

BRADY   How dare you attack the Bible?

DRUMMOND   The Bible is a book. A good book. But it's not the *only* book.

BRADY   It is the revealed word of the Almighty. God spake to the men who wrote the Bible.

DRUMMOND   And how do you know that God didn't "spake" to Charles Darwin?

BRADY   I know, because God tells me to oppose the evil teachings of that man.

DRUMMOND   Oh, God speaks to you.

BRADY   Yes.

DRUMMOND   He tells you exactly what's right and what's wrong?

BRADY   (*Doggedly*) Yes.

DRUMMOND   And you act accordingly?

BRADY   Yes.

DRUMMOND   So you, Matthew Harrison Brady, through oratory, legislation, or whatever, pass along God's orders to the rest of the world! (*Laughter begins*) Gentlemen, meet the "Prophet From Nebraska!"

BRADY'S *oratory is unassailable; but his vanity—exposed by* DRUMMOND'S *prodding—is only funny. The laughter is painful to* BRADY. *He starts to answer* DRUMMOND, *then turns toward the spectators and tries, almost physically, to suppress the amused reaction. This only makes it worse.*

BRADY   (*Almost inarticulate*) I—Please—!

DRUMMOND (*with increasing tempo, closing in*) Is that the way of things? God tells Brady what is good! To be against Brady is to be against God!

More laughter.

BRADY (*Confused*) No, no! Each man is a free agent—

DRUMMOND   Then what is Bertram Cates doing in the Hillsboro jail? (*Some applause*) Suppose Mr. Cates had enough influence and lung power to railroad through the State Legislature a law that only *Darwin* should be taught in the schools!

BRADY   Ridiculous, ridiculous! There is only one great Truth in the world—

DRUMMOND   The Gospel according to Brady! God speaks to Brady, and Brady tells the world! Brady, Brady, Brady, Almighty!

DRUMMOND *bows grandly. The crowd laughs.*

BRADY   The Lord is my strength—

DRUMMOND   What if a lesser human being—a Cates, or a Darwin— has the audacity to think that God might whisper to *him*? That an un-Brady thought might still be holy? Must men go to prison because they are at odds with the self-appointed prophet? (BRADY *is now trembling so that it is impossible for him to speak. He rises, towering above his tormentor—rather like a clumsy, lumbering bear that is baited by an agile dog*) Extend the Testament! Let us have a Book of Brady! We shall hex the Pentateuch, and slip you in neatly between Numbers and Deuteronomy!

At this, there is another burst of laughter, BRADY *is almost in a frenzy.*

BRADY (*Reaching for a sympathetic ear, trying to find the loyal audience which has slipped away from him*) My friends— Your Honor—My Followers—Ladies and Gentlemen—

DRUMMOND   The witness is excused.

BRADY (*Unheeding*) All of you know what I stand for! What I believe! I believe, I believe in the truth of the Book of Genesis! (*Beginning to chant*) Exodus, Leviticus, Numbers, Deuteronomy, Joshua, Judges, Ruth, First Samuel, Second Samuel, First Kings, Second Kings—

DRUMMOND   Your Honor, this completes the testimony. The witness is excused!

BRADY (*Pounding the air with his fists*) Isaiah, Jeremiah, Lamentations, Ezekiel, Daniel, Hosea, Joel, Amos, Obadiah—
There is confusion in the court. The JUDGE *raps.*

JUDGE You are excused, Colonel Brady—

BRADY Jonah, Micah, Nahum, Habakkuk, Zephaniah—
BRADY beats his clenched fists in the air with every name. There is a rising counterpoint of reaction from the spectators. Gavel.

JUDGE (*Over the confusion*) Court is adjourned until ten o'clock tomorrow morning!
Gavel. The spectators begin to mill about. A number of them, reporters and curiosity seekers, cluster around DRUMMOND. DAVENPORT *follows the* JUDGE *out.*

DAVENPORT Your Honor, I want to speak to you about striking all of this from the record.
They go out.

BRADY (*Still erect on the witness stand*) Haggai, Zechariah, Malachi . . .
His voice trails off. He sinks, limp and exhausted into the witness chair. MRS. BRADY *looks at her husband, worried and distraught. She looks at* DRUMMOND *with helpless anger.* DRUMMOND *moves out of the courtroom, and most of the crowd goes with him. Reporters cluster tight about* DRUMMOND, *pads and pencils hard at work.* BRADY *sits, ignored, on the witness chair.* MEEKER *takes* CATES *back to the jail.* MRS. BRADY *goes to her husband, who still sits on the raised witness chair.*

MRS. BRADY (*Taking his hand*) Matt—
BRADY looks about to see if everyone has left the courtroom, before he speaks.

BRADY Mother. They're laughing at me, Mother!

MRS. BRADY (*Unconvincingly*) No, Matt. No, they're not!

BRADY I can't stand it when they laugh at me!
MRS. BRADY steps up onto the raised level of the witness chair. She stands beside and behind her husband, putting her arms around the massive shoulders, and cradling his head against her breast.

MRS. BRADY (*Soothing*) It's all right, baby. It's all right. (MRS. BRADY *sways gently back and forth, as if rocking her husband to sleep*) Baby . . . Baby . . . !

The curtain falls

ACT THREE

The courtroom, the following day. The lighting is low, sombre. A spot burns down on the defense table, where DRUMMOND *and* CATES *sit, waiting for the jury to return.* DRUMMOND *leans back in a meditative mood, feet propped on a chair.* CATES, *the focus of the furor, is resting his head on his arms. The courtroom is almost empty. Two spectators doze in their chairs. In comparative shadow,* BRADY *sits, eating a box lunch. He is drowning his troubles with food, as an alcoholic escapes from reality with a straight shot.* HORNBECK *enters, bows low to* BRADY.

HORNBECK   Afternoon, Colonel. Having high tea, I see.

> BRADY *ignores him.*
> Is the jury still out? Swatting flies
> And wrestling with justice—in that order?

> HORNBECK *crosses to* DRUMMOND. CATES *lifts his head.*
> I'll hate to see the jury filing in;
> Won't you, Colonel? I'll miss Hillsboro—
> Especially this courthouse:
> A melange of Moorish and Methodist;
> It must have been designed by a congressman!

> HORNBECK *smirks at his own joke, then sits in the shadows and pores over a newspaper. Neither* CATES *nor* DRUMMOND *have paid the slightest attention to him.*

CATES   (*Staring straight ahead*) Mr. Drummond. What's going to happen?

DRUMMOND   What do you think is going to happen, Bert?

CATES   Do you think they'll send me to prison?

DRUMMOND   They could.

CATES   They don't ever let you see anybody from the outside, do they? I mean—you can just talk to a visitor—through a window —the way they show it in the movies?

DRUMMOND   Oh, it's not as bad as all that. (*Turning toward the town*) When they started this fire here, they never figured it would light up the whole sky. A lot of people's shoes are getting hot. But you can't be too sure.

At the other side of the stage, BRADY, *rises majestically from his debris of paper napkins and banana peels, and goes off.*

CATES (*Watching* BRADY *go off*) He seems so sure. He seems to know what the verdict's going to be.

DRUMMOND   Nobody knows. (*He tugs on one ear*) I've got a pretty good idea. When you've been a lawyer as long as I have—a thousand years, more or less—you get so you can smell the way a jury's thinking.

CATES   What are they thinking right now?

DRUMMOND (*Sighing*) Someday I'm going to get me an *easy* case. An open-and-shut case. I've got a friend up in Chicago. Big lawyer. Lord how the money rolls in! You know why? He never takes a case unless it's a sure thing. Like a jockey who won't go in a race unless he can ride the favorite.

CATES   You sure picked the long shot this time, Mr. Drummond.

DRUMMOND   Sometimes I think the law *is* like a horse race. Sometimes it seems to me I ride like fury, just to end up back where I started. Might as well be on a merry-go-round, or a rocking horse . . . or . . . (*He half-closes his eyes. His voice is far away, his lips barely move*) Golden Dancer. . . .

CATES   What did you say?

DRUMMOND   That was the name of my first long shot. Golden Dancer. She was in the big side window of the general store in Wakeman, Ohio. I used to stand out in the street and say to myself, "If I had Golden Dancer I'd have everything in the world I wanted." (*He cocks an eyebrow*) I was seven years old, and a very fine judge of rocking horses. (*He looks off again, into the distance*) Golden Dancer had a bright red mane, blue eyes, and she was gold all over, with purple spots. When the sun hit her stirrups, she was a dazzling sight to see. But she was a week's wages for my father. So Golden Dancer and I always had a plate glass window between us. (*Reaching back for the memory*) But—let's see, it wasn't Christmas; must've been my birthday—I woke up in the morning and there was Golden Dancer at the foot of my bed! Ma had skimped on the groceries, and my father'd worked nights for a month. (*Re-living the moment*) I jumped into the saddle and started to rock— (*Almost a whisper*) And it *broke*! It split in two! The wood was rotten, the whole thing was put together with spit and sealing wax! All shine, and no substance! (*Turning to* CATES) Bert, whenever you see something bright, shining, perfect-seeming—all gold, with purple spots—look behind the paint! And if it's a lie—show it up for what it really is!

A RADIO MAN *comes on, lugging an old-fashioned carbon microphone. The* JUDGE, *carrying his robe over his arm, comes on and scowls at the microphone.*

RADIO MAN (*To* JUDGE) I think this is the best place to put it—if it's all right with you, Your Honor.

JUDGE There's no precedent for this sort of thing.

RADIO MAN You understand, sir, we're making history here today. This is the first time a public event has ever been broadcast.

JUDGE Well, I'll allow it—provided you don't interfere with the business of the court.

The RADIO MAN *starts to string his wires. The* MAYOR *hurries on, worried, brandishing a telegram.*

MAYOR (*To* JUDGE) Merle, gotta talk to you. Over here. (*He draws the* JUDGE *aside, not wanting to be heard*) This wire just came. The boys over at the state capitol are getting worried about how things are going. Newspapers all over are raising such a hullabaloo. After all, November, ain't too far off, and it don't do any of us any good to have any of the voters gettin' all steamed up. Wouldn't do no harm to just let things simmer down. (*The* RADIO MAN *reappears*) Well, go easy, Merle.

Tipping his hat to DRUMMOND, *the* MAYOR *hurries off.*

RADIO MAN (*Crisply, into the mike*) Testing. Testing.

DRUMMOND *crosses to the microphone.*

DRUMMOND (*To the* RADIO MAN) What's that?

RADIO MAN An enunciator.

DRUMMOND You going to broadcast?

RADIO MAN We have a direct wire to WGN, Chicago. As soon as the jury comes in, we'll announce the verdict.

DRUMMOND *takes a good look at the microphone, fingers the base.*

DRUMMOND Radio! God, this is going to break down a lot of walls.

RADIO MAN (*Hastily*) You're—you're not supposed to say "God" on the radio!

DRUMMOND Why the hell not?

The RADIO MAN *looks at the microphone, as if it were a toddler that had just been told the facts of life.*

RADIO MAN   You're not supposed to say "Hell", either.

DRUMMOND *(Sauntering away) This* is going to be a barren source of amusement!

BRADY re-enters and crosses ponderously to the RADIO MAN.

BRADY   Can one speak into either side of this machine?

The RADIO MAN *starts at this rumbling thunder, so close to the ear of his delicate child.*

RADIO MAN *(In an exaggerated whisper)* Yes, sir.   Either side.

BRADY attempts to lower his voice, but it is like putting a leash on an elephant.

BRADY   Kindly signal me while I am speaking, if my voice does not have sufficient projection for your radio apparatus.

RADIO MAN nods, a little annoyed. HORNBECK *smirks, amused. Suddenly the air of the courtroom is charged with excitement.* MEEKER *hurries on—and the spectators begin to scurry expectantly back into the courtroom. Voices mutter: "They're comin' in now. Verdict's been reached. Jury's comin' back in."* MEEKER *crosses to the* JUDGE'S *bench, reaches up for the gavel and raps it several times.*

MEEKER   Everybody rise. *(The spectators come to attention)* Hear ye, hear ye. Court will reconvene in the case of the State versus Bertram Cates.

MEEKER crosses to lead in the jury. They enter, faces fixed and stern.

CATES *(Whispers to* DRUMMOND*)* What do you think? Can you tell from their faces?

DRUMMOND is nervous, too. He squints at the returning jurors, drumming his fingers on the table top. CATES *looks around, as if hoping to see* RACHEL—*but she is not there. His disappointment is evident. The* RADIO MAN *has received his signal from off-stage, and he begins to speak into the microphone.*

RADIO MAN *(Low, with dramatic intensity)* Ladies and gentlemen, this is Harry Esterbrook, speaking to you from the courthouse in Hillsboro, where the jury is just returning to the courtroom to render its verdict in the famous Hillsboro Monkey Trial case. The Judge has just taken the bench. And in the next few minutes we shall know whether Bertram Cates will be found innocent or guilty.

The JUDGE *looks at him with annoyance. Gingerly, the* RADIO MAN *aims his microphone at the* JUDGE *and steps back. There is hushed tension all through the courtroom.*

JUDGE (*Clears his throat*) Gentlemen of the Jury, have you reached a decision?

SILLERS (*Rising*) Yeah. Yes, sir, we have, Your Honor.

MEEKER *crosses to* SILLERS *and takes a slip of paper from him. Silently, he crosses to the* JUDGE'S *bench again, all eyes following the slip of paper. The* JUDGE *takes it, opens it, raps his gavel.*

JUDGE   The jury's decision is unanimous. Bertram Cates is found guilty as charged!

There is tremendous reaction in the courtroom. Some cheers, applause, "Amens." Some boos. BRADY *is pleased. But it is not the beaming, powerful, assured* BRADY *of the Chautauqua tent. It is a spiteful, bitter victory for him, not a conquest with a cavalcade of angels.* CATES *stares at his lap.* DRUMMOND *taps a pencil. The* RADIO MAN *talks rapidly, softly into his microphone. The* JUDGE *does not attempt to control the reaction.*

HORNBECK (*In the manner of a hawker or pitchman*)
Step right up, and get your tickets for the Middle Ages!
You only *thought* you missed the Coronation of Charlemagne!

JUDGE (*Rapping his gavel, shouting over the noise*) Quiet, please! Order! This court is still in session. (*The noise quiets down*) The prisoner will rise, to hear the sentence of this court.
(DRUMMOND *looks up quizzically, alert*) Bertram Cates, I hereby sentence you to—

DRUMMOND (*Sharply*) Your Honor! A question of procedure!

JUDGE (*Nettled*) Well, sir?

DRUMMOND Is it not customary in this state to allow the defendant to make a statement before sentence is passed?

The JUDGE *is red-faced.*

JUDGE   Colonel Drummond, I regret this omission. In the confusion, and the—I neglected—(*Up, to* CATES) Uh, Mr. Cates, if you wish to make any statement before sentence is passed on you, why, you may proceed.

Clears throat again. CATES *rises. The courtroom quickly grows silent again.*

CATES (*Simply*) Your Honor, I am not a public speaker. I do not have the eloquence of some of the people you have heard in the last few days. I'm just a schoolteacher.

MRS. BLAIR   Not any more you ain't!

CATES (*Pause. Quietly*) I *was* a schoolteacher. (*With difficulty*) I feel I am . . . I have been convicted of violating an unjust law. I will continue in the future, as I have in the past, to oppose this law in any way I can. I—

CATES *isn't sure exactly what to say next. He hesitates, then sits down. There is a crack of applause. Not from everybody, but from many of the spectators.* BRADY *is fretful and disturbed. He's won the case. The prize is his, but he can't reach for the candy. In his hour of triumph,* BRADY *expected to be swept from the courtroom on the shoulders of his exultant followers. But the drama isn't proceeding according to plan. The gavel again. The court quiets down.*

JUDGE   Bertram Cates, this court has found you guilty of violating Public Act Volume 37, Statute Number 31428, as charged. This violation is punishable by fine and/or imprisonment. (*He coughs*) But since there has been no previous violation of this statute, there is no precedent to guide the bench in passing sentence. (*He flashes the automatic smile*) The court deems it proper—(*He glances at the* MAYOR)—to sentence Bertram Cates to pay a fine of—(*He coughs*) one hundred dollars.

The mighty Evolution Law explodes with the pale puff of a wet firecracker. There is a murmur of surprise through the courtroom. BRADY *is indignant. He rises, incredulous.*

BRADY   Did Your Honor say one hundred dollars?

JUDGE   That is correct. (*Trying to get it over with*) This seems to conclude the business of the trial—

BRADY (*Thundering*) Your Honor, the prosecution takes exception! Where the issues are so titanic, the court must mete out more drastic punishment—

DRUMMOND (*Biting in*) I object!

BRADY   To make an example of this transgressor! To show the world—

DRUMMOND Just a minute. Just a minute. The amount of the fine is of no concern to me. Bertram Cates has no intention whatsoever of paying this or any other fine. He would not pay it if it were one single dollar. We will appeal this decision to the Supreme Court of this state. Will the court grant thirty days to prepare our appeal?

JUDGE   Granted. The court fixes bond at . . . five hundred dollars. I believe this concludes the business of this trial. Therefore, I declare this court is adjour—

BRADY (*Hastily*) Your Honor! (*He reaches for a thick manuscript*) Your Honor, with the court's permission, I should like to read into the record a few short remarks which I have prepared—

DRUMMOND   I object to that. Mr. Brady may make any remarks he likes—long, short or otherwise in a Chautauqua tent or in a political campaign. Our business in Hillsboro is completed. The defense holds that the court shall be adjourned.

BRADY (*Frustrated*) But I have a few remarks—

JUDGE   And we are all anxious to hear them, sir. But Colonel Drummond's point of procedure is well taken. I am sure that everyone here will wish to remain after the court is adjourned to hear your address. (BRADY *lowers his head slightly, in gracious deference to procedure. The* JUDGE *raps the gavel*) I hereby declare this court is adjourned, sine die.

There is a babble of confusion and reaction. HORNBECK *promptly crosses to* MEEKER *and confers with him in whispers. Spectators, relieved of the court's formality, take a seventh-inning stretch. Fans pump, sticky clothes are plucked away from the skin.*

MELINDA (*Calling to* HOWARD, *across the courtroom*) Which side won?

HOWARD (*Calling back*) I ain't sure. But the whole thing's over!

A couple of HAWKERS *slip in the courtroom with Eskimo Pies and buckets of lemonade.*

HAWKER   Eskimo Pies. Get your Eskimo Pies!

JUDGE *raps with his gavel.*

JUDGE (*Projecting*) Quiet! Order in the—I mean, your attention, please. (*The spectators quiet down some, but not completely*) We are honored to hear a few words from Colonel Brady, who wishes to address you—

The JUDGE *is interrupted in his introduction by* MEEKER *and* HORNBECK. *They confer sotto voce. The babble of voices crescendos.*

HAWKER   Get your Eskimo Pies! Cool off with an Eskimo Pie!

Spectators flock to get ice cream and lemonade. BRADY *preens himself for the speech, but is annoyed by the confusion.* HORN-BECK *hands the* JUDGE *several bills from his wallet, and* MEEKER *pencils a receipt. The* JUDGE *bangs his gavel again.*

JUDGE   We beg your attention, please, ladies and gentlemen! Colonel Brady has some remarks to make which I am sure will interest us all!

A few of the faithful fall dutifully silent. But the milling about and the slopping of lemonade continues. Two kids chase each other in and out among the spectators, annoying the perspiring RADIO MAN. BRADY *stretches out his arms, in the great attention-getting gesture.*

BRADY   My dear friends . . . ! Your attention, please! (*The bugle voice reduces the noise somewhat further. But it is not the eager, anticipating hush of olden days. Attention is given him, not as the inevitable due of a mighty monarch, but grudgingly and resentfully*) Fellow citizens, and friends of the unseen audience. From the hallowed hills of sacred Sinai, in the days of remote antiquity, came the law which has been our bulwark and our shield. Age upon age, men have looked to the law as they would look to the mountains, whence cometh our strength. And here, here in this—

The RADIO MAN *approaches* BRADY *nervously.*

RADIO MAN   Excuse me, Mr.—uh, Colonel Brady; would you . . . uh . . . point more in the direction of the enunciator . . . ?

The RADIO MAN *pushes* BRADY *bodily toward the microphone. As the orator is maneuvered into position, he seems almost to be an inanimate object, like a huge ornate vase which must be precisely centered on a mantel. In this momentary lull, the audience has slipped away from him again. There's a backwash of restless shifting and murmuring.* BRADY'S *vanity and cussedness won't let him give up, even though he realizes this is a sputtering anticlimax. By God, he'll make them listen!*

BRADY (*Red-faced, his larynx taut, roaring stridently*) As they would look to the mountains whence cometh our strength. And here, here in this courtroom, we have seen vindicated—(*A few people leave. He watches them desperately, out of the corner of his eye.*) We have seen vindicated—

RADIO MAN (*After an off-stage signal*) Ladies and gentlemen, our program director in Chicago advises us that our time here is completed. Harry Y. Esterbrook speaking. We return you now to our studios and "Matinee Musicale."

He takes the microphone and goes off. This is the final indignity to BRADY; *he realizes that a great portion of his audience has left him as he watches it go.* BRADY *brandishes his speech, as if it were Excalibur. His eyes start from his head, the voice is a tight, frantic rasp.*

BRADY   From the hallowed hills of sacred Sinai . . .

He freezes. His lips move, but nothing comes out. Paradoxically, his silence brings silence. The orator can hold his audience only by not speaking.

STOREKEEPER   Look at him!

MRS. BRADY (*With terror*) Matt—

There seems to be some violent, volcanic upheaval within him. His lower lip quivers, his eyes stare. Very slowly, he seems to be leaning toward the audience. Then, like a figure in a waxworks, toppling from its pedestal, he falls stiffly, face forward.

MEEKER *and* DAVENPORT *spring forward, catch* BRADY *by the shoulders and break his fall. The sheaf of manuscript, clutched in his raised hand, scatters in mid air. The great words flutter innocuously to the courtroom floor. There is a burst of reaction.* MRS. BRADY *screams.*

DAVENPORT   Get a doctor!

Several men lift the prostrate BRADY, *and stretch him across three chairs.* MRS. BRADY *rushes to his side.*

JUDGE   Room! Room! Give him room!

MRS. BRADY   Matt! Dear God in Heaven! Matt!

DRUMMOND, HORNBECK *and* CATES *watch, silent and concerned —somewhat apart from the crowd. The silence is tense. It is suddenly broken by a frantic old* WOMAN, *who shoves her face close to* BRADY'S *and shrieks.*

WOMAN (*Wailing*) O Lord, work us a miracle and save our Holy Prophet!

Rudely, MEEKER *pushes her back.*

MEEKER (*Contemptuously*) Get away! (*Crisply*) Move him out of here. Fast as we can. Hank. Bill. Give us a hand here. Get him across the street to Doc's office.

Several men lift BRADY, *with difficulty, and begin to carry him out. A strange thing happens.* BRADY *begins to speak in a hollow, distant voice—as if something sealed up inside of him were finally broken, and the precious contents spilled out into the open at last.*

BRADY (*As he is carried out; in a strange, unreal voice*) Mr. Chief Justice, Citizens of these United States. During my term in the White House, I pledge to carry out my program for the betterment of the common people of this country. As your new President, I say what I have said all of my life. . . .

The crowd tags along, curious and awed. Only DRUMMOND, CATES *and* HORNBECK *remain, their eyes fixed on* BRADY'S *exit.* DRUMMOND *stares after him.*

DRUMMOND   How quickly they can turn. And how painful it can be when you don't expect it. (*He turns*) I wonder how it feels to be Almost-President three times—with a skull full of undelivered inauguration speeches.

HORNBECK   Something happens to an Also-Ran.
Something happens to the feet of a man
Who always comes in second in a foot-race.
He becomes a national unloved child,
A balding orphan, an aging adolescent
Who never got the biggest piece of candy.
Unloved children, of all ages, insinuate themselves
Into spotlights and rotogravures.
They stand on their hands and wiggle their feet.
Split pulpits with their pounding! And their tonsils
Turn to organ pipes. Show me a shouter,
And I'll show you an also-ran. A might-have-been,
An almost-was.

CATES (*Softly*) Did you see his face? He looked terrible. . . .

MEEKER *enters.* CATES *turns to him.* MEEKER *shakes his head:* "I don't know."

MEEKER   I'm surprised more folks ain't keeled over in this heat.

HORNBECK   He's all right. Give him an hour or so
To sweat away the pickles and the pumpernickel.
To let his tongue forget the acid taste
Of vinegar victory.
Mount Brady will erupt again by nightfall,
Spouting lukewarm fire and irrelevant ashes.

CATES *shakes his head, bewildered.* DRUMMOND *watches him, concerned.*

DRUMMOND   What's the matter, boy?

CATES   I'm not sure. Did I win or did I lose?

DRUMMOND   You won.

CATES   But the jury found me—

DRUMMOND   What jury? Twelve men? Millions of people will say you won. They'll read in their papers tonight that you smashed a bad law. You made it a joke!

CATES   Yeah. But what's going to happen now? I haven't got a job. I'll bet they won't even let me back in the boarding house.

DRUMMOND   Sure, it's gonna be tough, it's not gonna be any church social for a while. But you'll live. And while they're making you sweat, remember—you've helped the next fella.

CATES   What do you mean?

DRUMMOND   You don't suppose this kind of thing is ever finished, do you? Tomorrow it'll be something else—and another fella will have to stand up. And you've helped give him the guts to do it!

CATES (*Turning to* MEEKER, *with new pride in what he's done*) Mr. Meeker, don't you have to lock me up?

MEEKER   They fixed bail.

CATES   You don't expect a schoolteacher to have five hundred dollars?

MEEKER (*Jerking his head toward* HORNBECK) This fella here put up the money.

HORNBECK   With a year's subscription to the Baltimore *Herald,*
We give away—at no cost or obligation—
A year of freedom.

RACHEL *enters, carrying a suitcase. She is smiling, and there is a new lift to her head.* CATES *turns and sees her.*

CATES   Rachel!

RACHEL   Hello, Bert.

CATES   Where are you going?

RACHEL   I'm not sure. But I'm leaving my father.

CATES   Rache . . .

RACHEL   Bert, it's my fault the jury found you guilty. (*He starts to protest*) Partly my fault. I helped. (RACHEL *hands* BERT *a book*) This is your book, Bert (*Silently, he takes it*) I've read it. All the way through. I don't understand it. What I do understand, I don't like. I don't want to think that men come from apes and monkeys. But I think that's beside the point.

DRUMMOND *looks at the girl admiringly.*

DRUMMOND   That's right. That's beside the point.

RACHEL *crosses to* DRUMMOND.

RACHEL   Mr. Drummond, I hope I haven't said anything to offend you. You see, I haven't really thought very much. I was always afraid of what I might think—so it seemed safer not to think at all. But now I know. A thought is like a child inside our body. It has to be born. If it dies inside you, part of you dies, too! (*Pointing to the book*) Maybe what Mr. Darwin wrote is bad. I don't know. Bad or good, it doesn't make any difference. The ideas have to come out—like children. Some of 'em healthy as a bean plant, some sickly. I think the sickly ideas die mostly, don't you, Bert?

BERT *nods yes, but he's too lost in new admiration for her to do anything but stare. He does not move to her side.* DRUMMOND *smiles, as if to say: "That's quite a girl!" The* JUDGE *walks in slowly.*

JUDGE   Brady's dead.

They all react. The JUDGE *starts toward his chambers.*

DRUMMOND   I can't imagine the world without Matthew Harrison Brady.

CATES   (*To the* JUDGE) What caused it? Did they say? (*Dazed, the* JUDGE *goes off without answering.*

HORNBECK   Matthew Harrison Brady died of a busted belly.

DRUMMOND *slams down his brief case.*

HORNBECK   You know what I thought of him,
And I know what you thought.
Let us leave the lamentations to the illiterate!
Why should we weep for him? He cried enough for himself!
The national tear-duct from Weeping Water, Nebraska,

Who flooded the whole nation like a one-man Mississippi!
You know what he was:
A Barnum-bunkum Bible-beating bastard!

DRUMMOND *rises, fiercely angry.*

DRUMMOND   You smart-aleck! You have no more right to spit on his religion than you have a right to spit on *my* religion! Or my lack of it!

HORNBECK (*Askance*) Well, what do you know!
Henry Drummond for the defense
Even of his enemies!

DRUMMOND (*Low, moved*) There was much greatness in this man.

HORNBECK   Shall I put that in the obituary?

DRUMMOND *starts to pack up his brief case.*

DRUMMOND   Write anything you damn please.

HORNBECK   How do you write an obituary
For a man who's been dead thirty years?
"In memoriam—M.H.B." Then what?
Hail the apostle whose letters to the Corinthians
Were lost in the mail?
Two years, ten years—and tourists will ask the guide,
"Who died here? Matthew Harrison Who?"
A sudden thought.
What did he say to the minister? It fits!
He delivered his own obituary!
He looks about the witness stand and the JUDGE's *bench, searching for something.*
They must have one here some place.
HORNBECK *pounces on a Bible.*
Here it is: *his* book!
Thumbing hastily.
Proverbs, wasn't it?

DRUMMOND (*Quietly*) "He that troubleth his own house shall inherit the wind: and the fool shall be servant to the wise in heart."
HORNBECK *looks at* DRUMMOND, *surprised. He snaps the Bible shut, and lays it on the* JUDGE's *bench.* HORNBECK *folds his arms and crosses slowly toward* DRUMMOND, *his eyes narrowing.*

HORNBECK   We're growing an odd crop of agnostics this year!

DRUMMOND's *patience is wearing thin.*

DRUMMOND (*Evenly*) I'm getting damned tired of you, Hornbeck.

HORNBECK   Why?

DRUMMOND   You never pushed a noun against a verb except to blow up something.

HORNBECK   That's a typical lawyer's trick: accusing the accuser!

DRUMMOND   What am I accused of?

HORNBECK   I charge you with contempt of conscience!
Self-perjury. Kindness aforethought.
Sentimentality in the first degree.

DRUMMOND   Why? Because I refuse to erase a man's lifetime? I tell you Brady had the same right as Cates: the right to be wrong!

HORNBECK   "Be-Kind-To-Bigots" Week. Since Brady's dead,
We must be kind. God, how the world is rotten
With kindness!

DRUMMOND   A giant once lived in that body. (*Quietly*) But Matt Brady got lost. Because he was looking for God too high up and too far away.

HORNBECK   You hypocrite! You fraud!
With a growing sense of discovery.
You're more religious than *he* was!

DRUMMOND *doesn't answer.* HORNBECK *crosses toward the exit hurriedly.*
Excuse me, gentlemen. I must get me to a typewriter
And hammer out the story of an atheist
Who believes in God.

He goes off.

CATES   Colonel Drummond.

DRUMMOND   Bert, I am resigning my commission in the State Militia. I hand in my sword!

CATES   Doesn't it cost a lot of money for an appeal? I couldn't pay you . . .

DRUMMOND *waves him off.*

DRUMMOND   I didn't come here to be paid. (*He turns*) Well, I'd better get myself on a train.

RACHEL   There's one out at five-thirteen. Bert, you and I can be on that train, too!

CATES (*Smiling, happy*) I'll get my stuff!

RACHEL   I'll help you!

They start off. RACHEL *comes back for her suitcase.* CATES *grabs his suit jacket, clasps* DRUMMOND'S *arm.*

CATES (*Calling over his shoulder*) See you at the depot!

RACHEL *and* CATES *go off.* DRUMMOND *is left alone on stage. Suddenly he notices* RACHEL'S *copy of Darwin on the table.*

DRUMMOND (*Calling*) Say—you forgot—

But RACHEL *and* CATES *are out of earshot. He weighs the volume in his hand; this one book has been the center of the whirlwind. Then* DRUMMOND *notices the Bible, on the* JUDGE'S *bench. He picks up the Bible in his other hand; he looks from one volume to the other, balancing them thoughtfully, as if his hands were scales. He half-smiles, half-shrugs. Then* DRUMMOND *slaps the two books together and jams them in his brief case, side by side. Slowly, he climbs to the street level and crosses the empty square.*

The curtain falls

Further Suggestions for Study

1. What do you consider to be the significance of the title?
2. How do the fictional additions of Rachel and the Reverend Jeremiah Brown add to the dramatic effectiveness of the play?
3. Describe any character encountered in your personal reading who had similar courage to that of Bert Cates.
4. Which laws do you think the general public ignores? What would happen if they were repealed?
5. What do you consider to be the advantages and disadvantages of religious or political instruction in the schools?
6. William Jennings Bryan, the counterpart in real life of Matthew Harrison Brady, once maintained that a teacher acts *in loco parentis* (in place of the parent) and that a teacher should therefore teach what the parents wanted their children to learn. Defend your agreement or disagreement with Bryan's proposal.
7. In what ways does the play depict Drummond as basically a religious person?
8. In what ways was the judge entitled, in point of law, to rule all expert testimony on evolution as "irrelevant"?
9. How exactly do the authors turn an "ideas" play into a dynamic, human document?
10. Consult the Canadian or the United States Bill of Rights. In what ways do they guarantee Drummond's statement that "Anyone . . . has the right to think"?

Suggested Reading

Center of the Storm: Memoirs of John T. Scopes, John Scopes and James Presley, Holt, Rinehart and Winston.
Clarence Darrow for the Defense, Irving Stone, Doubleday.
Critical reviews of the motion picture of *Inherit the Wind*:
Time, October 17, 1960, page 95.
Saturday Review, October 8, 1960, vol. 43, page 30.
Newsweek, October 17, 1960, vol. 56, page 114.
Life, September 26, 1960, vol. 49, page 77.
Coronet, July 1960, vol. 48, page 12.
America, October 15, 1960, vol. 104, page 101.
Senior Scholastic, September 1960, vol. 77, page 40.